# Coaching for Careers

# Coaching in Practice Series

The aim of this series is to help coaching professionals gain a broader understanding of the challenges and issues they face in coaching, enabling them to make the leap from being a 'good-enough' coach to an outstanding one. This series is an essential aid for both the novice coach eager to learn how to grow a coaching practice, and the more experienced coach looking for new knowledge and strategies. Combining theory with practice, the series provides a comprehensive guide to becoming successful in this rapidly expanding profession.

***Published and forthcoming titles:***

Bluckert: *Psychological Dimensions to Executive Coaching*

Bluckert: *Gestalt Coaching: Right Here, Right Now*

Brockbank and McGill: *Coaching with Empathy*

Brown and Brown: *Neuropsychology for Coaches: Understanding the Basics*

Driver: *Coaching Positively: Lessons for Coaches from Positive Psychology*

Hawkins: *Creating a Coaching Culture*

Hay: *Reflective Practice and Supervision for Coaches*

Hayes: *NLP Coaching*

McGregor: *Coaching Behind Bars: Facing Challenges and Creating Hope in a Women's Prison*

Paice: *New Coach: Reflections from a Learning Journey*

Pemberton: *Resilience: A Practical Guide for Coaches*

Rogers: *Building a Coaching Business*

Sandler: *Executive Coaching: A Psychodynamic Approach*

Vaughan Smith: *Therapist into Coach*

Vaughan Smith: *Coaching and Trauma: Moving Beyond the Survival Self*

Wildflower: *The Hidden History of Coaching*

# Coaching for Careers

## A Practical Guide for Coaches

*Jenny Rogers*

 Open University Press

Open University Press
McGraw-Hill Education
8th Floor, 338 Euston Road
London
England
NW1 3BH

and Two Penn Plaza, New York, NY 10121-2289, USA

First published 2019

Copyright © Open International Publishing Ltd, 2019

All rights reserved. Except for the quotation of short passages for the purposes of criticism and review, no part of this publication may be reproduced, stored in a retrieval system, or transmitted, in any form or by any means, electronic, mechanical, photocopying, recording or otherwise, without the prior written permission of the publisher or a licence from the Copyright Licensing Agency Limited. Details of such licences (for reprographic reproduction) may be obtained from the Copyright Licensing Agency Ltd of Saffron House, 6–10 Kirby Street, London EC1N 8TS.

Senior Commissioning Editor: Hannah Kenner
Head of Open University Publishing: Laura Pacey
Editorial Assistant: Karen Harris
Content Product Manager: Ali Davis

A catalogue record of this book is available from the British Library

ISBN-13: 9780335248254
ISBN-10: 033524825X
eISBN: 9780335248261

Library of Congress Cataloging-in-Publication Data
CIP data applied for

Typeset by Transforma Pvt. Ltd., Chennai, India
Printed and bound by CPI Group (UK) Ltd, Croydon, CR0 4YY

Fictitious names of companies, products, people, characters and/or data that may be used herein (in case studies or in examples) are not intended to represent any real individual, company, product or event.

# Praise for this book

*"This is a must-have resource for all coaches to support clients in career and job transition."*

Terry H. Hildebrandt, PhD, MCC, MCEC, Director of
Evidence Based Coaching, Fielding Graduate University, USA

*"The clearest, wisest guide I have yet read on coaching towards success in the complex world of work."*

Sarah Gillett CMG CVO,
Former ambassador, and coach in-training

*"Jenny continues to set the bench mark for what it means to be a great coach. An inspiring read for anyone interested in coaching."*

Kate Stephens, CEO, Smart Works Charity

*"The wealth of Jenny's own experience and the depth of her expertise gives her the authority to teach us all and we are grateful to her for the extent of our continued learning."*

Catherine Devitt CEO, Meyler Campbell

*"This is far more than a superbly comprehensive set of tools and techniques for career coaching – although it definitely is that. This is a masterful narration of the whole story of career coaching at a much deeper level."*

Jane Cook, Head of Leadership and Coaching, Linden Learning

*"An experiential step-by-step guide to working with clients who are exploring real issues around their work, career, and life, to bring out their best selves. One of the best in furthering your learning and growth as a coach."*

Diane Brennan, DBH, MCC, Director of Leadership & Organizational
Development University of Arizona and Past President of the
International Coach Federation (2008)

*"A thorough overview of the skills and knowledge required by career coaches. This not only defines the coach's professional toolkit, but reveals the very best practice in career coaching."*

John Lees, author of How to Get a Job You Love

# Contents

Series preface      x

**Introduction**      1

*The evolution and rewards of career coaching*

**1 The career landscape**      5

*The history of careers as a concept; the changing world of work: the demographic, technological and economic changes that are producing a volatile climate; myths and half-truths about careers; why it is important for us as coaches to look at our own assumptions about jobs and work*

**2 Special skills of the career coach**      16

*Career coaching needs all the basic coaching skills but used with more intensity and more sophistication: empathy, listening, challenging, managing and containing strong emotion and knowing how to give information and feedback in ways that minimize the chances of the client rejecting it*

**3 Preparing**      33

*Why it matters to define your market; setting fees and managing price resistance; getting over your fear of selling; how to have the 'chemistry conversation'*

**4 Getting started: the first session**      42

*Why clear contracting matters; tools and techniques for assessing the present, including the client's personal life and exploring the 'backstory': how their childhood influenced the person they are today, setting goals*

**viii** CONTENTS

## 5 Brand identity    58

*The critical importance for clients of differentiating themselves; how to use the idea of 'brand' and 'brand essence'; psychometric questionnaires and how they can help; the strengths-based approach, pluses and minuses; where 360 feedback may contribute valuable data; how to identify transferrable skills*

## 6 The client in words: their CV/résumé    77

*The true purpose of a CV and the common mistakes that clients make, including the 'safe pair of hands' trap; different styles and types of CV: how to help clients choose the right format and to compose a powerful covering letter*

## 7 The search    93

*Old and new methods of job search compared; how to help clients get over their reluctance to network and to search the 'invisible market' and to get the best out of agencies and consultants*

## 8 Coaching for interviews    107

*The irrational and unpredictable nature of job interviewing and how to prepare clients for anything they meet; image and why it matters; how to help clients with nervousness; how to coach them through a failsafe way of answering questions through using storytelling techniques*

## 9 Not just an interview: more scrutiny for the client    125

*The origins of assessment centres and why they make for better hiring decisions; how to prepare the client for what they might encounter, including giving a presentation, going through a role play and completing tests or personality questionnaires; giving clients feedback on sensitive topics*

## 10 What's the point of it all? Working with clients on life purpose    137

*It is demanding to work with clients who ask, 'what's my life purpose?' when it is unlikely that there are easy answers; why this work may evoke the coach's own struggle to answer the same question; some approaches that will help along with specific 'exercises'*

## 11 Decision time                                      153

*All career coaching clients will face decisions at some point: accept a job or refuse? Resign? Go freelance?; why it matters to resist over-swift thinking and what will work instead; how and why the coach may be able to increase the client's skill as a negotiator; how to work with the client on exiting with aplomb and to start well in a new job*

References                                              173
Index                                                   175

# Series preface

When we published our first title in the *Coaching in Practice* series, way back in 2007, only an exceptionally wise person could have predicted the rapid expansion of coaching. Then, it was hard to find reliable initial training and even harder to find anything more advanced. Then, it was unclear whether it was truly possible to make a career out of coaching and the number of people working as coaches was comparatively small. Today all that has changed, much of it for the better. There are many excellent training courses. Nationally and internationally recognized qualifications have expanded in both scope and rigour.

As a supervisor I am a personal witness to the viability of coaching as a lucrative career. There are tens of thousands of people calling themselves coaches: the word has even been adopted to cover activities as varied as parent coach, finance coach, career coach and even, as I saw in a recent article, flirting coach. Executive coaching is now an attractive second career for increasing numbers of people looking for new ways of growing their interest in the development of people.

Yet while there are many books that cater for the beginner coach, including my own book, also published by Open University Press, *Coaching Skills: The Definitive Guide to Being a Coach*, it is still the case that there are relatively few that explore and deepen more specialist aspects of the role. There is more interest in questions of ethics and boundaries, for instance in the shadowy line between therapy and coaching. There is better understanding of the mysteries of the coach–client relationship and of what makes it work – or not. There is more acceptance of the idea that every coach needs a supervisor.

This is the territory that we cover in this series. The titles range from the practicalities of developing and running a coaching business to the history of coaching, and to books that expand the range of tools, techniques and approaches that a coach might try with teams as well as with individuals. Underlying themes are, in many titles, about the psychology of human change and why it matters so much in coaching. As I know from personal experience of running initial coach training courses, it is often hard to find enough time to cover all of these vital topics in sufficient depth.

The series is called *Coaching in Practice* because the aim is to unite theory and practice in an accessible way. The books are short, designed to be easily understood without in any way compromising on the integrity of the ideas they explore. All are written by senior coaches, in every case with many years of hands-on experience.

This series is for you if you are undertaking or completing your coaching training and perhaps in the early stages of the unpredictability, pleasures and dilemmas that working with actual clients brings. Now that you have passed the honeymoon stage, you may have begun to notice the limitations of your approaches and knowledge. You are eager for more information and guidance. You probably know that it is hard to make the leap between being a good-enough coach and an outstanding one. Or perhaps you are a much more experienced coach thirsty for more help and challenges. You may also be one of the many people still contemplating a career in coaching. If so, these books will give you useful direction on many of the issues which preoccupy, perplex and delight the working coach.

Jenny Rogers
Series Editor

# Introduction

This book is for any coach who wants to understand and get better at career coaching. It offers a stage-by-stage guide to how to do it. You may be a full-time executive coach, a personal coach, an associate with an outplacement company, an internal coach with a large organization, a volunteer at a charity that offers help on getting people back into the workforce, or perhaps you are an HR professional. You probably already have at least some knowledge and experience of coaching in this area but I find that it is rare for a coach to feel confident about the whole career coaching cycle – the focus of this book.

In my own case, career coaching crept up on me as a specialism. I began as an executive coach at a time nearly 30 years ago when few people knew what coaching was, other than recognizing its role in sport. It was common to see puzzled expressions when I said what I did for a living. This was especially true if I mentioned working with clients in sectors that had nothing to do with my own earlier experience as a television producer with the BBC. I remember my dad, then in his 80s, and having worked all his life in the coal industry, earnestly asking me how I could possibly coach, for instance, the manager of a coalmine, when I clearly knew nothing about coal or mining. My reply was that if managers of mines needed technical help then they could readily find a mentor but that my role would be to work with them on how effectively they were managing their people and themselves, themes which are universal; you wouldn't need a degree in geo-engineering to do it.

This sunny belief that as coaches we could work with anyone from any sector on anything at all was the unspoken default in those more settled times. But gradually, the organizational brokers, the people who chose and paid for coaches, were becoming pickier. With coaching a newly attractive second career for so many people and with so many coaches now hunting for work, they could afford to be selective. They asked tougher questions about your experience of their sectors, they wanted to know how many people you had coached who were just like the potential client they had in mind, they were looking for reputation and specialist expertise, including of career coaching. More and more of my own work began to involve clients who needed specific help on career direction, writing a CV or preparing for an interview.

As the financial crisis of 2008 started to grip public and private sectors alike, I noticed a change in the issues that clients were bringing. People who had looked forward to safe, steady careers in one organization or sector, found that their jobs were in jeopardy and that they needed to re-examine all of their assumptions about what made for satisfying work. Some welcomed the upheaval as a valuable

**2** COACHING FOR CAREERS

chance to rethink their lives, others were bewildered and frightened, doubting that their skills had the magic of 'transferability'. Young graduates were questioning whether their degrees were the passport to success that they had been promised. Mass redundancies were no longer surprising, though virtually always a shock to those on the receiving end. This turbulence has not gone away; if anything it has increased, a topic I look at in Chapter 1.

From the beginning of my coaching career I had espoused the value of taking a whole-life perspective, sometimes to the surprise of clients who had expected that the focus of our work would be purely on their professional issues. Now, I was finding that clients not only made no resistance to looking at their personal lives, they also embraced the topic eagerly because it is so obvious that career needs to be seen in the context of everything else that is going on in your life. That legendary 'ladder' might have been snatched away but it gave clients the chance to reconsider work as just one part of leading a fruitful life. More and more clients found their way to me where career was straightforwardly the presenting problem and not just a vague buzz in the background.

In parallel with this, and certainly a factor in why so many people felt that they needed external help, organizations were getting more rigorous in their promotion and selection processes. There were some high-profile employment tribunals that embarrassed a good many well-known organizations by exposing the inadequacies of the traditional panel interview. Then, too, the pressure to survive in a newly competitive environment made it even more imperative for employers to appoint the right person and the cost of making a mistake at selection became obvious. All of this put pressure on candidates, some of whom could not understand why they were repeatedly rejected for shortlisting, despite apparently having everything that the job needed, or if shortlisted, were failing to give a good account of themselves at interview.

I found that clients were looking for coaching because they had already exhausted all the obvious sources of help. They had asked for feedback and had often found that it was either not offered at all or else they had been fobbed off with unhelpful platitudes. They had consulted family, colleagues and friends, they had read the books and looked on the internet yet they were still stuck. This was where I came in.

Then, as now, the request for coaching typically took two forms. There were the clients who knew that there was something awry with the way they were handling job interviews and were looking for a single session. I learnt to be cautious about whether this was what they really needed. Some people were telling themselves that it didn't matter whether they wanted the job or not because they were 'getting practice at being interviewed'. They needed to understand that their lack of motivation would be instantly apparent to the employer, so this tactic was self-defeating and in the end, chronically disheartening. The introductory 'chemistry conversation' between coach and potential client may often suggest that the client needs a different kind of session first, one that identifies what it is that they really want. Sometimes when that question is answered, there is no need for interview coaching. When the client is clear that this is a job they are truly keen to get and have already been shortlisted, plus they have failed to get similar jobs in the recent past, then a one-off interview coaching session is probably all that is necessary.

At the other end of the spectrum are the people who want and need a comprehensive programme often because they have been made redundant, have been forced to move to a new area because of their domestic circumstances or have fallen seriously out of love with whatever job they are currently doing. This coaching programme will start with assessing their current situation and will then go on to consider their 'brand', including their personality and skills and how they express all of this in their CV/résumé. Many clients are uninformed about the best ways to look for a job because they are still assuming that the visible job market of advertisement and websites is how they will find the perfect fit, so as a topic this might easily absorb a whole coaching session. At this stage, thanks to your work together, the client will have clarity about who they are, what they want, what they offer and how to search effectively for a new role, so when they get shortlisted, it will be much easier to prepare them for interviews and assessment centres. Once they get the job offer, as their coach you may be able to add considerable value by working with them on how to decide whether the answer is yes or no, then if it is yes, how to negotiate the best deal and then how to make a positive start in the new job. When this is your approach to career coaching it could easily absorb many sessions, perhaps 12 hours or more, and hugely increase the client's chances of getting the job they want. I deal step by step with all of these topics in this book.

## A note on the case studies

Confidentiality is essential in coaching. The many case studies and examples I give in this book are all composites or fictional, though each one represents the typical people and situations that any career coach is likely to encounter.

## The rewards

The coaching profession itself is changing. The all-purpose coach is now a rarity. Clients look for people with specialist expertise. This might be by sector, by seniority and type of role, by age or by the type of issue that clients bring. I see this in my own work as a supervisor to other coaches where currently I work with coaches who specialize in these areas: clients returning to work after parental leave, jobless young graduates, marketing directors, owners of small and medium-sized businesses, media executives, hedge fund managers, head teachers, military personnel, MBA students and doctors. Virtually all of the clients with whom these coaches are working will have career issues at some point and increasingly often, career is actually the presenting issue.

**4** COACHING FOR CAREERS

Career coaching is rewarding. It is rewarding financially because it is one of the few areas of coaching where individuals will invest in themselves rather than expecting funding from employers. It is gratifying to earn good money but what matters more, certainly to me, is knowing that I am making a difference and this is much easier to see when the topic is career. In so many other kinds of coaching the link is maddeningly opaque between what we do and establishing exactly how the client benefits. In writing this book my aim is to increase your confidence and capability to undertake this challenging and deeply rewarding work. I should very much like to hear how you get on. Please email me with any comments, suggestions or questions: jenny@JennyRogersCoaching.com.

# 1   The career landscape

As I look at my schedule for the next few weeks, I am always pleased to see that I have several people who are coming for career coaching. I never know what people will bring but it is always intriguing:

> *Dale's* task is to convince an employer that he is serious about not wanting another chief executive role in healthcare and to find what he calls a 'no fuss 9–5 job running a smallish hospital department instead'.
>
> *Louis* has spent 18 years fitting occasional work as a freelance web designer around his role as the main carer for his six children. He is 55 and wonders if it is too late to relaunch himself in a totally different career, saying, 'My confidence is at rock bottom'.
>
> *Ibukun* has made endless job applications without success. At the charity where I am a volunteer interview coach, she tells me about her long and dangerous journey across Africa when she was only 10 years old, her self-funded first-class degree from a British university, her divorce from an abusive man and her intense wish to find a job where she could eventually qualify as an HR specialist. She has taught herself fast touch typing, is tri-lingual, is fluent in two Nigerian languages and also has impeccable English. Childcare and the demands made by her degree course have meant that she has not had anything more than patchy paid employment for six years.

## What is a 'career'?

The word *career* itself has been sniffed at suspiciously. Isn't it the case that middle-class people have careers whereas working-class people just have jobs? According to this way of thinking, a career is something involving personal choice, vocation and job satisfaction whereas a job is just a grim necessity. This in itself feels like a misguided distinction. I remember here a particular staff member at the British Council HQ reception desk just off Trafalgar Square in London. He several times described to me his pride and pleasure in making people from all over the world feel welcome, telling me how he loved his job – yet he had what many people would

**6** COACHING FOR CAREERS

see as a humble role. And I have worked with countless people in highly paid, high-status jobs who were deeply miserable. I see career as a neutral word that simply describes someone's journey through a variety of jobs and types of work which may or may not be well paid or satisfying and which may or may not involve progression in status or money.

In practice I find little difference between the coaching I do for the well educated and well paid and what I do as a charity volunteer where I am working with people who have often been sorely disadvantaged by life events. The same questions press, the same worries niggle, the same hopes and fears are present, there is the same range of attitudes and abilities. The differences lie in the context and the resources that are available rather than in the nature of the issues that people bring.

## The career landscape

Theories about career abound in the academic literature: careers as fitting square pegs into square holes, careers as social constructs, careers as life stages, careers as manifestations of chaos theory, careers as embodiments of family history, careers as excellent examples of gender and cultural bias. Some of these ideas have translated into practical tools that a career coach can use; many remain interesting philosophical notions. Some are challenging, for instance, whether we exaggerate the amount of personal control we have over any of our career decisions when so many of them are in fact triggered by external events, often global and technological in origin, over which we have no control whatsoever. Probably we do exaggerate, but perhaps this is a useful delusion to have. All these theories faithfully reflect the times in which they were produced. Julia Yates' book *The Career Coaching Handbook* (2014) has a neat summary if you are interested in learning more about the theoretical background.

### How it used to be

Nineteenth-century English fiction gives clues about how work used to be seen. It is striking how little attention is paid to the idea of a job as something that is intrinsically rewarding. In these novels, there are a few characters with work that resembles present day employment yet the way of life they describe could hardly be more different. The poor worked on the land and lived in tied cottages at the whim of their landlord or were drawn to the cities where badly paid work was dirty and dangerous. Vast numbers of people, in the cities or in rural areas, worked 'in service', that is as servants to those who were better off. The poorer you were the more likely it was that you would work gruellingly long hours with no respite and little financial reward.

Upper-class prosperity was built on land ownership and inheritance so jobs were an irrelevance unless you were unfortunate enough to be a younger son or to belong to a family that had inexplicably lost its money. Professional jobs did not automatically bestow status. If you were a doctor, you struggled to be regarded as the social equal of the landowners or prosperous entrepreneurs who were your patients, not surprising perhaps at a time when the practice of medicine was safe but largely ineffectual. Women with any pretention to 'gentility' were prevented from working at all. Jobs in government were emerging but the people who hold them are depicted strolling to their civil service offices in the middle of the morning and leaving at around four in the afternoon. Their jobs were largely sinecures and obtained through personal connection with no competition. Work, such as it was, filled the gaps between hunting, dancing, drinking and other pleasant kinds of socializing. The books are full of clergymen who have no interest in religion and army officers who have no interest in soldiering. Merit and performance were irrelevant. The idea of work that is a vocation or that fulfils a life purpose is rarely featured, though a striking exception is Dr Lydgate in George Eliot's magnificent novel *Middlemarch* published in 1871 but set 40 years earlier. Lydgate's obsessive commitment to his job, driven by his interests in social justice and scientific evidence, is regarded as eccentric and reckless by many of the other characters.

The upheaval of wars in the 20th century, compulsory schooling with free education, raising the school leaving age, universal suffrage and better healthcare all made this way of life untenable – and by the 1940s it had vanished.

### Mid-20th century

A young person leaving school or college in the mid-20th century would have found that jobs were plentiful and the choices were easy because there weren't that many. Depending on where you lived and the social status of your parents, you slid into doing work that your parents and possibly also your grandparents would have recognized and sometimes it would be the same work: the son of a factory worker was expected to become a factory worker. Perhaps you headed for unskilled or semi-skilled work in an office or shop. It may have been dull but it was secure and reasonably well paid and there was camaraderie with your fellow workers. If you were among the privileged small percentage of your age cohort who secured a university place, which in the UK at least was free at that time, you became a teacher, a doctor, a lawyer or one of the other familiar professional roles, or possibly a trainee manager in one of those factories, offices and shops. It was common to stay in one company or one sector for your entire working life but then you could look forward to retirement with a decent pension, living in the house that you had bought at an affordable price or rented cheaply from your local authority.

As a school leaver or at the end of your university course you might have some time with a person known as a 'careers advisor' or 'vocational guidance officer'. If you were lucky you might meet a thoughtful practitioner who would be friendly, challenging, take an interest and encourage some searching thinking as well as giving you valuable information which was otherwise only obtainable by doing a tedious

**8** COACHING FOR CAREERS

library search in person. If you were unlucky, you met a bored individual whose questions were perfunctory and who languidly offered a few scrappy pamphlets. Training was offered for 'career counsellors' and the consumers of their work were assumed to be young people. Although there are hundreds of self-help books with career themes, even now little has been written for people working with adult clients in mid or later career.

### The situation for women

A woman colleague retiring from the BBC in the late 1970s circulated a memo she had carefully preserved from the day she had joined 40 years previously. It informed her that were she to get married, she would have to resign. She did get married but kept her marriage and her one pregnancy a secret (how she did this I have no idea) and never told a soul that she was a married working mother. She sent this memo to every woman in the department to remind us of our own good fortune. The idea of the male breadwinner had been deeply embedded into social norms: the 1901 census shows that only 10 per cent of married women were in paid employment and it had nudged up just a few percentage points in the 1931 census. Like the BBC, many organizations insisted that being a married woman was incompatible with work, even in professions such as teaching that were dominated by women. Benefits went to men; women were assumed to be 'dependants'. 'Married woman' and 'housewife' were used as interchangeable terms.

## The changing world of work

How different all of this is now. The post-war boom in the birth rate, rising numbers of divorces, and the acute need for labour in an expanding market made these assumptions unsustainable and now there are as many women as men in the labour force. Heavy industry is a fraction of what it used to be in most first world countries and in the UK the number of people in the gig economy is roughly the same as the number in what is left of manufacturing. Pension schemes have been closed because we are living too long to make them viable. About 1 in 12 of us works in insecure jobs where we are either self-employed or working on so-called *zero-hours contracts* where the employer can dictate when and how often we work.

Routine work is handled by computers and 'the office' is rapidly becoming an outmoded concept when so much of what used to be 'office work' can be done from anywhere. University degrees mean less when up to 40 per cent of 18-year-olds are entering higher education, and some degrees and some universities are valued a great deal more highly than others and now, in the UK at least, with the cost of a degree zooming upwards, enrolments are going down. Higher education is expensive, leaving graduates with a substantial debt to repay; housing is unaffordable for young people unless they have parents who can unload some of the equity in their homes. For many young people it is common after university to return to living with parents and to do a few years in a McJob, serving hamburgers, making coffee

THE CAREER LANDSCAPE **9**

or folding clothes in Gap. Adolescence can seem infinitely prolonged when this is the scenario. Far from stepping straight into a reasonably well-paid job, a spell as an intern on little or no money is now one of the best ways into a professional career and that will often depend on how well connected your parents are.

Being made redundant used to be a matter of shame, suggesting that 'redundancy' was a face-saving disguise to allow a poor performer to escape with a decent financial settlement. There are still plenty of cases where this is true, but it is far more common for whole cohorts of people to lose their jobs because global or online competitors have eaten into the company's market, the financial forecasts were way too optimistic or new regulations made the product too expensive. It is not at all uncommon for me to work with clients who have experienced redundancy more than once in their careers.

There are striking differences between people in professional roles and people in low-skilled or semi-skilled jobs. Around 1990, long hours started becoming the preserve of professional jobs. People in these jobs are now widely assumed to be willing to work 12-hour days without complaint, to be available online around the clock and through weekends especially if they work for a global company where different time zones and cultural norms have to be accommodated, while the other staff skip away at five. The gap between the well paid and the low paid has widened. A chief executive may be earning many thousands of times more than the people on whatever the equivalent is of the shop floor, whereas in the middle of the 20th century these differentials were relatively small.

The job market has changed structurally with many of the in-the-middle jobs disappearing. Technology has made it possible for us as customers to do much for ourselves that previously had to be done by other humans. We use self-checkouts in supermarkets, fill our own petrol tanks, file our own taxes, book our own airline tickets, print our own photos. Shopping for almost everything can be done online. Robotics and Artificial Intelligence will erode many jobs that previously could only be done by a person. Empty high street shops are the norm and it is clear that no company is too big to fail. To survive, there is pressure to reduce costs and if it can be made more cheaply in Asia, it will be. In the UK, if farm workers from Eastern Europe can be hired to pick fruit at lower costs then this is what will happen. Mass movements of people mean that we are a greatly more diverse society than we were 70 years ago with all the pluses and minuses that this involves.

There is a cost to these changes and we see it in the end of political and economic certainty and the advent of social upheaval: astonishing election results, a hollowing-out of the middle ground politically, the advent of 'fake news' on a grand scale and a great deal of ill-tempered debate.

### The rise of the centenarian – and the falling birth rate

In first world countries there are other striking changes. A hundred years ago British men could expect to live to about 51 and women to 55. A child born in Britain today has a 50 per cent chance of living to past 100 years thanks to improvements in

## 10 COACHING FOR CAREERS

public health such as vaccination programmes, anti-smoking campaigns, antibiotics and better treatment of heart disease. By the year 2080 there could be 21,000 centenarians whereas in 1920 there were a mere 200. How to pay for the care needed to support the enormous increase in people living to very old age is a problem that has so far resisted solution. Marriage is declining whereas cohabitation increases. More women are deciding against having children and in some countries there will be a net decline in population. The longer we live the more likely we are to change partners so blended families will become even more common and the loneliness of so many older single people a massive challenge to mental health services.

In their book, *The 100-Year Life* (2016), Lynda Gratton and Andrew Scott predict some of the consequences, suggesting that because it will be so difficult to fund a pension, people will work into their 70s and 80s, health permitting, staying younger for longer. As the authors say, deadpan, the age at which people have their first coronary will go on rising. It will be commonplace for four or even five generations to be alive at the same time, so although people may have fewer children there will be more grandparents and great-grandparents in their children's lives.

At the same time as older people are living for longer, fertility rates are falling all over the world. As prosperity increases, people have fewer children. Contraception becomes widely available, the risk of children dying in infancy recedes and in a non-agrarian economy, it becomes less and less acceptable to employ children as workers, so the case for having a big family disappears. If this trend continues, some populations will not renew themselves. With fewer productive young people available, this, again, will change the nature of work and the workforce.

## Privilege is not for everyone

Today, longevity is increasing but so is the gap between the privileged and the underprivileged. While I was thinking about this chapter, I had two coaching encounters in the same week. These brought the contrast home:

*Victor* was born Vittorio to an Italian family with very little money in the Clerkenwell district of London. His parents were determined that he should go to university, and he did. He is in his early 70s and still working three days a week as CEO of the specialist printing business he founded 35 years ago. He is in a happy second marriage to a woman nearly 20 years younger and now wants to step away from his current role, maybe becoming Chairman. The immediate prompt has been a medical investigation even though he has been pronounced fit and indeed he is slim and physically active, telling me that on many weekends he and his wife cycle at least 60 miles in and around London. He is close to the four children from his first marriage and enjoys his ten grandchildren. He has what he describes as a 'neglected' talent for photography and is considering enrolling for a one-year part-time course at one of London's premier art colleges. He is an enthusiastic and thoughtful client, telling me that he wishes he'd known about 'this coaching thing' years ago.

My most recent sessions with *Rachel* have been dominated by concerns about her mother. Like Victor, Rachel's mother, Edie, is in her early 70s and came from a family with little money. But there the similarities end. She has lived all her life in an isolated English village, left school at 15 and had the first of her five children at 17. She has lived alone since the death of her husband ten years ago. She is overweight, has type 2 diabetes, has chronic circulatory problems that are affecting her feet and she takes medication for depression. She rarely ventures out unless Rachel or one of her other adult children is there to manage it. These are some of the things that Edie has never done: had any higher education, had a paid job, been to London, driven a car, taken cash from an ATM, used a self-checkout in a supermarket, belonged to an exercise class, purchased goods online, set up a direct debit, used a computer. Rachel has bought Edie a smartphone and patiently explained how to use it, but says that her mother is 'afraid' of it and most of the time it is either switched off or out of battery.

## The hidden rules of success

Everyone who is successful in their career would like to believe that they have made their own good fortune. Yet when you interrogate the careers of highly successful people, you will virtually always find an invisible history of help: parents who could afford private education; learning early in life about codes of behaviour, language and dress and how they apply to elite environments; having powerful people in their wider networks who could tell themselves that they were innocently 'talent-spotting' when picking young people for patronage. The writers Sam Friedman and Daniel Laurison expose how this works in their book, *The Class Ceiling: Why it Pays to be Privileged* (2019). They give the example of a leading British accountancy firm where apparently nebulous concepts such as 'having polish' are actually specific but unspoken rules associated with shared backgrounds, dress, humour and lifestyle. When you do not come from a social class that makes all of this easy, the sense that you do not fit can be overwhelming, something that I have

**12** COACHING FOR CAREERS

heard many hundreds of times from clients who may well decide to opt out, feeling that the effort is exhausting and ultimately could still result in failure. The book backs the idea that elite careers are built on the support of others.

The financial crisis of 2008 and the austerity that has followed have punished the less well off. Women and young people are also disproportionately affected by these changes: for instance, women are still far more likely than men to pick up the caring responsibilities for elderly parents that would previously have been handled by the state. Gaps between rich and poor seem to be increasing, something we can see in the shocking sight of so many children already obese at 10 years old, typically from money-poor households. These children are headed for a significantly shorter lifetime while their slimmer and more affluent peers forge ahead in every way. Food banks, free school meals and school breakfast clubs can sometimes be the only way that some families can survive. The English town of Stockton has the dubious privilege of holding the record as one of the worst examples of health inequalities in the UK. In Stockton there is an 18-year difference in life expectancy between the poorest and the most affluent, with ill-health starting in early middle age for the poorest. We have to assume that this gap will widen.

In her novel *Unsheltered* (2018), the American writer Barbara Kingsolver explores what some of the consequences could be. The book is set in 2016 in the run-up to the US presidential election of that year. One set of characters inhabits a house that is literally falling down because it was built without foundations, a metaphor for contemporary America. Tig, the youngest adult in the story, and maybe it is significant that she is described as extremely short in stature, represents the generation who will have to deal with the consequences of climate change, of the mass movements of desperate people across continents, of the social disruption caused by inequality and of the knowingly false promises of politicians who appeal to our meanest resentments. Tig espouses the view that the days of plenty are over and that the wish of every parent, that their child should have more than they did themselves, is a fantasy. The newest generation will have to learn to live with less, to be ingenious, to recycle and upcycle, to conserve their resources and to share, because 'wanting too much stuff is toxic'. Is this the dream of a naïve idealist or is it a plausible scenario? The novel has no answers to this question.

## Secrets of career success

This turbulent world will have consequences for employment. As people get richer they want to consume more services, but many of these will be provided to the affluent by those significantly less privileged people obliged to find work in the gig economy. This is shifting the focus to the value of intangible assets. In previous decades what was valued was the knowledge and skill that you acquired in earlier career, with a heavy emphasis on initial qualifications, whereas now what is needed is continuous updating, mental flexibility, the crucial importance of knowing how

THE CAREER LANDSCAPE **13**

to network and understanding that reputation is everything, including a reputation for diligence, fairness, getting things done and the ability to create and be part of a team. Self-employment may be risky but it also brings freedom and can be lucrative – as long as you know how to manage a business; entrepreneurial skills are a vital asset. Whereas in the last century it was desirable to be a long-stayer in a single organization, now such a choice will raise eyebrows. It no longer surprises me to hear clients express restlessness after three or four years in one job.

Working life will be extended, so physical and mental health, fitness, a strong and constantly renewing friendship circle and personal happiness become critically important. Lack of emotional intelligence is already a barrier to finding and keeping a good job and is likely to become even more so in the future. Personal presentation will matter more, though it already matters when there is evidence that senior people tend to be taller and that good-looking people get promoted more readily than those who are less lucky in this respect.

## Popular myths about careers

It is worth all of us in career coaching looking carefully at our own assumptions about what career actually means before we ask clients the same question. Are we as coaches guilty of unconsciously sharing popular myths about careers? Some of these myths or half-truths are ones that I hear in my coaching room every month, for instance:

- I can be master of my career
- There's a perfect job waiting for me somewhere and I deserve to have it
- If I have a dream, it can come true
- I'm too old to find another job
- It's down to the organization to manage my career
- There should be a perfect match between what I need and what the organization needs
- If I get more qualifications I will get a better job
- A career plan is possible.

As coaches we will be doing clients a favour to explore the assumptions they are making and then to ask how many of these assumptions are borne out in reality. Ambiguity is now the name of the game. Far more is down to chance, luck and to peculiar, unexpected events than anyone might like to believe. The client who believes in making their own luck will do better than the one who hopes against hope that someone will spot their brilliance.

No amount of dazzling career coaching will find a job for the person who insists that somewhere there is the ideal job for them in an area where all those jobs have disappeared. In an era when some of the biggest organizations are rightly worried about survival, it is hard for them to behave well in general, let alone

**14** COACHING FOR CAREERS

to look out for an individual. Equally, the behemoths of high tech have so many well-qualified candidates burning to work for them that they can afford to act carelessly, taking the view, *plenty more where they came from*. While age prejudice is certainly a reality, what counts as 'old' will depend as much on the individual, their health, the vibrancy of their connections to the contemporary world, as on their chronological age.

Qualifications do help, especially in early career and for some careers they are mandatory, but more qualifications are only rarely the solution to flagging prospects. What they may do is reignite a passion for a particular subject or increase self-confidence – a different aim. Getting qualified may also be essential once a client has already decided on a different career path. I think here of my brother-in-law who became a minister of religion after a successful career in education but this was a vocation, a belief that he was called to do it and a path he had long followed in a lay capacity; training, passing tough assessments and then ordination was the essential gateway to a new role.

Another set of assumptions might be that there are given stages in career as in life: early career should be about finding out what you might be good at – or as a kind of apprenticeship phase; middle career is about building on what you are good at and later career is about stepping back into a well-earned and well-funded retirement where you devote yourself to voluntary work. Quite apart from the fact that these ideas miss out women's role as childbearers, today, careers may zig-zag with a long period of experimentation at any stage not just at the start, with moves from freelance into conventionally paid work and back out again, phases of shared parenting and part-time working where either partner might be the major breadwinner, serious angst in middle age with a strong desire to change careers completely and a portfolio career at any point. I have yet to meet a single client who had a long-term career plan that came to pass.

This turbulent scene is sometimes described with the acronym VUCA, meaning volatile, unpredictable, chaotic and ambiguous, and indeed that is what it seems to be.

## What career coaches need to know

It is often asserted at coach training events that coaches don't need specialized knowledge because our role is not to be advisors or mentors. In practice coaches do need deep and specialized knowledge of all sorts, for instance of organizational behaviour and of human psychology, especially the psychology of change. If you want to do well in career coaching you need to be across the subject. Quite apart from the skills you need, you should be up to date on employment trends in the industries or sectors where you have a client base and be well informed on a range of psychometrics even if you decide not to pursue qualifications in them. You need to be willing to explore concepts such as 'gravitas' with clients who have been told that they lack it, digging into what this actually means in practice in their organizations, when it is often code for a particular kind of conversational exchange, accent, dress and values. You need to know how recruiters work and how employers think. It is extremely helpful to have been an employer yourself and to have seen how it works from the other side of the interview table. You need to understand where people typically go wrong in crafting their CVs and in job interviews; you need to be familiar enough with negotiating principles to be able to advise clients on how to get the best possible deal if they get a job offer. I cover these subjects in this book but a book is no substitute for the in-depth knowledge that the everyday experience of career coaching will bring.

You may like to know what happened to the three clients I described at the top of this chapter:

It took *Dale* only six weeks to find a new job. He says, 'I walk to work, I leave at 5.30. I spend lots of time with my wife, we have proper holidays, I'm doing a good job that I enjoy. I'm earning a lot less but we have more than enough for our needs anyway. No regrets!'

*Louis* had a piece of luck: an uncle unexpectedly left him some money. It was enough to make a long-held idea spring to life. Louis turned out to have a passion and a talent for project management. As he said, 'If you can get six kids to school on time every day with a decent breakfast in their bellies and all the right kit, you can do anything.' He and his wife released some equity by downsizing and began a series of property ventures where Louis was an active project manager, redesigning the properties, dealing daily with builders and has created a modest portfolio that is now bringing in some income.

*Ibukun* and I had just 90 minutes together and agreed that we would spend the minimum amount of time on job interview prep as this was an area where she already felt confident. Instead we sketched out a short-term plan for her next steps. Ibukun got an offer – an admin job on the minimum wage but it was in a large company. She contacted their HR department and did a number of informally conducted research interviews (Chapter 6) with their staff. She began writing a well-considered blog on general HR issues and this soon attracted the attention of her colleagues. Within a year Ibukun had moved into a junior HR role where she is now doing a part-time course, sponsored by her employer, to get herself fully qualified.

It was a privilege to work with these three very different clients. The one thing they all had in common was their motivation: one of the essential conditions for success in any kind of coaching, but absolutely critical in career coaching.

# 2 Special skills of the career coach

It may seem as if career coaching doesn't involve anything special in terms of the skills it needs. In some senses this is true. It's likely that in one form or another you will have encountered all the skills that I describe in this chapter. Basic coach training touches on most of them. The difference with career coaching is two-fold: you may need them more frequently and you may need to use them with greater intensity and sophistication:

> *Nick* is 56 and has just lost his job as a middle manager with a hotel chain. It is a crisis that has taken him by surprise. He has three children who are still in education and a wife with serious health problems. The family is dependent on his income. He worked as a chef in his 20s but feels it is too late to reconnect with the restaurant world; he is out of touch and feels too old for the physical demands of the chef role. What should he do? In the first session with his coach he breaks down, saying he is overwhelmed by fear and anxiety.
>
> *Ava* is obviously employable because she has no difficulty getting on shortlists. But after the seventh rejection at interview she is feeling despairing and depressed. She describes the forthcoming eighth interview as 'a bridge I absolutely must cross' and has approached a coach for help.
>
> *Sharon* stole a cheque at work. She and her husband have severe financial and marital problems and she gives this as the reason for making what she describes as 'a silly one-off mistake'. The police were not involved but she was dismissed for gross misconduct. She has had a long period of unemployment and feels increasing desperation about work, money and her marriage. Now a local charity is sponsoring three coaching sessions for her.

Scenarios of this type will be familiar to most career coaches. In the run of more generic coaching, I notice that there is often less sense of urgency, there seems to be less at stake, however committed the client is to their agenda. In career coaching there is often intensity and sometimes, as in the scenarios above, there is anguish.

## Empathy

Empathy is the foundation of all coaching. If for any reason empathy is lacking, coaching cannot work. Innumerable studies from the world of therapy, close cousin to coaching, have shown convincingly that empathy is what makes the difference to whether therapy succeeds or fails – the school of therapy, its theoretical base and the techniques used by the therapist come a long way behind. I believe that the same is true of coaching. But here is the dilemma: you cannot 'do' empathy to a client. It can sometimes be faked but synthetic empathy is not convincing for long.

The more intense the feelings of the other person, the more intense your own instinctive reaction is likely to be. But empathy is not the same as sympathy. When you feel sympathy you feel emotionally involved, the other person's distress makes you anxious, you may be tempted to join in and to offer solutions. Empathy gives us the ability to understand how others feel but compassion is what gives us the desire to relieve it. This is not the same as pity. Pity is closely associated with condescension. You feel more powerful, you bestow your pity. When this happens the person who is pitied feels patronized and diminished rather than helped. Empathy is about putting yourself in the other person's place, seeking to understand how they experience the world without wanting them to follow your advice. Coaching is about choosing change and empathy provides the essential precondition.

As a coach you are inviting the client to be open, vulnerable and undefended, and you will match this in your own behaviour. Being undefended is something that most of us find to be difficult if not impossible as the default in our everyday lives: we have fine-tuned our defences and this is why we can get locked into a blinkered view of the world. If we have already experienced hurt and disappointment, and all of us have, we will go a long way to avoid experiencing it again. To be undefended in front of a stranger is asking a lot, but the more quickly you encourage the client to do this, the more successful the coaching is likely to be. I like the word that therapists use when they talk about creating *containment* for the client as a way of generating the safe space where real work can be done.

Empathy is underpinned by congruence. This means that your words, your gestures and posture, your voice, language and your inner worlds are totally aligned. You see lack of congruence when someone who is clearly angry and is showing their anger through shouting, roars, 'I'm not angry!' You might see it in a coach who says the right words but whose tone of voice seems offhand and whose body betrays boredom.

Empathy starts with noticing. First, it's self-awareness in the moment: how tired or energized are you? Have you been able to set your own preoccupations and distractions to one side? Where are you on that spectrum of anxious–confident about seeing this client? What you see as commendable calm, the client might see as cold and forbidding. It is equally possible to overdo warmth where it might seem to convey a craven need to be liked or a secret wish for the drama of tears. I once had a coach myself whose favourite question was 'How does that makes you feel?'

## 18 COACHING FOR CAREERS

It seemed that she was never happier than when I was upset. In the end this behaviour became distracting and, ultimately, annoying.

Then, what do you notice about the client? Does their facial expression betray eagerness, happiness, tension, gloom? How about their dress: tidy and together or dishevelled and scruffy? As the session continues you will be constantly monitoring body language, yours and theirs. This is absolutely not in order to do that naïve 'mirroring' so popular on a certain kind of simplistic management development course where you aim to do some kind of stilted copying of the other person.

The capacity for empathy is inborn but it is a learnt behaviour combining unconscious emotional responses with the executive function of thinking. It takes discipline and practice to do it well. The essential step is to switch off judgement. How do you do this? We are all judgemental to some extent, we have to be because there is no time for nuanced weighing up of every person and situation. But as a coach you have the luxury of being able to choose. Forget any idealistic notions you may have about being free from prejudice: this is impossible. Human beings are hardwired to be prejudiced. As herd animals it has been and continues to be part of our survival mechanisms. But we can face up to the prejudices that we have. See prejudice for what it is: fear of the 'Other', which may or may not be justified. Face up to your preconceptions. When you meet and work with someone apparently representative of a group whose opinions and values you dislike, bias can be replaced by curiosity, judgement by inquiry and by asking yourself, *What makes this unique individual tick?*

### The limits of empathy

The danger in writing and teaching about empathy in coaching is to overlook its limits. We can forget that its essence is a process involving two people. It is simultaneously emotional and cognitive. If you are speaking to someone whose attention drifts to their watch or to some fascinating other person just over your shoulder, it is more or less impossible to carry on talking. The feeling of profound disconnection is instant. This phenomenon is usually discussed in relation to the coach as a stern warning that the client will pick up on even the tiniest cues that could indicate lack of attention. But it applies just as much to the client. If the client is not returning your empathetic signals you will find that your relationship withers straight away, another proof that you cannot 'do' empathy. There could be a myriad reasons why this happens: the client is tired, unwell or distracted, the client does not rate or like you, the client does not want to be there – or possibly the client just can't do empathetic behaviour.

It is dismaying as a coach when any of these things happens. Some time ago I was asked to coach a distinguished CEO. His difficulties included harsh criticisms by staff of his allegedly 'remote' personal style. He seemed willing enough to engage in coaching while constantly expressing polite puzzlement about what on earth it was and why his Chairman and his HR director had thought I could help since I was not an expert in his field. Ever courteous, he insisted that we stagger on through six sessions during which time he was head-hunted for and got a similar job in the US. I was never able to feel any genuine connection to him other than the intellectual challenge of striving for a way to reach him and ended every session feeling exhausted and disappointed with myself. My attempts to raise it with him and to query whether it was worth continuing the coaching went nowhere.

## Listening

Poor listeners are such poor listeners that they are supremely unaware of how poor their listening is. Others can mime listening, head nicely cocked on one side, nodding and murmuring, 'I hear what you say', a sure sign that they have not heard. It is easy to mishear, add fancy interpretations of our own and to misremember vital pieces of information. We get involved in the story and in effect have stopped doing the kind of listening that is needed for coaching. It takes training, feedback, endless practice and tough self-discipline to be able to listen successfully for the whole of a 90- or 120-minute coaching session, ideally without writing down a single note until after the client has left, but that should be the aim.

There are a number of ways to make the task easier. Start by having the intention to listen with focus, setting your own agenda to one side and especially vow that you will stop worrying about what question you should ask next. Listen for the headlines in what the client is saying. Next, check how often you are intervening. This means you are listening at two levels simultaneously: you are in the conversation and you are monitoring how it might look and sound if you were the legendary fly on the wall. If you judge that you are doing too much of the talking, then stop. The moment you notice that the client has been talking uninterruptedly for a while, it is probably time to intervene. What is the cause of your silence? Do you hesitate to interrupt, even though you know that you should, because it might seem rude? Have you got confused with the ins and outs of the client's story? If so, it is time for a summary.

## Summarizing

You can only give an accurate summary if you have been listening. Committing yourself mentally to summarizing frequently will help keep you focused. Summarizing is evidence to the client that you have been listening but only if you do it carefully. This means starting by asking permission:

> May I interrupt here? I'd like to summarize what you've said to make sure I'm understanding it. . .

Then you give a brief, accurate precis of what the client has said, using their vocabulary and without adding any opinions or interpretations of your own. It doesn't matter whether you agree or disagree. You end by asking:

> Have I got that right?

**20** COACHING FOR CAREERS

Asking this last question virtually always releases new information. The client has felt validated and now they are ready to go deeper. If you have got some vital aspect wrong, then the client can put you right. This apparently simple technique communicates acceptance and respect. If you want to add a different opinion, you can do it later, but by summarizing you are showing the client that they have been heard. When we feel heard, we are much readier to listen.

## The critical importance of language

The language you use is critical to creating that climate of trust. Keep to open questions which will begin *What. . .* or *How. . .* and avoid anything that begins with a verb such as *have, did, was, is, wasn't, isn't, could,* as this kind of question always contains a hidden instruction that comes from your agenda. *Have you asked your colleague? Would it be a good idea to try. . .? Do you ever. . .?* It is virtually always better to ask a version of the same question which starts with *what, who* or *how:*

> Who else needs to be consulted?
>
> What's your concern about this?
>
> What ideas do you have about solutions?
>
> How might you set about the first steps?

. . . with added words which ask for more information:

> Tell me more about that.

Avoid questions beginning *why*. They can come across as a reproach. A client once told me that after only one session he had fired a previous coach who overused this question, telling me that this man's opening question had been, 'Why did you delay for so long in finding a career coach?' The client said to me, 'I wanted to say *Because I had very good reasons which I am unlikely to divulge to you when you ask me such a rude question,* but of course I just gave some non-committal reply and decided there and then to end it at a single session – and did'.

Effective listening means noticing the rhythm of the client's language, noticing repeated words, noticing the words that name emotions, noticing the hesitations, the emphases, and distinguishing these from what is just noise. Never assume that you know what it means when the client uses a popular metaphor such as feeling they have a *dark cloud* hanging over them or that they are *working in a toxic culture*. Some metaphors are so powerful that they will jolt you by the way they convey the distress that the person has felt. Recently a client told me that he felt like 'an untethered balloon', a startling simile that perfectly conveyed the fragility and loss of control that he was experiencing. A colleague who had been deeply unhappy in her job for some time described her misery and isolation with this shocking simile, saying, 'It was like being the only Jew in a Nazi organization'. Listen for such metaphors and similes. They provide essential clues to the client's inner world. Enquire into the metaphor:

| | |
|---|---|
| Client | I get a horrible knot in my stomach when I think about networking. It frightens me. |
| Coach | You get a knot . . . tell me what that knot is like. |
| Client | It's like a nasty string of chewing gum that's got tangled up. I can't digest it, it makes me feel ill. |
| Coach | A nasty string of chewing gum, that's a vivid phrase. . . What would you like to do with that tangled nasty string of chewing gum? |
| Client | I'd like it to dissolve and go away. . . |
| Coach | Well let's see if we can get it to dissolve by looking in a bit more detail at what frightens you. |

## Managing strong emotion in the coaching room

For many of us, our identity is bound up in work. Work gives life meaning; it provides daily structure, an easy way to find friends and to feel that we belong; work absorbs a huge amount of our waking hours; getting paid is factual recognition of what other people believe we are worth – so it is no surprise that any threat to that identity can feel like a crisis and with crisis goes strong emotion. I have worked with clients where the whole of their first session was punctuated by tears and many where people struggled to contain their feelings of betrayal, shock, anxiety, disappointment, self-recrimination and rage.

It is likely that you will hear stories that astonish in the managerial clumsiness and brutality they have involved:

*Polly* is 23 and has a master's degree with distinction from the London School of Economics. Initially she felt lucky to have found an intern job with a political lobbying firm, even though the work was poorly paid. She describes

# 22 COACHING FOR CAREERS

daily humiliations at the hands of her boss who routinely shouts at her, refers to her in meetings as 'the girl' and sometimes makes sexually charged comments about her appearance. It has become unbearable to stay, even though she has no idea where to go next

*Odette* was stopped by a security guard as she entered the building. She was asked for her pass and told to wait in reception. The Chairman's PA came down, looking embarrassed and nervous, to tell her that unfortunately the Board had decided to terminate her contract as chief executive. She was to go home and await a phone call to discuss terms while her personal belongings would be boxed up and sent to her by taxi.

Sometimes there is no sudden shock, just a slow process of stress and attrition, for instance where a company makes its financial difficulties plain and then announces a tortuous selection–deselection process. This rarely feels anything but gruelling and unfair to participants, whether they are eventually confirmed in their jobs or designated for redundancy. The sense of personal rebuff can be overwhelming, for instance if someone has been temporarily promoted, the job is advertised and the sitting candidate does not get the job. Even in the many cases where the process is transparently fair and handled with sensitivity, the person on the 'losing' side can feel bruised and rejected.

## What to do

Ask what the client needs from you. The majority will say that they need to tell you their story. You are not a family member, not a friend, not a colleague and yours may be the one place where they can say what has happened without interruption, embarrassment or unwanted advice-giving. There is comfort for clients just in knowing that they have been heard. You and the client will need to judge where that fine line is between re-telling the story and re-awakening pointless anger. Feeling angry means being in a state of helplessness and although anger can give a degree of energy for change, it's not a state where sensible decisions can be made. The past has happened, it can't be revoked or made to disappear. Moving on is healthier.

Here are some coaching behaviours to avoid:

- Joining in: you cannot coach if you are as upset as the client
- Getting into an elaborate debate about the fairness or unfairness of what has happened and especially not starting a discussion about how the client contributed to their own misfortune: that might be useful later, but not in the heat of the client's strong feelings at that moment

SPECIAL SKILLS OF THE CAREER COACH **23**

- Talking about what happened to you that was similar: it's not about you and the client may think that you are trying to outdo them in a *who's-had-the-worst-experience* competition
- Offering well-meant clichés such as 'cheer up', 'everyone makes mistakes' as these imply that the client's feelings are not legitimate.

What works instead is to pay close attention, summarizing every now and then and offering comments like, 'That sounds really grim' or 'I'm so sorry you had to go through that' or 'Anyone would find that challenging'. Crying will stop if you just listen quietly with tissues to hand.

Your aim is to normalize the emotion and if it feels appropriate you might refer people to well-known models such as Elizabeth Kübler Ross's change curve where responses to difficult change can take the pattern of initial denial followed in turn by anger, 'bargaining', a feeling of depression or paralysis then acceptance. (If you are unfamiliar with this model there is a good description on Wikipedia https://en.wikipedia.org/wiki/Kubler-Ross_model.) Ask the client where they believe they are in this cycle. This might be especially useful if you notice the client returning obsessively to the specific circumstances of their crisis: the clumsy way they were given the bad news, feelings of 'if only', a wish for revenge or of avoiding taking the practical steps that would help restore their equanimity. Although you should remember that normally you only know one side of the story, you will probably want to acknowledge poor standards of behaviour on the part of the organization when it seems clear that this is indeed what has happened.

It may be especially important to keep up contact between sessions, using text and email, as people can feel bereft, especially if they have been forced into an abrupt separation from their former colleagues and workplace. I aim to keep up a steady flow of enquiries, suggestions for reading, offers to look at new versions of a CV and anything else that I believe might help the client to feel less alone. Enquire into symptoms: loss of appetite, self-medicating with alcohol or opioid drugs, sleeplessness and touchiness are all common. Coach around these disclosures in the usual way, especially by asking what the client has found to be helpful in the past, encouraging them to keep their social lives vibrant, to make sure they get some exercise and to consult their doctor if their symptoms seem persistent and intrusive.

In reflecting much later on how coaching had helped him in the exceptionally trying circumstances of losing his job, one client's comment to me on what had helped was this:

> 'You weren't dismayed by my dismay nor did you wave it away, but your whole response was to convey quiet optimism and hope. I clung to that even at the very point where it must have looked to you as if I would never get over my sense of hopelessness.'

## 24 COACHING FOR CAREERS

### *Kindness*

Everywhere you go at my local teaching hospital you will see a reminder of the Trust's four values: Safety, Kindness, Teamwork and Innovating. When I see one of these bold notices, it strikes me anew as at once unusual and wonderful because it includes kindness. Kindness! Of course there should be kindness in clinical care, but how often do we experience it rather than the brisk 'caring' of people who cannot disguise their busyness? I have certainly experienced kindness as a patient at this hospital: a comforting touch and reassuring words just before being given an anaesthetic; holding my hand when recovery from surgery seemed frustratingly slow; keeping the pharmacy open so that I could collect an urgently needed drug.

I now think of kindness as essential to coaching and sincerely hope that it is something that my own clients feel that they experience from me. It is different from, though closely allied to, empathy. An article in the *British Medical Journal* (2008) by Dr Eileen Palmer, the medical director of a hospice, describes the beautiful end-of-life care experienced by her father and then by her partner. She says it was 'an invisible, untaught web of kindness and generosity', commenting that in assessing professional performance in such stressful situations, the two questions that really matter are, 'Did I hear what matters most for this person right now?' and 'Was I kind?' In bringing questions to my own coaching supervisor, these are the two that are always uppermost in my mind.

## Giving information

Career coaching is not some special form of training with a class of one. If the client has any suspicion that this is what is in your mind, they will resist, sometimes by just abandoning their coaching programme even when it has already been paid for in full:

> *Roxanne* has submitted a video recording as part of her journey towards a coaching qualification. She is working as an associate of a large outplacement company and this is the client's third session. He arrives late with a perfunctory apology. No sooner has he sat down than Roxanne is standing commandingly at a flip chart waving her pen at the client then talking as she scribbles a list of 'Essential points about networking'. In effect she is giving a little lecture with a few pauses for 'questions' that the client ignores. As the session continues, the client edges his chair further and further away, begins some noisy rooting about in his bag and takes out his phone, openly reading from it while Roxanne appears not to notice. After 45 minutes, he abruptly stands up and says he has just had an urgent message and has to leave. Roxanne never sees this client again.

I was Roxanne's supervisor and in discussing this humiliating event, Roxanne revealed that the outplacement company insisted on their coaches following a set timetable. Session 3 had to be about networking and Roxanne, new to the company and anxious to impress, had prioritized her wish to be seen as a conscientious associate over the needs of her client. It was more than possible that this client already had all the information he needed about networking or else that he did need the information but was alienated and offended by the way she had offered it to him.

Over the 40 or so years that coaching has been around as a profession, a consensus has emerged about its essentially non-directive nature. All coach training includes teaching on the way that giving advice is counterproductive. You will never know the other person as well as they know themselves. It is impossible to know everything about their circumstances, no matter how open they are with you. Giving advice means that you pose as cleverer, wiser and more grounded than the other person. The human brain sees this as an attack. The amygdala, the brain's alarm system, sends the hormone cortisol to the prefrontal cortex, shutting down thinking. The client's energy goes into resistance, even if this is expressed with tremendous politeness or not actually expressed at all. As a beginner coach you learn to keep your own agenda out of the way and to manage your anxiety about being seen to do a good job. Coaching is about the client becoming more resourceful, more confident, better able to make prudent choices and clients do this by coming to their own conclusions, not by adopting yours. The client is the one who lives with their decisions, not you.

All of this applies to career coaching. The difference is that the more career coaching you do, the more you will acquire expertise in the subject matter, for instance, on creating a CV, getting through interviews successfully, dressing the part or working with recruitment consultants. This is different from and in addition to the expertise that you have in coaching itself. You have a duty of care to make this informational expertise available to clients. But how do you do it in a way that does not trigger resistance?

## Reframing 'advice' as 'information'

I reframe 'advice' as 'information'. This may seem like a semantic quibble but I believe it is more than that. The coach who gives advice says 'Do it my way'. The coach who gives information says, 'Here is something to consider, it's up to you how you use it.' Although you will indeed acquire expertise in career coaching, there are few definites. Who is to say that there is one best way to write a CV or to dress for an interview? There are far too many variables to offer that degree of certainty and for that reason alone your information needs to be offered as just an opinion that can and should be challenged.

**26**  COACHING FOR CAREERS

Make this explicit by labelling everything you do, starting by asking permission:

> There's some general guidance on how to tackle assessment centres – OK to describe it?

Then check on how much the client already knows.

> How much do you already know about this? I don't want to waste our time by telling you things where you already have all the information you need.

Never miss out this step as it will stop you embarrassing yourself by offering a client information on a subject where it is always possible that they know more than you do:

> *Olivia* is 17 and is getting some career coaching paid for by parents who are anxious for her to get a place at Oxford or Cambridge. Olivia's coach is a Cambridge graduate herself and prides herself on keeping up with the latest trends in university admission processes. Just in time she remembers to ask, 'What do you already know about Oxbridge entrance?' Olivia replies that her school runs regular workshops on the topic, she has been to open days at both universities and has already had extensive coaching on Oxbridge interviews from several of her teachers. Olivia's real concern is how to tell her parents that neither Oxford nor Cambridge feels right for her and that her heart is set on getting a place at Bristol.

Depending on the answer, you can then flex what you offer by asking follow-up questions about which aspect the client needs to concentrate on and what level of depth they need. We coaches can enjoy passing on what we know. We feel we are serving the client when we do it and often we are right: we are. But we can also be in danger of finding it all so thrilling that we don't know when to stop.

There are two ways to make the information more useful to the client. First, ask them how they would like to get the information:

> Would you like the headlines first or do you like to get information step by step?

Then, as you give the information in the style the client has requested, stop, with real pauses at regular intervals to check on what questions the client has.

Assume that they will have questions and possibly also objections because what you are telling them may not fit with their own experience or preconceptions. This is very different from the usual way that professionals give information to clients, where the information is typically offered in a fast, continuous stream with token pauses preceded by 'Any questions?' before plunging on again. Good questions here might be:

> How does this fit with what you already know/your own experience?
>
> How much sense does this make?
>
> What questions do you have so far?

Since the danger is usually of saying too much rather than too little, pay attention to how the client seems to be responding and say something like:

> There's a lot more I could say about this, but perhaps that's enough?

To make it clear that the final choice is the client's, I will often give several examples, told as mini-stories of how other clients have tackled similar problems. So rather than endorse one style of CV I will offer brief case studies of how different, carefully anonymized, clients made their choices of CV and will follow this up by emailing at least three sample CVs for the client to ponder.

### Disagreeing

There will be times when you have to disagree. At the most extreme, you may need to speak up straightforwardly when the client proposes something that you know to be factually inaccurate, against the law or that will put them or other people at risk. Make your point straightforwardly followed immediately by emphasizing the client's right to challenge you back.

*Glyn* has told his coach what he earns. A potential employer has asked for details of his current salary package as part of his CV. The coach notices that Glyn has added 10 per cent to his salary on the draft CV he shows her. Calmly she says, 'Glyn, this is different from the amount you told me.' 'Yes,' he says, 'I think I'm worth it, and it will help me negotiate a higher salary'. The coach is careful to keep her face friendly but serious while she tells Glyn that he risks losing any job he is offered because new employers routinely check salary with previous employers. 'Don't do it,' she says, adding, 'but of course it's your decision.'

## Giving feedback

Recently a former client recommended me to a colleague whom she judged needed career help. She inadvertently copied me on the original email, including the comment, 'If you work with her you'll find she's very direct!' The recipient did choose me and later I asked him how he had interpreted this statement. He smiled, saying, 'That you didn't do coaching bullshit and were probably exactly what I needed'.

Mmm. That was OK then, but it might not have been. Here is the issue. In 'ordinary' coaching you may be able to get around the question of giving feedback because the only kind you may need to offer is the mild sort routinely taught on coach training programmes. This is usually described as 'feedback in the here and now' and it means that you offer low-risk comment on the client's mood, posture and language, such as 'I notice you seem very animated when we talk about x and less so when we talk about y.' Even this can feel tricky at first because it goes beyond what is common in polite discourse.

Feedback in career coaching may need to be more robust and more frequent. That sounds fine in theory but in practice I know from my own work as a coach to senior executives and as a supervisor of other coaches that feedback is more often boasted about in the abstract than practised in reality. Coaches seem to be no different from everyone else in their reluctance to give properly structured feedback. In my supervision work with other coaches, we often explore what it is that has held the coach back from giving the client necessary and vital feedback on aspects of their behaviour that show up in the coaching and that are faithful if muted reflections of similar behaviour at work.

The reasons seem to be that we hesitate because we lack confidence in our own judgement – *perhaps I'm wrong, who am I to criticize or praise?* This may be an especial temptation when the client is senior and well-known: we can be overawed by their apparent eminence. Sometimes we are afraid of damaging the relationship by hurting them because they seem so vulnerable. Or we hesitate because what needs to be said is so very personal and we don't know how to do it. When this happens we back away or take refuge in convoluted statements in which some genuine feedback is so deeply buried that the client will miss it, or else we offer faint hints that are easily misinterpreted or ignored.

None of these is a good reason for opting out of giving feedback in career coaching and you will often have a duty to do it. It is highly likely that the client will expect you to give detailed feedback for instance on their CV/résumé, on their job-searching strategy and on how they prepare for interviews. You simply can't dodge it: if you do, you will be letting clients down.

Start by assessing your motive. The only acceptable motive is to benefit the client. If there is any smidgeon of feeling that you want to punish the client or emphasize your superiority then hold back. If it feels difficult to do, ask yourself what feels difficult. Often the assumed difficulty will be that you doubt that client's

SPECIAL SKILLS OF THE CAREER COACH **29**

capacity to deal with what you have to say, but this is in itself a patronizing assumption. How do you know? The client is free to accept, reject, get upset or angry just as you have the freedom to respond to how they respond.

## A safe and easy way to give feedback

Feedback is not the same as criticism. Feedback is given calmly for the benefit of the receiver, it is specific, does not contain generalizations, it is two-way and future focused. If you follow these six steps it is hard to go wrong:

1. Ask permission: *Is it OK to offer you some feedback?*
2. Look for what is working as well as for what is not working.
3. Describe what you have seen or heard, owning your own opinion, using phrases like *I noticed, I observed, I heard*, keeping judgement out of it. So say, 'I noticed you touched your face two or three times' rather than 'You looked unconfident because you were touching your face a lot'.
4. Describe the impact on you including a phrase like . . .*and I wondered. . . As I was watching and listening the impact on me was that I wondered if you had lost confidence for a moment in what you were saying and I got a bit distracted.*
5. Ask the client for their response: *How does that seem to you?*
6. Coach around whatever emerges remembering to ask, *So what might you need to do in future?*

### Positive feedback

Feedback is often discussed as if it is entirely about conveying critical messages. In reality it is just as useful, maybe more so, for underlining the positive, telling clients what is working. Using the feedback protocol distinguishes it from the faint praise or polite appreciation that often passes for 'feedback' in everyday life. These are phrases such as 'That was brilliant!' or 'You did fine!' By giving your comments a specific behavioural focus you are suggesting practical ways to develop by building on what is already successful. This is especially important when you are coaching clients around their interview technique (Chapter 8).

## Networking

Networking gets a bad press as a word. People associate it with being sycophantic and self-serving, with time-wasting or with getting drunk and over-eating at pointless meetings and conferences. Clients often need to reassess their views of it and to see it as positive and generous, a way of giving as much as of taking. As a coach you may need to do the same. I find that many of the coaches whom

**30** COACHING FOR CAREERS

I supervise do have a healthy network of other coaches, but may lack an up-to-date and reliable network of contacts with other professionals. This can matter because clients often need to be put into contact with people who have specialist expertise:

> *Stevie* arrived for her regular coaching session looking upset. 'Yesterday', says Stevie, 'I was told my job has to go. No warning. No reason other than the new owners of the business want to bring in their own people.' Stevie's coach abandons his plans for the session. After listening to Stevie's account of what has happened and asking her what has been proposed as a severance package, he says, 'Stevie, I think you need immediate legal advice. I get very good feedback on a particular lawyer specializing in employment issues.' The lawyer acts for Stevie and takes over all the negotiations with the employer, obtaining a 30 per cent increase in the monetary side of the package and a number of improvements in its other aspects including a deal that will give Stevie an extra six coaching sessions as well as paying for her legal fees.

Depending on your own interests and network you might be surprised by how often you can suggest a name to a client, explaining what this person does and how they can add value. I worked with a client whose career was being sabotaged by his severe phobia about dentistry. No dentist had seen his teeth for 30 years. They were crumbling so badly that he was ashamed to smile and had got into the habit of covering his mouth when he spoke. This became a crisis when his firm restructured and he had to apply for a different job in a different location where no one knew him. Coaching him around how to make a powerful bid for this job, I was able to suggest an excellent dentist, also a trained coach, who specialized in phobic patients. Bravely, and after much wobbling, the client did confront his fears, got new teeth, made an extraordinary leap in confidence – and got a new job.

When I make referral suggestions I make it clear that I have no business relationship with the people I recommend and for that reason often suggest more than one name. Where a client follows this up I always ask for feedback on how it has gone and modify my future recommendations accordingly. Here is a checklist of the type of expert whom I suggest you might find it useful to have in your address book, in order of importance in terms of the frequency with which you might need such a name.

## SPECIAL SKILLS OF THE CAREER COACH  **31**

| Other experts | Comments |
|---|---|
| Employment lawyer | A specialist in a bigger legal practice is more likely to have the expertise a client needs than a jobbing solicitor in a high-street firm |
| Financial advisor | It helps that this is a well-regulated sector, but check that the person you suggest is licensed |
| Recruitment or executive search consultant | This is a sector with many niche consultants (see Chapter 7) but you may know a generous individual who can offer guidance on how to find the right colleague even if this is in a competitor firm |
| Family lawyer | Unfortunately, career change often coincides with difficulties in personal relationships |
| Therapists | Names here might include family therapists, couple therapists and personal therapists |
| Presentation and voice skills | Most coaches can help with everyday problems in presentation skills but sometimes you might want to recommend a specialist where a client appears to have intractable problems that go beyond what you can do |
| Personal style | Style and colour advice is valued by clients, men and women alike, but make sure you recommend a person who gets consistently positive feedback as poor-quality advice is endemic in this field |
| Clinical professionals | Clients will already have a trusted general practitioner who can make referrals, but you may have useful additional contacts, for instance dentists, physiotherapists, osteopaths, psychiatrists, dermatologists and so on where a recommendation could be helpful |
| 'Creativity' coaches | People making major career shifts often want to explore neglected gifts such as writing, playing a musical instrument, photography or painting. Depending on your own interests you may be able to recommend a specialist coach here |
| Small business advisors | Most banks offer this service free, but the quality is variable. A small business coach might be a safer or additional choice |

**32** COACHING FOR CAREERS

| Other experts | Comments |
| --- | --- |
| Web developers | Clients setting up their own businesses will need a website. DIY software might be fine at the outset but such sites can look samey or just dull and an experienced professional is usually a better bet in the long term |
| De-cluttering advisors: house or wardrobe | Career change can trigger a wish to clear away clutter, physical as well as psychological |
| Well-being coaches: diet and nutrition, exercise, stress | Most clients will be able to find their own helpers here but you may know of someone with unusually successful approaches whom it is worth recommending |

See the skills I describe in this chapter as work-in-progress. For my own part it is a never-ending project. Should I ever get to the stage where I consider it finished, then it will be time to exit the scene.

# 3 Preparing

When I began as a coach nearly three decades ago, there was little competition. Those few of us in the market had a different problem – explaining what coaching was, and even more pressingly, what it was not: not therapy, not training, not consultancy, not mentoring. There was no training or supervision; we had to pick up whatever scraps of guidance we could wherever we could find them. Today there are tens of thousands of coaches and it has become a popular next career choice for people leaving conventional employment. There are so many training courses that it has become hard to distinguish the excellent from the charlatans. Corporate clients have responded by insisting on nationally and internationally recognized qualifications as an entry barrier and what they demand is rising all the time in terms of individual accreditation, supervision and hours or years of experience.

This puts a premium on investing in training, holding a recognized coaching qualification, getting regular supervision from a more experienced coach and continuing to attend professional development workshops. Where career coaching is concerned it is essential to keep your knowledge of the employment market up to date. What comments are clients getting on the CVs they have prepared with you? Is your advice about how to behave in a job interview proving valuable? Are there signs that psychometric questionnaires are being used more by recruiters and if so which ones, or that more organizations are running assessment centres and if so, what is their content? What about social media – are they becoming less important or more important in the recruitment process? Do you see trends in how clients talk about agencies and head-hunters? These fragments of feedback on your work and on market intelligence help guard against being innocently unaware that you are slipping slowly out of date.

**Your product**

The more competitive the world of coaching becomes, the more narrowly you may need to aim and the more carefully you need to define your market and do what is known as 'market segmenting'. The segments could define clients by any of these criteria: age; seniority; gender; sector; geographical area; profession; type of problem. Some ways of referring to market segments pass into popular speech, for instance Babyboomers, Gen X, Gen Y and Millennials are market segments defined by age.

**34** COACHING FOR CAREERS

You could have several different types of client who might each need something slightly different. You may be offering coaching alongside other kinds of allied work such as consulting, recruitment, facilitation and training. Or career coaching as one product may be combined with coaching people on their first hundred days in a new job or on handling stress, but the segments need to add up to a sensible business proposition where you are the unifying factor. How you do this will depend on where you believe you are credible because credibility matters to clients: have you worked in their world? Do you understand what it is like to be in their jobs? Have you already worked with people like them? What is it that is unique about you when compared with the competitor coaches that your clients might be considering? What deep knowledge do you have on specific topics? What gives you the edge?

### Your website

Virtually all clients will check out the recommendation from friends and colleagues by searching for you on the internet. They will expect to see you on social media, they will expect you to have a website and what they find will shape their view of you.

So many coaches have websites that make the mistake of talking in waffly, high-flown coaching jargon. They describe 'techniques', they boast about the coach's qualifications. None of this interests individual clients. Whereas the corporate buyer needs to know that you have had training in order to be reassured that you are not just a well-meaning and inexperienced amateur, I have never once been asked by an individual client whether I am 'qualified'. They don't care where you got your coaching qualification or whether you hold licences in psychometric questionnaires or about the PhD it took you such a long time to complete. When you put the emphasis on qualifications and techniques in your website copy you are acting like a seller not like a buyer; you believe that what you are selling is 'coaching' whereas what you are actually selling is the answer to a need. Commercial success is always about seeing the world from the buyer's perspective so it will make sense for your website to reflect what you know about how clients describe their problems:

> How do I get through this job interview when nervousness has got the better of me in previous interviews?
>
> I'm stuck in a job I hate but I've been in it for ages and I think this will put off a new employer. How do I get past this?
>
> I've lost my job. I didn't expect it, I didn't deserve this to happen to me and I've got no idea what to do.
>
> I've been repeatedly turned down for promotion even though I get very positive appraisals. What am I getting wrong?

Keep the website simple. Four pages is plenty at first: a home page that sets out your essential proposition and your own background, then a page each for services, client list (ideally with testimonials from named people) and contact details with an email link. Later you can add a blog or links to interesting articles and other resources.

## Pricing and price resistance

How do you set fees? Look first at what competitors are charging by asking corporate HR people what they are paying for coaching, asking other coaches what their fee range is and how they charge in different markets. Most fellow coaches will give this information readily. You should note that there is no such thing as a 'going rate' in coaching; it varies enormously depending on geographical area, sector, the experience and reputation of the coach and the seniority of the client. You may want to consider whether you charge by the hour and session or for a whole programme. In my own case I usually quote an upfront price for the whole coaching programme because I include unfettered email and phone access between sessions and because I believe that career coaching is best seen as a seamless process that unfolds as it goes on rather than as a series of potentially disconnected one-off sessions. The programme itself may vary from two to seven sessions or more, depending on the initial discussion.

### Price resistance

*Andrew* is nearing his 60th birthday and feels that he is too young to retire in the traditional sense, but no longer wants to continue his full-time work as a podiatrist. 'The work is physically and emotionally tiring', he says, 'and I think I need a total re-evaluation of my life, possibly a complete change of career.' Andrew approaches a coach recommended by a friend. The coach listens to what Andrew describes and says that usually this would take minimally a six-session programme and quotes her fee. Andrew whistles in amazement. 'I never thought it would be that expensive,' he says. 'Not sure I can afford it'.

I have known many coaches who get themselves into a tangle when this happens. Some see the sale slipping away and start to argue, defending their own prices. This may seem undignified to the client and will usually just increase their resistance. It is far better to agree that the fee might seem like a lot of money especially

**36** COACHING FOR CAREERS

if it has to be paid by an individual out of taxed income, and even more especially if you have to add VAT or whatever the sales tax is in your country. My own practice is that if the proposed fee proves to be too much, I can suggest a coach whose work is known to me and who charges less than I do. I follow this up with an email giving that coach's details but leaving the door open for the client to return to me if they wish.

Some potential clients for career coaching assume that they will have to pay for their coaching programme themselves. They have never tested this assumption by asking their boss if the company will pay. An enlightened organization understands that even if the expected outcome of the coaching is that the person leaves, it is still good practice to offer to fund it. The reason is that a restless employee is unlikely to be doing their best work and it is in everyone's interest that they should make a smooth transition to a different role.

Some coaches are not confident enough of their own expertise, they undervalue it and are too ready to compromise, for instance by offering to do just three sessions even though they know that double that number is what is really needed and are uneasily aware that this will mean that the work is likely to feel incomplete and unsatisfying. Others feel sorry for the client and offer an enormous discount. Think carefully before you offer a discount. Questions to ask yourself might be:

> Do I want to get the experience of working with this client because it will develop and stretch me?
>
> Will it add kudos to my brand to be able to say that I work with this client?
>
> Will it compromise the quality of the work if there are fewer sessions than instinct tells me that the client needs?
>
> How likely am I to feel exploited and resentful because I am working below my normal fee level?
>
> Do I have spare capacity where getting some work, even at a low rate, is better than getting none?
>
> Will it damage my brand if I am too cheap?

Many coaches fail to realize that they can be rejected because they are too cheap. In my early days as a coach I sometimes lost work by being too timid to quote a reasonable fee. People on big salaries can actually like the idea of paying a premium rate for their coaching: it matches their view of themselves as worthy of their own generous financial rewards.

Clients who themselves charge hourly fees will expect a similar rate per hour to their own. Anything that falls too far below that may suggest that your work is inferior.

This is another good reason for being clear about your target market. If you need to earn a decent living from coaching, you will make this unlikely if you are

PREPARING **37**

aiming your efforts exclusively at people on modest incomes. However, I have learnt to be cautious about making assumptions here: someone you think is affluent may turn out to be struggling financially, whereas someone you assume to be hard up may be well able to afford your fees. I had offered a heavily discounted fee to a client who had described herself as a 'housewife'. In our first session she told me about her wealthy husband and her pride at living in a road famous for having some of the most expensive houses in the UK.

Expect to get some confusing initial answers to all these questions: a period of trial and error is inevitable but in the longer term it will provide valuable learning because, hard though it can be to accept, the market decides and we all have to listen to what it thinks of us. Note: my book *Building a Coaching Business: Ten Steps to Success* (2017) deals with all aspects of setting up and running a coaching business, including how you establish your business brand plus the daunting but eminently resolvable question of how you find new clients.

## The 'chemistry' conversation

A potential client has made contact. The coaching relationship begins from this moment. Usually it will start with a discussion about whether or not you want to work together. This is not just a formality.

Coaching is an overcrowded profession so the 'look-see' or 'chemistry' conversation has become standard practice. If you see this process as some kind of audition you are putting yourself at a disadvantage from the start. The true purpose of the conversation is matching. The point is that it is a two-way process: you are choosing the client every bit as much as they are choosing you. Is this your kind of client? Do you have the expertise that they need? If you are known to be in demand or to work with apparently impressive and senior people, the conversation may seem much more as if the client is a petitioner humbly begging to work with you. If you are relatively new to coaching, the client may feel that they have the upper hand.

### Fear of selling

Many coaches have a fear of selling. They see it as manipulative, tacky and embarrassing. They dread looking desperate or greedy. It feels unfamiliar and uncomfortable. The solution is to reframe your view of the process. You will always be talking to someone who is, in sales jargon, a 'warm lead', that is someone who has already declared themselves interested. You will never be forcing anyone to buy. You will be working with integrity and from coaching principles, one of which is that people are resourceful and are able to make sound choices. You will be respectful because your aim is to meet a need. You will be willing to decline the engagement if anything about it does not feel morally right and

**38** COACHING FOR CAREERS

to live with your disappointment if a client whom you liked has decided not to work with you.

In the conversation itself, your role is to be its facilitator just as you facilitate the process in the coaching itself. You are helping the client to uncover what it is that they really need. You have had this kind of discussion many times before, the client has not. If you leave it to the client to manage the conversation you will probably find yourself either having a hazy chat about coaching in general, trying to do some sample coaching or else being unhelpfully pushed into 'selling' mode far too soon.

Start by double-checking that the client is still expecting to talk for the time you have agreed and by restating the purpose of the conversation: to assess match. Its first part should take 15 to 20 minutes. Your role is to ask the questions, to listen, to summarize and to explore. What does this client need?

> What's triggered the decision to look for career coaching?
>
> How far have you got in your own thinking about your next steps?
>
> What degree of urgency is there for you?
>
> What's your own sense of the areas where you specifically need help?
>
> Have you had a coach or mentor in the past? If so, what worked or didn't work in that relationship?
>
> What are you looking for in choosing a coach?

Your aim is to establish need and then what the client's criteria for buying actually are and only then, in the second part of the conversation, to shape what you say to fit those criteria, including how you work, what you charge, where you typically meet clients and how many sessions you estimate that the client needs to have. When this goes well, you and the client are quickly consulting your calendars and agreeing the date and time for your first session. If the client has doubts, or genuinely has other coaches on a shortlist, they may say, 'I'll get back to you', though note, if they do not choose you, this may turn out to be an empty promise.

## Reasons to say no

Part of the purpose of the conversation is to alert you to reasons to say no. For instance, the client may be a young graduate whose parents have contacted you. They are willing, indeed eager, to pay for the coaching. When you talk to the actual potential client you may sense a lot less urgency about career issues on their part. This was how one coach gave me a summary of the kind of conversation that can so easily happen:

| | |
|---|---|
| Coach | Your Mum and Dad are concerned about you and your career and they've suggested that career coaching might help. |
| Young grad | Yeah, they're always worried one way or another that's what parents do isn't it! I'm living at home again – it's cool man! No more exams! |
| Coach | But are YOU worried? |
| Young grad | Nah! Not really – I'm picking up bar work and that pays for my own drinks. Got plenty of time to think about proper jobs. I'm only 22. |
| Coach | OK, well I think I'd better report back to your parents that now may not be the best time. |
| Young grad | I'd be willing to give it a go. . . |
| Coach | Mmm. It's more than just giving it a go so let's leave it at that for the time being. |

Any scenario where someone else wants the client to have coaching should be approached with caution. Most will turn out to be benign; the person who makes the approach is acting as a well-informed go-between. But sometimes this is not the case:

*Adnam* is approached by the HR director in a retail bank about coaching a manager who is one of several candidates for a job. Something in this conversation alerts Adnam to the notion that all is not what it seems. A little probing soon reveals that Adnam's potential client has a long record of problematical behaviour and is most unlikely to be successful in the interview, after which this person will be made redundant. If he says yes, Adnam will be engaging in a process that he knows to be morally wrong. His own reputation, unfairly of course, will suffer because 'his' client will not get the job, however excellent the coaching. Adnam says politely that he cannot take the assignment but offers to work with the client later if indeed he is made redundant. He never hears again from the HR director. On reflection, Adnam feels relieved. He does not want to work with a company that is behaving in such a duplicitous way with its staff.

**40** COACHING FOR CAREERS

In a turbulent economy, firms go bust, merge, get acquired, relocate and shed jobs. The HR department may suggest coaching for the more senior people destined to lose their jobs. Most people in this situation are shocked, even when they have seen it coming, but they quickly realize the value of having a coach who can offer immediate perspective and help. Some are too bewildered and upset to engage, it's too soon, they are just not ready. When the conversation reveals that this is the case, suggest that you and the client schedule a date to talk again in a few days when they may be clearer and calmer about what they need, letting your HR contact know that this is how you have left it.

Just occasionally you may encounter a client where the chemistry conversation reveals someone with an inability to take responsibility for themselves and for their careers. Such clients are in a dark place where their bitterness and disappointment are overwhelming. Sometimes you may suspect that they also have mental health problems. What may happen is that in the chemistry conversation the client repeatedly expresses high levels of fury, distress or helplessness that seem out of proportion to the situation, often aimed at an employer who has allegedly betrayed promises, for instance of a promotion or of a continuing career. If this really is the case then the outlook for any coaching is poor. They need a different kind of help.

Occasionally there may be clients who are looking for you to behave like the careers teachers they believe they remember from school where the teacher did all the thinking and apparently had magical powers of diagnosis. These clients may have a work history that seems disjointed and unsatisfying. They often describe themselves as miserable and disoriented. You may or may not feel that you can work with clients like these but you need to explore their expectations carefully and to challenge any lack of realism when you believe that this is what you are meeting. Explain that it is not your role to pronounce on career direction nor to suggest specific jobs because you could never know the client as well as the client knows themselves. It's not about job-matching, given the enormous range of jobs available. Where the client expresses overt dismay that this is not your model of career coaching, assuming for the moment that it is not, this should trigger a further round of discussion where the topic is how your own version of career coaching works and how willing the potential client is to engage in it.

One further reason to decline a career coaching engagement is that the budget is too small for the work that you believe to be necessary but the potential client tells you that there is no room for negotiation and you can see no reason to offer a discount. This may be equally the case when the organization is footing the bill or when individuals are paying for themselves.

Between the initial conversation and your first session, suggest that the client sends you anything that they think it will be helpful for you to see. Many people have taken a variety of psychometric questionnaires during their careers. If they can access them, ask the client to scan or forward the results. A CV is always useful because it shows you how the client sees themselves as well as giving you an account of their career so far. Some people may have survey feedback from colleagues as well as appraisal data. It all adds to the unfolding picture of the client.

You may also want to send the client your own questionnaires or forms to fill in, including some of the typical 'exercises' that you plan to use in the first session – the subject of the next chapter.

# 4 Getting started: the first session

The first session is the foundation of everything that follows. You will be getting to know each other and your job is to accelerate the process of creating trust, encouraging the client to be as open as possible. You will be clarifying the client's overall goals for the coaching programme, deepening what you heard in the chemistry conversation while being aware that goals will frequently change shape during the time you are working together. You will be contracting about how you work. You will be asking the client to assess what they feel their current state is, not just at work but in their personal lives too because no one ever makes a career decision in a vacuum. There is a lot to do, and even if you normally work in 60- or 90-minute blocks, I recommend making this first session 2 hours if at all possible. How to do it is what this chapter is about.

## The welcome

One of the most striking differences between coaching and its close cousin disciplines is its far greater emphasis on the kind of personal connection that signals, *we are equals in this conversation.* I have never yet given a coaching session that has failed to start with some social chit chat and the offer of refreshment. It makes such a difference to start with warmth, to enquire about the client's journey, to hang their coat up carefully, to take them to where you will be working, to point out where the bathroom is and to offer tea, coffee or water. I am aware when I offer these simple comforts that I am drawing helpfully on the well-understood rituals of host and guest. It is easy to overlook how important this is: some clients may be apprehensive, for instance wrestling with how candid to be with you or worrying about how far what is about to happen may feel embarrassing.

You will have heard in the chemistry conversation about the client's immediate reasons for seeking career coaching but it will make sense to ask:

> What else has happened since we spoke (or met)?
>
> What further thoughts have occurred to you?

The more the client described a crisis in that conversation the more important it can be to ask these questions and the more likely it is that there will have been developments that could change the shape of the session. For instance, a client who has been made redundant might have a date planned with the lawyer who will represent their interests with the employer and wants to run through with you what it will be vital to say.

Touch on the overall goals you will have heard in the chemistry conversation, reassuring the client that the point of this first session is to expand and refine the goals and that you will return to this as part of the wrap-up process in the final 15 minutes. Tell the client that this session may not feel like 'coaching' because its purpose is to understand the present scenario and that you will impose more obvious control over it through your own questioning and 'exercises' than they are likely to experience later on in the coaching programme.

## Contracting

You do need to do some contracting in this first session though in effect you will be re-contracting continually through the entire programme, responding adaptably to the client's needs, stated and unstated. This opening round need not be laborious and it need take no more than ten minutes. The words you speak will be less important than the client's actual experience of whether what you claim matches what you do. All contracting should be an evenly balanced and flexible two-way conversation, not a set of pronouncements from the coach.

If you did not ask in the chemistry conversation whether the client has had a coach before, now is the time to do so. The purpose of the question is to learn what worked for the client and what didn't and how far this matches your own beliefs and practice. Many people have had previous experiences of coaching, therapy or mentoring and it is always instructive to explore how this went and what the client liked or disliked:

> A bit too much focus on 'how did that make you feel?' OK as far as it went but there's more to life than just emotion.

> I really liked her – she was generous with her experience and often went the extra mile by sending me handouts and so on after the sessions.

> A tad mechanical – it was just about behaviour change and it got a bit superficial after a bit.

Having had these replies, explore how this might affect how you work together and don't be afraid to challenge or discuss if the client seems to be asking for something that you know you cannot supply. Most clients take confidentiality for granted but it still matters to say that what is said in the room stays in the room. This may trigger a discussion about ethics, for instance if the client already

**44** COACHING FOR CAREERS

knows that they want to leave their job but believes that the organization wants to keep them:

> *Marissa* has told her organization that her request for coaching is part of 'a personal development plan'. What she has not said is that this plan involves exiting the organization. She has chosen her coach specifically because she sees from the coach's website that he specializes in career issues. She expresses some disquiet about this apparent 'deception'. Marissa's coach comments calmly that how or if to raise her wish to leave should become part of their joint agenda but that a healthy organization encourages people to move on when it is the right time so he does not see any moral problem. He adds that the wish to change jobs is usually clearer to colleagues than many clients believe and that a plan to leave is unlikely to be a surprise to anyone who knows Marissa well.

Make the usual statements about what the limits of confidentiality are. Normally such limits will be about the danger of harm to self or others. My own clients typically brush this caveat away. In nearly 30 years of practice with many hundreds of clients I have only ever had to act on this warning twice, so the duty to say it is probably more about the coach's need for self-protection than anything the client might need to hear.

Briefly revisit your agreement about the number of sessions you will have, sketching out how you think the content of the coaching might unfold, based on what you know so far about what the client has said they need. Touch on the length of the sessions and how you will invoice, ending this phase of the session with the question, 'Anything else that you think we should discuss?'

## Assessing the present

How does the client feel about their present or most recent job? This is more than just a routine question. The answers will contain clues about what motivates them, their personality and what they need from the future. Does this client spring out of bed on a Monday morning joyously anticipating the week ahead or do they wish they could have a Duvet Day, avoiding what has become an unpleasant environment?

One way to do this is to send the client a questionnaire in advance. This has the plus of starting the client thinking and can give helpful structure to the conversation in the session itself. This one is loosely based on the kind of survey that is commonly used in employee engagement questionnaires.

| How far do you agree with these statements? | 1 = not at all, 5 = fully | | | | |
|---|---|---|---|---|---|
| | 1 | 2 | 3 | 4 | 5 |
| I respect the organization | | | | | |
| I use all my skills | | | | | |
| I have a positive relationship with my boss | | | | | |
| My work matters | | | | | |
| I have a high level of freedom in my work | | | | | |
| I have at least one colleague who is a friend | | | | | |
| I get frequent feedback on my work | | | | | |
| My ideas are taken seriously | | | | | |
| I feel I am developing and growing as a human being | | | | | |
| The organization keeps me fully informed on its plans | | | | | |

Ask the client to talk you through how they have responded. Usually the discussion will highlight what is important to the client either because it is missing in their present role or because it is something that is working well and that they prize. You may also like to ask the client to rank these factors in order of their priority for them.

If you prefer to avoid forms and set structures, you can just ask a free-form question in the session itself. Say something like:

> Talk me through how you feel about your present job. Let's start with the pluses.

When a client is deeply unhappy with their current role they may struggle to find anything positive in their reply. If so, ask if it has always been miserable, as often it has not, and ask them to say what the job felt like when it still seemed like a reasonably good fit. Then do the same for the minuses:

> What are the downsides?

**46** COACHING FOR CAREERS

Expect a wide range of replies to both questions:

> This is my dream job. I love it; I never expect to find anything ever again that fits me so well. I can't believe I've been told I'm redundant – and it's all been so brutal.

> It was a mistake ever to take this job. I only did it because I was on the rebound from failing to get the promotion I wanted and I left my previous job in a huff. I hate every minute I'm at work.

> Everything would be fine if it weren't for my boss. She's the boss from hell: dictatorial, rude, demanding. I spend my day trying unsuccessfully to avoid her. I have no freedom, she's looking over my shoulder all the time.

Changing jobs by leaving an organization is an upheaval and is rarely without at least some negative consequences. It is always worth checking whether it might be possible to improve job satisfaction by seeking an internal promotion or by just changing the design of the current job. Check, too, whether the downsides might be a temporary blip or whether it is likely that some of its unpleasant features could change, for instance that a despised boss might move on quickly. Ideally in any job move the push and pull factors are in equilibrium. If there is more push than pull, that is, the client is frantic to run away from their current role because they are finding it unendurable, then they are at risk of making a poor choice where a new job is concerned or even of following the risky strategy of resigning before they have found something else.

As a follow-up either to the questionnaire or to the pluses and minuses conversation, ask,

> What would need to happen to persuade you to stay where you are?

## The question of 'fit'

Another way of looking at the present is to ask what level of fit there is between the client's enthusiasms, their skills and what the organization needs. Ideally these need to lie snugly together (see Figure 4.1).

Where we lose our enthusiasm for a job because it has become mundane or because our interests are zooming off in a different direction, we may still have the skills that the organization wants but we feel increasingly disaffected (see Figure 4.2).

> *Liz* has an apparently 'glamorous' job on a women's magazine. She respects her boss, files her copy on time, writes vividly and is popular with colleagues. But she describes herself as 'bored silly' with writing about fashion and

GETTING STARTED: THE FIRST SESSION  47

> beauty. 'It's all so trivial, it's too dependent on advertisers and their whims; I can do it in my sleep and sometimes I think I do. I just have to make a move otherwise I'll still be writing about lipstick ten years from now.'

A third possible scenario is the one where what the organization needs and what the client can offer have moved apart. This can sometimes be the case where people have been made redundant. Their skills used to be exactly what the organization needed, but this is no longer the case (see Figure 4.3).

**Figure 4.1** Fit with organization needs

**Figure 4.2** The client has lost enthusiasm

**Figure 4.3** The client's skills no longer fit

> *Elmer* has worked in admin roles throughout his career. He is diligent, loyal and meticulous. Unfortunately he feels increasingly daunted by the new computer programs he has been required to use. Training courses have left him feeling even more anxious and the gap between what the company needs and what he can offer is widening. In yet another round of cost-cutting Elmer's post is likely to be on the list for redundancy.

You might ask the client how they would draw their own diagram using this model.

## The decision environment

It would be a rare person indeed who ever makes a career decision without taking every other aspect of their life into account. A client whose health is fragile may not wish to move if it would mean that they would have to start again with a new set of doctors and may also have limited energy for the sort of job searching that involves exhausting travel. Someone whose marriage is disintegrating may be reluctant to make another major life change at the same time. People whose children are well settled in a carefully chosen school may be reluctant to budge beyond some rather small geographical radius. Elderly parents may need daily visits that cannot be delegated to anyone else. A client with substantial savings may be willing to take risks and may face redundancy with more equanimity than a client with few financial resources. Disclosing this information has another advantage: it helps create rapport because you will get a far more rounded picture of the client.

### Choosing 'exercises'

There will only be time to use one 'exercise' on this topic in the opening session. Choose whichever you feel will best suit the client, based on what you already know about them.

## GETTING STARTED: THE FIRST SESSION    49

The best-known exercise here is the venerable Balance Wheel, sometimes called the Wheel of Life or the Life Scan Wheel: an eight-wedge pie chart where you are invited to declare your satisfaction on a 1–10 scale with your work, physical environment, health, wealth, friends and family, partner, personal development and leisure. I will not reproduce it here. You can readily find free downloads through your browser, for instance https://www.thecoachingtoolscompany.com/products/wheel-of-life-coaching-tool.

### Emotional needs: how far are they being met?

There are many frameworks suggesting what our core needs are as human beings. They include Abraham Maslow's 'Hierarchy of needs' with basic survival at the bottom and self-actualization at the top. There is a good account of this influential theory and how it has changed over time at https://en.wikipedia.org/wiki/Maslow%27s_hierarchy_of_needs. Then there is Ryan and Deci's (2000) analysis suggesting Autonomy, Competence and Emotional Connection as our fundamental needs. The developer of the FIRO-B questionnaire, Will Schutz (1958), came to similar conclusions, calling his own definitions Inclusion (belonging) Control (power) and Affection (love). This simple grid incorporates several of these ideas in one place:

Human beings have emotional needs that must be met. How satisfied are you with your current life in relation to these needs? Choose red for highly dissatisfied, amber for so-so and green for very satisfied.

|  | Red | Amber | Green |
|---|---|---|---|
| Autonomy and control |  |  |  |
| Fun |  |  |  |
| Loving and being loved |  |  |  |
| Friends |  |  |  |
| Connection to your community |  |  |  |
| Safety and security |  |  |  |
| Direction, meaning and purpose in your life |  |  |  |
| Competence: using all of your skills |  |  |  |
| Status, feeling recognized and rewarded |  |  |  |

## 50 COACHING FOR CAREERS

- Which are the strong areas?
- Which are the weaker ones?
- Which might need immediate attention?
- What are the implications for your career and life?

Jo, an actor client complaining of 'lack of direction' completed this grid and pronounced herself woefully lacking in the areas of community, competence and meaning. Her TV, stage and film work, never plentiful, had dried up and she was half-heartedly working with a group of actor friends on a 'drama for schools' project. I asked her how many fellow-actors she knew who were making a good full-time living from stage and TV work. The answer was 'hardly any' and the few she did know were working for relatively small salaries on what she called 'Mousetrap jobs' – a reference to the long running Agatha Christie play that makes no pretence of being anything but cheerfully run-of-the-mill entertainment. Jo came to see that her drama work with schoolchildren had more than the seeds of everything she needed but it had to be treated more seriously with more commitment, energy and skill. Eventually she took over the artistic direction of this little troupe, turning it into a modestly successful commercial operation with deeply satisfying work, taking plays to schools in areas of social deprivation where children had never previously experienced live performance.

## The backstory

We all acquire attitudes in childhood and these shape our behaviour. We can be totally unaware of how profoundly we have been affected by what we hear, see and experience as children when we are not mature enough to assess or evaluate what the adults around us are doing and how their opinions of us influence our view of ourselves. I have come to see how essential it is to hear at the very least the headlines here. Did the client experience unconditional love from both parents? What challenges did they or their family face? How were these challenges met? If there was adversity and deprivation what form did it take and how did the client cope? What part did education play? Was this client the first to go to university in their family? In listening to the answers you will hear how the adult emerged and how their assumptions were created, for instance about the value and purpose of education and of working hard, their aspirations, their attitudes to conflict, their levels of self-esteem and their ability to create healthy relationships. Even

GETTING STARTED: THE FIRST SESSION **51**

though coaching does not generally seek answers to the question, 'why do I behave like this?' it is still useful to understand what the possible answers might be and it becomes clear to the client that you are prepared to enter such personal territory without fleeing in fright.

> *Oliver* is dismayed by the failure of his many attempts to find a better job. Meagre scraps of feedback from interviews suggest that he lacks personal impact. As a client I notice that he constantly adds self-deprecating comments whenever he describes his skills or achievements along with avoiding eye contact. Enquiring into his childhood reveals a prosperous family but a father so involved in his work that he was rarely home and a mother who, as he says, 'was a bit remote and didn't do affection'. He was sent to boarding school at 8 years old. As a little boy, Oliver learnt to protect himself from hurt and from the feeling that he was not loveable by adopting an over-modest demeanour, visibly shrinking when asked to do anything that looked like self-promotion. Exploring this in our first session was the beginning of learning how to project the hidden more confident and more effective person.

Ask, too, about the family employment history. What attitudes did the client hear about work? What jobs did parents, grandparents and great-grandparents do? In some professions there is a dynastic approach to career choice. For instance, doctors, lawyers and architects are many times more likely than other professions to have a family member who is or was in the same profession. The positive side of this approach to work is that the child grows up knowing what the job is really like. The negative side is the possibility of covert or overt pressure to follow a path for which the individual is wholly unsuited. Where a client describes many exam re-sits, constant worrying about whether they are good enough and uncertainty about their next career step in the profession, it is worth asking how their decision to enter it at all was made.

## How to introduce it

Say something like, 'I'm interested to hear about your early life. We're not doing psychotherapy here, but attitudes and beliefs that we develop in childhood have a way of persisting into adult life'. Don't say, 'Tell me a bit about yourself' or 'Tell me your life story'. These questions are too vague and most people will not know how to answer. Ask about the kind of environment the client's parents created, exploring what kind of attachment they created: warm and accepting at one end of the

## 52 COACHING FOR CAREERS

spectrum or coercive, cold and critical at the other? Which parent were they closer to? What values and beliefs about work did the client's parents describe and demonstrate? How far did gender play a part? How far was academic achievement valued? Did the client grow up with some kind of label attached to them, for instance in relation to siblings – 'You're the clever one, she's the pretty one?'

I find that it is always essential to look at what sayings, mantras and mottos the client's family espoused. Most of us are utterly unaware of the deep influence these sayings have and of how they shape attitudes and expectations, many of them negative: *mustn't grumble; life's not fair; who'd be interested in you; can't be helped; always do your best; if you want something doing, do it yourself; stand on your own two feet because no one else will do it for you; the world doesn't owe you a living; don't make trouble; it's not worth educating girls. . .*

This discussion will virtually always produce material that is directly relevant to the coaching:

As a naïve 16-year-old, *Josie* was told this by a tactless careers teacher: 'Unlike your brother you're not bright enough to go to university, but you'd make a good secretary'. Josie left school, did a secretarial training and got a job at the BBC. Through hard work and the good luck of having a boss who could see past stereotypes, she won a place on a production training course and became a respected radio producer. Now she is applying for promotion to a managerial job. Josie breaks down as she tells the coach her story, remembering that teenage girl. Her brother was 'the clever one', his career mattered because he was a boy, while she, Josie, was 'the practical one' and was expected to get married young and then to drop out of employment. 'I've always felt I wasn't good enough'. Not feeling good enough is one sure way to guarantee failure in the promotion process. Josie and her coach devote a whole session later in her coaching programme to starting the process of demolishing this belief, including looking at its more malign effects in her everyday life, such as her hesitant speech and the downward inflection of her sentences that it could be disastrous to display in a job interview.

*Bradley* knew from an early age that he was gay but as the child of fundamentalist Christian parents he decided that he had to keep his sexuality a secret even from close friends. He cultivated what he called 'a dull dog personality' at work and in his private life. In his late 20s he met the man who was to become his lifetime partner and came out, though not to his parents, and the 'dull dog' habit persisted. At work, he has got stuck at a far more junior level than his many gifts would suggest. The organization is now being wound up and Bradley has to look for another job. He says, 'I'm fed up with myself and frustrated. I've hidden the real me for so long, I really don't know who I am or what I have to offer'. This alerts Bradley's coach to the likelihood of needing to work more than usually hard at discovering the unique person underneath the layers of carefully cultivated greyness.

## What if. . .?

Some coaches worry that clients may baulk at talking about childhood but you will probably find that this concern proves groundless. It may say more about the coach than about the client. The coach dreads the client protesting on the grounds that talking about childhood is dangerously near to psychotherapeutic territory or that it might prove difficult to deal with a harrowing story. You will indeed hear some harrowing stories and it will help to know how to understand them, for instance through the lens of *attachment theory*. (There is a simple explanation of this on Wikipedia, https://en.wikipedia.org/wiki/Attachment_theory.) In her book *Where Did You Learn to Behave Like That?* Sarah Hill suggests that coaches should devote ample time to drawing out the client's story, claiming that in childhood, one way or another, we all experience what she calls *imperfect love*. Startling as this idea is at first, I have come to believe that she is right, even if the imperfections are minor. You might also want to get some training on the impact of childhood trauma, defined as any long-lasting negative experience, such as inadequate parenting, that permanently affects mind and body. There is no room to explore these ideas in this book but you could go to the website that my colleague Julia Vaughan Smith and I have developed, www.coachingandtrauma.com for some initial briefing and explanations. Vivian Broughton's book (2017) *Becoming Your True Self* is a useful introductory guide and Julia's book *Coaching and Trauma: Moving Beyond the Survival Self* (2019) explains applications to coaching.

A much greater risk than the danger of 'doing harm' is that once they get going, the client may want to talk and talk, possibly imagining that this is what you want them to do, taking up the whole session with the intricate ins and outs of their life history. This will rarely be a good idea, so your willingness to interrupt respectfully and firmly will be essential.

### Genograms

I have known some career and other coaches speak enthusiastically about using genograms. A genogram looks at a quick glance just like any other family tree, but it has a different aim. This is to reveal psychological and medical patterns between

**54** COACHING FOR CAREERS

generations. There is a range of standard symbols for instance to represent male, female, identical twins, adoptions, divorces and marriages. Genograms are mostly used by clinicians and family therapists but some coaches find that it is valuable to bring to the surface those hidden patterns of assumption, preferred jobs, disputes and disruptions that can have profound effects on attitudes to work. Specialist software makes it relatively easy to create a genogram. There is an introductory explanation at https://en.wikipedia.org/wiki/Genogram.

### Career history: identifying the 'thread'

The first session is the place and time for the client to talk you through their career so far. Your joint aim is to identify whatever thread of motivation runs through the client's decisions, including false starts, abandoned careers and the jobs that turned out to be rewarding. Start with childhood jobs: Saturday jobs at the local hairdressing salon or supermarket, then student jobs and go on to first full-time jobs, following through to the present.

The questions are the same for each job:

> What attracted you to this role?
>
> What was it like actually doing it, pluses and minuses?
>
> When you left, what was that decision about?

Even those childhood jobs may prove to have some clues about what the client enjoys.

> *Bryn* has had a successful career in forestry but he is finding its physical demands too difficult after orthopaedic surgery. His goal for coaching is 'to discover something that will give me the same satisfaction in later life'. He says, 'I never realized till we had this conversation how early all those things that matter to me showed themselves! I delivered newspapers, starting at aged 12, rain or shine for two years. I loved the open air, the freedom, the quiet streets, the closeness to urban wildlife – I often saw our local foxes – and I loved that feeling of having a responsible job and doing something that people needed.'

Expect to see that many people had early false starts. Their parents may have had rigid ideas about what their son or daughter should do. A significant number of my own clients have been born to immigrant parents who worked hard all their lives in relatively humble kinds of employment. These parents can be desperate for their children to have professional jobs, have made many sacrifices to pay

GETTING STARTED: THE FIRST SESSION **55**

for education and have often had extremely fixed ideas about suitable careers, in descending order of desirability: medicine, dentistry, the law, accountancy, pharmacy – careers that combine social status with stability and a good income. Sometimes it can feel impossible to disentangle yourself from the obligations that these choices create:

> *Amra* was the only child of immigrant parents from Pakistan. They ran a successful shop and made it their priority to buy Amra a good education. She became a doctor. At 38 she was struggling with stress and depression. During the discussion about her career path so far, Amra broke down as she described constant discomfort with her role as a haematology consultant. 'I've achieved everything my parents dreamed of for me, but I can't stand it. I wouldn't care if I never saw another patient again. Medicine was the wrong choice for me and I realized it even when I was a medical student but I felt obliged to plough on and not let people down. I'm good at the science but I don't like it. I can act being nice to patients, but every day I yearn for work to be over.'

Few people have ever considered their whole career so far in this way and it can be enjoyable as well as enlightening. Some questions to ask might include:

What themes do you spot in what you've just described?

What needs do you see that you have been serving?

What does this suggest that you must avoid at all costs?

In which contexts do you thrive?

What sort of people do you need around you to be at your best?

Which skills have you enjoyed using?

What skills might be emerging as areas that you might want to develop?

## Reviewing other data

Where you are working with middle aged or older people, it is more than likely that they will have had training involving personal development. The more senior they are, the more likely this is. Ask what courses the client has done and which, if any, had lasting impact and why. The real purpose of management development training may be self-insight: sometimes it will be the only time that people have heard honest feedback about their effect on others. Such events may also confirm or challenge people's career trajectories.

**56** COACHING FOR CAREERS

You will already have asked the client to send you any other information they have about themselves. This could include their current CV, a battery of psychometric profiles, appraisal data and feedback from colleagues. Where clients have sent these documents I take plenty of time to read them in advance, highlighting anything that seems intriguing or puzzling in order to prepare for exploring them with the client. Expect to spend ten minutes or more discussing what the client has offered through these documents. The questions here are:

> What did you learn about yourself?
>
> How valid do you feel these comments and interpretations are?

Expect a wide range of responses to this discussion:

> Can't remember a thing about all those questionnaires – do they make sense to you?
>
> It was a long time ago and I think I might have changed since then.
>
> Hit me like a sledgehammer – had never realized before that other people saw me as a controlling over-talker; I've had to learn how to moderate it.

Clients who have lost their jobs may have been given challenging feedback via appraisals or staff surveys. They may contest the views expressed. If so, just log it for now and suggest that you can explore its significance in a subsequent session.

This, however, is the time and place to discuss whether the client would like to take further surveys and questionnaires. If the answer is yes, then agree which might be useful and discuss how they will be administered.

## Goals

As you come to towards the end of the session, you will probably find that the conversation naturally leads to revisiting the goals the client described in the chemistry conversation. You will now have a much more layered and nuanced understanding of what the client needs. You will have heard how they feel about their current role, heard them describe their career pathway, listened to what they say about the non-work parts of their life and you will have some idea of how they see themselves. Apart from the issues that specifically concern career, you may have heard about other topics that need some coaching attention.

Briefly summarize what you have heard. The two most powerful goal-setting questions are these:

> If this coaching programme were to be fantastically successful, what would have changed for you?

And then the ultimate goal-setting question:

Given all of that, what do you need from me?

Asking the questions this way is a safeguard against making assumptions – and the more experienced you are as a career coach the greater the danger of thinking that you know what clients want because you see what appear to be so many of the same needs. I learnt this the hard way myself a few years back when I lazily made the assumption that a new client needed just the kinds of initial 'exercises' I describe in this chapter. I asked him for feedback at its end, when, with great politeness, he said, 'Well, my wife is a coach and she and I have already done all the things you and I have just done'. Ever since that chastening experience, a beginner mistake made when I already had many years as a coach, I have made sure that I ask the question, *What do you need from me?* not only at the outset of every coaching programme but also a variant of it at the beginning of every subsequent session.

# 5 Brand identity

Of all the myths about looking for a job, the most unhelpful is that you need to be the most sober, the most cautious and the dullest version of yourself, whether this is when you apply for the job or when you present yourself at the interview. Naturally this is not how the idea is expressed. People talk about 'looking like a solid citizen' or seeming 'a safe pair of hands'. Like most myths there is some truth in it as employers can be easily frightened by excess and extremes. But, unfortunately, many people muff their chances, either at the initial recruitment stage or at the interview, by draining the colour from their applications and CVs – and missing the point. The point is to differentiate yourself, though of course you must do this in a positive way.

One cause of this misunderstanding is that many clients start out with the wrong question: 'Who will have me?' This is a defensive question that assumes that it will be difficult and that caution is therefore necessary. The right questions are 'Who am I?' and 'What do I really want?'

Beginning the process of finding reliable answers to these questions is what this chapter is about – and doing it through using the concepts of 'brand' and 'brand identity'. Looking at brand has two sides: the first is the client's inner person, who they are psychologically and how they see themselves, including their strengths and weaknesses. The second is the outer person: how others see them and the skills and knowledge they deploy in their lives and jobs. This chapter looks at both.

## The brand idea

You may meet the occasional client who objects to the whole notion of being a 'brand'. It reminds them of pretentious marketing jargon or of the disreputable methods that some companies use to persuade us to buy overpriced products that we don't need. If you encounter this client then you will need to find some other way of introducing the same ideas.

I start by asking people which products they seek out, even when it is not necessarily convenient or cheap to do so, and which competing products they avoid at all costs. The answers usually reveal that they are making fine discriminations in a crowded marketplace, often choosing on the basis of intricately calculated criteria:

> I will brave the crowds at Primark to buy underwear because it's well made and a third the cost of similar things at Marks & Spencer.

BRAND IDENTITY **59**

> My local wet fish shop for fish despite the queues and the much higher than supermarket prices because the fish is always fresh, they only buy from sustainable sources and the staff are always cheerful, very knowledgeable about cooking methods.
>
> I avoid every single one of the major coffee chains. Instead I look for the locally run coffee shop where there will usually be a distinctive vibe and a personal touch.

I usually then invite the client to briefly discuss how the companies concerned have differentiated themselves and how sometimes it seems that they have done this without spending anything on advertising. We then discuss 'brand promise': often expressed as a brief statement in shops or on packaging: the commitment to enduring values that the company says it will never compromise. This is because the most successful brands talk not just about *what* they make or do but about *why* they are in business at all: a link to their moral purpose. A brand promise does not mean that these organizations never have PR disasters from time to time, because they all do, but it does make it more likely that recovery will be quicker and easier. All brands, however successful, have downsides. A brand may seem arrogant, expensive, narrow in its thinking, careless about quality – and yet still be successful. This is the brand paradox: that a brand cannot appeal to everyone. A successful brand is as clear about who is NOT its customer as it is about the customer it wants and cherishes.

You may also want to discuss failing brands – and there are always plenty of current examples. The reasons for failure may vary, but most commonly it is that the brand could not compete in an overcrowded market – usually because it failed to differentiate itself.

## People are brands

After we have discussed the principles of branding, I move to the idea of *people as brands*. However popular certain famous individuals may be, there is always a downside. The more celebrated the person the more obvious their downsides are. You can think highly of a celebrity while being perfectly aware of their negative side. A talented actor may seem incapable of sexual fidelity, an admired member of the British royal family may be dutiful but dull, a colourful politician may not bother to disguise his impulsiveness, a highly paid model may be notorious for her tantrums. When a career is in the ascendant, the talents and strengths outweigh the negatives. Weaknesses may also be allowable when it is clear that they are under control.

Where coaching clients have struggled to get shortlisted or, if shortlisted, to win the job, it is often the case that their personal brand has been unclear or else positively misleading:

**60** COACHING FOR CAREERS

> *Simon* is a nurse, a man in a profession dominated by women. He wants to move to a more senior managerial role in the nursing hierarchy. His current 'brand' statements emphasize his warmth, his care for patients and his commitment to high clinical standards. He is puzzled by his failure to make headway in his ambitions. In discussion he tells me that he is trying to come across as 'soft and cuddly'. While he is indeed a likeable man, he is not in any way 'cuddly', in fact he is fierce, loud, funny, persistent and dynamic. He has some track record in his organization as an accomplished advocate for nurses' rights. His claims about quality and care for patients are what any employer will take for granted in a senior nurse.

Simon needs to see that if people want the kind of person he has been trying to project, then this is not his job. If he did somehow manage to fool the appointing managers, it is most unlikely that either he or they would be happy in the longer term. In effect he needs to rebrand himself.

## How psychometrics can help the brand discussion

After their initial training many coaches ask whether they should get themselves licensed to administer psychometric questionnaires/assessments. There can be understandable reluctance to do this when you have already spent a substantial sum on qualification training. You have to be certain that you would recoup the investment in time and money. Then, assuming you do decide to invest, which instruments should you opt for given that there are hundreds available, many of dubious quality?

### The case for

I imagine the scene:

| | |
|---|---|
| Coach | So what kind of a person are you? |
| Client | Err. . . |

Or later in the same conversation:

| | |
|---|---|
| Coach | What strengths do you believe you have? |
| Client | Umm. . . |

Most people cannot answer these questions easily. Modesty may get in the way. Or even immodesty. Or delusion. Much more likely, people do not have a readily accessible structure for describing themselves so if you ask these questions you will more often than not get waffly answers.

Fortunately, psychometricians have done the thinking for us and have provided reliable frameworks for such discussions. The best psychometrics offer shortcuts to self-awareness. When we are in a state of naïve ignorance we can assume that everyone else is just like us. A good psychometric can show us that this is not the case and that other people's behaviour, values, strengths and views of the world are radically different from our own. Understanding this can explain why we don't always get what we want or why we experience others as infuriating, along with why we may be seen by others as infuriating. Where the topic is career, psychometrics can be enlightening about the contexts and roles in which the client would thrive and those where they would be miserable. The best offer a safe way to have what might otherwise be a difficult conversation:

> *Maxine's* coach is spending a whole session on debriefing three psychometric assessments. One is a Jungian personality questionnaire (The Myers Briggs Type Indicator) that suggests that Maxine has a strong preference for privacy, for cool, objective analysis and for the tangibility of the here and now rather than the big-picture fuzziness of an unknowable future. The second is an instrument focusing on interpersonal style (the FIRO-B) that reveals Maxine's low need for inclusion in group activities, her choosiness about close relationships and her high need for control and autonomy. The third assesses Maxine against 16 personality traits and suggests a conscientious, hard-working, quiet person with a dislike of abrupt change. She scores highly for stress. Maxine looks dismayed at first but then her story pours out. She feels ill-suited to her current role where all the emphasis is on strategy and what Maxine describes as 'noisy brainstorming with people who love the sound of their own voices'. She has little autonomy. She expresses fear that her stress levels might get out of control. This is a pivotal conversation that enables her to steer away from another role just like the one she already has and to be proud of what she can offer in a different kind of organization and job.

These profiles can become part of the coach–client vocabulary, a helpful way of understanding conflicts with colleagues or family, offering perspective as well as a way of finding swifter answers to career dilemmas than might otherwise be the case. So a client who is dubious about a job offer might be able to explore their doubts through the lens of their psychometric results: is this really the job for a

**62** COACHING FOR CAREERS

person who has these traits? If the answer is yes, it is a good match, then what are the hesitations about?

### The case against

You can be a competent coach without ever using a single psychometric assessment. It is possible to get too evangelical about psychometric instruments and to claim more for them than they can do. No single questionnaire is perfect nor can truly peer deep into the psyche of any individual human being because as a species we are just too complex and too clever. Many questionnaires are poorly constructed or else the reports they produce contain lofty pronouncements about the person with far more certainty than could ever be justified.

Some clients will be wary or even hostile. They may half remember reading a negative article that has led them to conclude that 'it's all psychobabble' or have had a disappointing experience in the past where the interpretation was crudely done. The questionnaires are reports on yourself, so if you really want to skew the results you sometimes can through the way you fill them in. Some clients attribute more power to the process than it actually has: they are afraid that the questionnaire may reveal a secret weakness. It has to be said, too, that there are coaches who like the mystique and the power they believe it can offer because these hide their own lack of confidence.

### Making the choice

Even with all these caveats, I am a strong believer in the value of psychometrics. I find that most clients welcome the insights that they can provide. The art is to match what the client needs with what is available and with your own levels of knowledge. The range of products is wide, including personality, motivation, vocational interests, ability, strengths, and values. This table lists the instruments that I have found consistently valuable.

| | Examples | Comments |
|---|---|---|
| Jungian personality type | Myers–Briggs Type Indicator (MBTI)<br><br>Jung Type Indicator<br><br>Keirsey Temperament Sorter | Reveals which one of 16 possible 'types' you are based on 4 dimensions or 'preferences': Introversion/Extraversion; Sensing/Intuition; Thinking/Feeling, Judging/Perceiving. This popular strengths-based approach is also useful for teams; needs subtlety in interpretation to avoid stereotyping or blandness; impressive research behind it |

| Trait-based personality questionnaires | The 16 PF<br><br>'Big Five' questionnaires such as the NEO<br><br>Wave<br><br>The Hogan suite of 3 questionnaires<br><br>The OPQ (Occupational Personality Questionnaire) | Rates you on a 1–10 scale according to how much or little of a behavioural trait you have. Produces an individually based profile more obviously judgemental than those produced by Jungian questionnaires. Much excellent research lies behind the best of these questionnaires |
|---|---|---|
| Team roles | Belbin | A way of understanding informal roles in teams: every role adds value |
| Motivation and interpersonal style | FIRO-B | Reveals how much or how little need we have to belong (Inclusion), to have power (Control) and to love and be loved (Affection). Simplicity is deceptive: can hit clients hard and needs great care in interpretation |
| Career | Career Anchors | Based on the assumption that we have one over-riding motivator that guides and governs our career choices. There are eight possible choices. Discovering which one is at the top for you can be enlightening, explaining discomfort with earlier or current career choices |
| Conflict management | The Thomas–Kilmann Conflict Mode Instrument (TKI) | Analyses your preference for five possible ways of managing conflict where there is no one 'ideal' way. The assumption is that we may over or underuse any of the styles, each of which has its place in negotiating conflict, depending on the situation |

I make use of all these instruments, but the four I use with almost every client where career is the focus are the MBTI, the FIRO-B, Career Anchors and some version of the 'five factor' approach to personality. For more information on how to use Jungian instruments you might read my book *Coaching with Personality*

**64** COACHING FOR CAREERS

*Type: What Works* (2017) that has a chapter explaining the essence of some of the questionnaires listed above. My books on the MBTI (2007a and 2007b) and the FIRO-B (1997) co-authored with Judy Waterman, give explanatory profiles that coaches can use with clients.

An insightful way of thinking about career was developed by John Holland (1919–2008), a gifted American psychologist whose work first appeared in the 1960s. Holland's essential idea was that 'the choice of a vocation is an expression of personality': people were suited to jobs in types of working environment that reflected their personal interests. He identified six such environments and personalities:

- Realistic: the doers, people who like to work with their hands
- Investigative: the thinkers who like to work on their own and to observe and experiment with data
- Artistic: the creatives who work with ideas and things
- Social: the helpers who enjoy relationship-based work
- Enterprising: the persuaders who enjoy work with ideas and people
- Conventional: the organizers who like data, rules, structure and control.

Holland's work permeated career counselling as it was then called and many career interest inventories are based on it, including the excellent SuperStrong, a short, quick-to-take version of the original Strong Interest Inventory first developed in the 1920s (www.vitanavis.com). Results show as a kite-shaped hexagon, a reflection of which blend of interests will be right for an individual with suggested career interests along with personal styles around leadership, work, risk-taking and team orientation.

Holland's work has been criticized for appearing simplistic when so many jobs resist straightforward classification. Just getting your results on such inventories does not always seem to correlate with job satisfaction, nor give immediate help on how to identify your strengths. My personal top three are Creative, Social and Enterprising with my results suggesting careers in writing, teaching and training, speaking, coaching, social sciences and performing arts: exactly the careers and interests I have in fact followed. My own view is that middle aged and older people are as unlikely to be surprised as I was by their results on a Holland inventory and I don't use it with them for this reason. But the younger the client, the more valuable the insights it can provide.

### The 'Big Five'

Psychometrics are improving all the time and the best instruments have decades of respectable research behind them. One development has been a so-called *meta-analysis* combining insights from other questionnaires, suggesting that there are five dominant factors in human personality: *Openness, Conscientiousness, Extraversion, Agreeableness* and *Neuroticism.* These are easy to remember with the acronym OCEAN. You may see these referred to as 'The Big Five'. The question-naires ask how far you share the traits associated with the five factors.

The Five Factor model combines the work of several psychometricians, but it is still based on self-report, so as with others, can be open to falsification. I like the free version of this questionnaire, the IPIP-NEO at http://www.personal.psu.edu/~j5j/IPIP/ and have found it to give consistently reliable results as here:

> *Edwin* has been forced out of his job as medical director in a large hospital. A new chief executive said he wanted to make his own appointment and this is the reason that Edwin will give to the world. Underneath this there is a different story. When Edwin completes the IPIP-NEO it is the foundation for understanding how the vague hints that he received about being a 'difficult' colleague could manifest themselves in his behaviour. He has high scores for Conscientiousness and Neuroticism, low scores on Openness and Extraversion, medium scores on Agreeableness. Edwin's Conscientiousness can mean that he over-emphasizes rules, overworks and can seem rigid. Low scores on Openness explain his aversion to change and his belief that ideas about service improvement are 'impractical and fluffy'. His constant anxiety makes him hypervigilant and under stress he retreats into a shell of privacy where he finds it difficult to ask for help or to collaborate with colleagues. At first a reluctant coachee, he gradually becomes an enthusiast. The blunt portrait that emerged through the IPIP-NEO is a revelation and a turning point. 'Yes, this is me' he says, 'prickly and defensive; the managerial responsibility of the job overwhelms me and I need to look at why before I start looking for something else'. Edwin made a successful return to his earlier career as a surgeon where the role felt familiar and more straightforward and where part-time working reduced the stress that had become insurmountable in his medical director role.

## Getting the best out of psychometrics

To get the best out of psychometrics there are some guidelines that will help. First be clear why you want to use them at all. The only good reason is for the added insights that they can give and this is a decision that is best made on a case by case basis, ideally a joint decision between you and the client. Training helps and the more complex the underpinning theoretical framework, the more essential it is. Popular instruments such as the MBTI are plagued by phony copycat question-naires and by untrained interpreters. When you have both these factors present, a poor-quality instrument used by a coach who doesn't know what they don't know, the results are at best meaningless, at worse damaging to all concerned.

**66** COACHING FOR CAREERS

Choice of instruments can be confusing. Publishers understandably sing the praises of their own offerings and it can be challenging to see past the hype. If you are new to this field, ask other coaches what they find valuable and why. Cost is a factor, not just for training but for buying the questionnaire itself. The cheap 'paper and pencil' forms of administration have dwindled in availability and the cost of web-based reports has risen so you will need to recoup this out of your fee or make it an added extra, something that most clients intensely dislike. Look for peer-reviewed research and scrutinize the publisher's website to see what they say about their target market and how good a fit this is with your own client base. Where a questionnaire interests you, take it yourself and hire a qualified fellow professional to do the feedback. Pay attention to the experience of answering the questions and then to the quality of the report, if there is one, and to the clarity and usefulness of the insights that emerge. If the experience leaves you with that 'so-what?' feeling then why would it be any different for your clients?

I strongly advocate using more than one questionnaire, ideally at least three, each chosen for the different lens it can offer. When you do this you will need to devote at least two hours and possibly a half day to the discussion and debrief. Take your time with the interpretation, working through the material steadily, involving the client step by step. Keep theoretical explanation to a minimum. Ask about the experience of filling in the questionnaire and listen quietly to any anger or dismissive comments that the client expresses, answering courteously with factual corrections if they are needed. All profiles and results are speculative and should be treated as hypotheses, despite the over-insistent way in which some reports are written. Your own comments need to stress the tentative nature of the portrait that emerges:

> Your results suggest [whatever they suggest] but how do you respond to that?
>
> You say this does seem like you – can you give some examples of how this might play out in everyday life?
>
> Where is this not true for you?

The client is their own best judge of how well any profile fits them and we should be ready to abandon any preconceived ideas we may have about the client. Sometimes the client responds with rejection; they don't see themselves as being anything like the person described. Sometimes they agree with the interpretation but dislike it.

In a career coaching programme, there are other questions which it is vital to ask:

> What does all this suggest about the environments where you will thrive?
>
> Which types of role are likely to be a good fit for you?
>
> What does it imply about situations that you should avoid at all costs?

As a follow-up to a session that can be intense, involving – and potentially contains a lot of information that can disappear from memory quickly – I often ask clients to spend time on reflection, re-reading reports and notes, then to write up what they see as the main points to emerge, sending me a copy. I stress that there is no need to make this a piece of fine prose. Rather it is a working document that will filter into the brand discussion, and will influence how they approach the task of job searching, how they write their CV and how they present themselves in person to potential employers.

## The strengths approach

A significant shift in thinking, writing and practice emerged in human psychology towards the end of the 20th century. Whereas previously the emphasis had tended to be upon a doleful tale of distress and dysfunction, now there was something called *positive psychology*. There was an interest in what made us happy rather than what made us sad, in strengths rather than in weaknesses, in virtues rather than in sins. Positive psychology became a 'movement' associated with the work of Martin Seligman and Mihaly Csikszentmihalyi (2014) but in truth these ideas had been gathering force long before through the 'human potential' movement of the 1970s and in the work of the humanistic psychotherapist Carl Rogers – and many others. Carl Rogers' ideas (1956), specifically his belief in 'unconditional positive regard' from practitioner to client, have been profoundly influential. You could say that the whole modern approach to coaching is in itself a manifestation of the same ideas, built as it is on the foundation assumptions of respect, choice and resilience.

I like the strengths approach as a valuable part of the brand discussion. There are a number of ways you can tap into this thinking. You can use one of the many surveys, debriefing them as you would any other questionnaire, for instance the modestly priced introductory version of the Strengths Profiler (www.strengthsprofile.com), a British instrument that assesses 60 potential strengths and usefully categorizes your own into four categories. These are:

- Realized strengths: the ones you use and enjoy, associated with things you do well and that are energizing; likely to be an important part of your brand.
- Unrealized strengths: strengths that you have but use less frequently and that you could use more frequently; potentially a development area.
- Learnt behaviours: strengths you can draw on but do not enjoy, so will be more of a struggle; probably need to be dialled down at least a little as part of your brand thinking.
- Weaknesses: tasks that need strengths that you find draining and do not enjoy will draw out your weaknesses; avoid situations and jobs where these strengths are needed.

## 68 COACHING FOR CAREERS

There is a case in coaching for using approaches that involve physically handling materials and many of the people who sell questionnaires also sell sets of cards. The virtue of this kind of activity is that it is a counter to the tendency to over-verbalize and over-intellectualize and it can cut to the heart of what matters. I occasionally use the set of Strengths Cards published by Mindspring (https://mindspring.uk.com). They are based on Martin Seligman's free Values in Action survey (www.viacharacter.org).

The strengths are clustered under six headings called Virtues:

> **Wisdom and Knowledge:** creativity, curiosity, judgment, love of learning, perspective
> **Courage:** bravery, perseverance, honesty, zest
> **Humanity:** love, kindness, social intelligence
> **Justice:** teamwork, fairness, leadership
> **Temperance:** forgiveness, humility, prudence, self-regulation
> **Transcendence:** appreciation of beauty and excellence, gratitude, hope, humour, spirituality

The cards are postcard size, with a pleasant photograph on one side and an explanation of what the strength means on the other. I hand the pack to the client and say:

> Here are 24 cards, each with one character strength on it. Have a quick look through and then pick your top eight. Then I'd like you to whittle that down to your top five, the ones that you feel really reflect the strengths you are proud of.

When the client has made their choices, I ask them to talk me through what these strengths mean to them in practice.

### Weaknesses of the strengths-based approach

Both the Strengths Profiler and the Seligman/Mindspring approach like their rivals such as the Clifton Strengths Assessment have weaknesses. First, they label strengths using abstract words that client and coach may struggle to turn into everyday experience or to translate into something they can use in a CV or at an interview. My client Philip read his report with bafflement, saying that he had no idea what was meant by 'Narrator' or 'Catalyst' and we spent a fruitless 20 minutes trying to decode the words into something that connected with him before deciding that other approaches would work better.

Handling pretty postcards may feel to some clients like being back at school or on a training course where such techniques can bring life and activity to theoretical ideas but are heartily disliked by some participants for their apparent childishness. I can find no convincing evidence that the strengths approach increases confidence or competence, in fact some reviewers, notably Tomas Chamorro-Premuzic (2016) have concluded that there is a danger of creating delusions of excellence among people who are what he calls 'C and D players' or of encouraging the overuse of strengths to the point where they become derailers.

All that being said, there are many situations and clients for whom they are just right, achieving insights that may be elusive through other means:

> *Kirsty* is a young ordained theologian working at the HQ of her denomination. She did outstandingly well at university and was persuaded into her current job by a senior member of her church. The emphasis of the job is on policy. Kirsty has already told me that she finds what she calls 'politicking and in-fighting' wearisome and dismaying, saying that she sees a lot of it and would have expected people in a Christian organization to behave better. Yes, she does well at the strategic thinking that her job needs but she does not enjoy it. She picks five cards: Humility and Modesty, Hope, Love and Being Loved, Social Intelligence and Spirituality. She fans them out in her hand. 'I'm stunned', she says. 'How could I have been so naïve? I'm in the wrong job!' In discussion it is clear that Kirsty's brand is about close, loving, one-to-one relationships based on reliable intuition about the emotional needs of others; it is about her lack of ego, her optimism and the simplicity of her faith. Her job needs leadership but this was not one of the cards she picked: 'I don't want to be a leader!' Within a year Kirsty has negotiated a two day a week contract with her current employer and has become a hospital chaplain for the rest of the week, with a plan to become a full-time pastor in due course, and with the possibility of a career break if and when she has children.

## Values

Most approaches to strengths are actually just another way of looking at personal values but it may need discussion with the client to draw this out. The danger is of falling into a wishy-washy recital of pious statements, for instance about 'integrity' or 'authenticity', which most of us would sign up to without ever truly putting them to the test in terms of whether they actually guide our behaviour. Personal values matter because they are linked to the idea of brand promise: principles that

COACHING FOR CAREERS

represent personal moral priorities you would compromise only with the greatest reluctance. This is what commercial organizations mean by *brand values*, a commitment to principles that every customer should experience in every interaction with the brand, in person, online and in the products or services themselves.

It takes courage to make a public commitment to these values. As the English writer and poet John Milton notably proclaimed in 1644 at the height of the English Civil War, 'I cannot praise a fugitive and cloistered virtue, unexercised and unbreathed, that never sallies out and sees her adversary', in other words that virtue is easy when there is no challenge. Personal values act like a moral compass; they help us to make decisions in ethically complex situations. In career terms it matters to know what these values are because they help answer the questions:

> What really motivates you? Why do you work at all? In what circumstances would you put self-interest aside? Are the values that you espouse an exact match to what you actually do in practice?

A client who can identify their brand values has an advantage: they can make sure that such values are stated straightforwardly in their CV/résumé and then reflected in everything about how they present themselves through the written word and in person:

> *Antony* works in the prison education service and is hoping to make a move into another adult education role. He quickly identifies his personal brand values as *commitment to learning, kindness, fairness* and *resilience*. He says, 'Developing others and developing myself are really important to me, it's why I'm in teaching; I believe everyone can learn and develop. Kindness means that I always look beneath the surface of challenging behaviour – and we see a lot of that in prisons – to the damaged person underneath. I aim to be scrupulously fair but that means to myself as well as to others, so I'm not easily manipulated. Fairness also has relevance to social justice and that matters hugely to me and it's why I've been doing the work I do. Resilience: I've taken a lot of knocks in my own life but I can and do bounce back. It's tricky to live up to these principles, but my aim is to hold myself to account for them. I know I will bring them to any job that I do.'

## Getting feedback

The effectiveness of coaching is improved immeasurably when you add to the client's story by bringing other people's views into the frame and this assumes much greater significance when there are career issues. We humans vary hugely in our levels of self-awareness and it is a rare person indeed who truly sees themselves as others see them. Nearly always we have blindspots and treasured fantasies about ourselves. We frequently fail to understand how transparent we are to others. In a commercial environment the necessary counterbalance to any brand delusions can be brutally corrected by the market: customers like it or they don't. This does not and cannot happen in the same way with people. It is unusual to work in an environment where people know how to give and receive feedback and often it is not given at all or given too late and too harshly, sometimes only at the point where people are dismissed over their conduct or made redundant This is why you may want to initiate a process where other people's views become part of the client's brand thinking.

## 360 feedback

Many organizations now commission 360-degree feedback for senior staff, normally a questionnaire where people are asked to rate a colleague on a five-point scale against a number of behaviours considered to be crucial for job success. There is usually an additional section with space for narrative comments. It is worth asking clients if they have been the subject of such a survey in the recent past.

I am sceptical about the value of these questionnaires even though some feedback is better than none. Their air of scientific objectivity is misleading as there is no way of establishing whether respondents are using the scales in the same way or understand the items to have the same meaning. There is a bias to the positive as by and large people don't want to be mean about a colleague, often resulting in a so-what bland, nicey-nicey feel. The main strength of the report will be in the free-form comments but these are often just single sentences, headlines that give no clues about the behaviour the colleague has seen and that has led them to whatever conclusions they have drawn. For all these reasons I find that clients tend to dismiss or forget these reports, especially if they have been part of an appraisal, seeing them as tiresome pieces of bureaucracy, though sometimes when you look closely you can find a gem or two.

Instead, or in addition, you may want to suggest alternatives. Ideally I will carry out a structured process of interviewing up to ten of the client's colleagues, mixing direct reports with boss and peers, asking everyone the same open questions about leadership style, influencing style, communication and other skills, strengths and weaknesses. I guarantee the respondents confidentiality. I then write up a candid report that is seen solely by the client. This process has obvious weaknesses: it is expensive for the client to commission because it is time consuming for the coach who carries it out. It depends on your ability as the feedback-gatherer to absorb what are often contradictory views, to stay neutral and to write the report in a way that the client can hear without defensiveness. I believe that the limitations of the methodology are cancelled out by the vivid evidence that you collect

## 72 COACHING FOR CAREERS

of the client's actual behaviour. You will be able to report on strengths that the client may be taking for granted as well as on weaknesses, some of which the client may dimly recognize without understanding just how much potential they have to annoy.

### Debriefing 360 feedback

Handle the debrief with extreme care and with plenty of time. I will usually allocate two hours for it. Even when people guess what others might have to say, there is shock in seeing it written down or in realizing how powerfully their colleagues could be misinterpreting motives and behaviour. I never send the report in advance because I prefer to see the client's reaction at first hand. I ask them to scan it quickly, ask for an immediate reaction and then take it steadily step by step, paragraph by paragraph, discussing as we go:

> How far do you recognize this?
>
> What's your response?
>
> What are the implications for you?

Some people can only see the negatives; some dismiss the negatives saying that they do not respect people who can make such comments. Some clients are hurt and indignant, some are reassured by all the positives; some are solemn. I stress that feedback is not an instruction to change and that it is an advantage to know what perceptions others have of you because they will have these perceptions whether or not you are aware of them.

If for whatever reason it is not possible to get feedback this way then encourage the client to do it for themselves. The risk is that people will be far less open than they tend to be when talking to a neutral third party or when just filling in an anonymized questionnaire, especially if they are more junior, where they might fear reprisals, but at least the client is hearing it without an intermediary. Spend ten minutes or so rehearsing the client about the importance of writing everything down exactly as it is said and of staying neutral: no simpering denials where strengths are concerned or defensive splutterings when a weakness is mentioned, just a polite 'thank you' or a request for further clarity.

Some clients do it by email, some ask people if they will give 20 minutes for a phone or face-to-face conversation. The questions are simple:

> In working with me, what would you say my strengths are?
>
> Can you give me some specific examples of time or place where you've seen this?
>
> What are my less strong points?

BRAND IDENTITY **73**

Can you give me some specific examples, again of times and places where you've seen this?

What advice would you give me about how to build on my strengths/address my weaknesses?

Ask the client to bring all their notes to your next session and then conduct the debrief in the same step-by-step way that you would use if you had gathered the feedback and written a report yourself.

## Transferrable skills

Successful brands will often spend some time looking at what it is that they do uniquely well – the area sometimes called *core competencies*. A competency is defined as underpinning knowledge combined with attitudes and behaviour to produce a skill that we can do consistently well. This is different from the inner pondering that characterizes psychological drivers, character strengths and values.

Many clients worry about how transferrable their skills really are. When you have stayed in one organization for a long time you may believe that you can only be successful in the environment where people know and tolerate you. Mostly this is untrue; the skills are transferrable so the problem is self-confidence not skill. Another self-imposed limiting belief is to accept that you have technical knowledge and skills (reading balance sheets, legal obligations, coding, technology and so on) without realizing that you will probably also have many so-called 'soft skills', the ones that are associated with emotional intelligence such as the ability to persuade, to manage conflict, to coach, to inspire.

### A framework for identifying skills

Where clients are baffled about where to start with the task of identifying their transferrable skills it can help to give them a prompt. Here is one such framework:

| Thinking | Analysing data, researching, spotting trends, forecasting |
| --- | --- |
| Problem-solving | Defining the issue, assessing, researching, forming conclusions, making recommendations |
| Communicating in writing | Writing clearly and grammatically, adjusting tone for different audiences, persuading |

**74** COACHING FOR CAREERS

| Communicating verbally | Speaking articulately and persuasively, adjusting style appropriately, leading groups |
|---|---|
| Influencing | Listening attentively, advocating, explaining, teaching, mediating, dealing with conflict respectfully, coaching and mentoring |
| Managing change | Staying flexible and open-minded, getting involved, dealing with resistance, living with ambiguity |
| Organizing, making things happen | Planning, prioritizing, giving instructions, following through, dealing with detail, doing whatever needs to be done, meeting deadlines |
| Leadership and management | Creating a vision, giving feedback, motivating, delegating |
| Teamwork | Collaborating, sharing information, acknowledging others' strengths, ability to work with wide range of other temperaments and personalities |
| Self-management | Aware of own strengths and weaknesses and ability to manage them, working independently, openness to feedback, showing prudent self-confidence |

Few of us are 100 per cent brilliant in all of these areas. You might ask clients to go through this list rating themselves on a ten-point scale, highlighting the skills where they believe they excel, and asking them for examples of where they have made a difference using these skills.

## Wrapping it all up

As we near the end of this process I refer back to the discussion we had about brand. My questions are:

> What problems can you reliably promise to solve for an employer?
>
> What do employers get if they get you? What's the essence of your personal brand?
>
> What's your brand promise or brand essence, the principles you will never compromise?

# BRAND IDENTITY

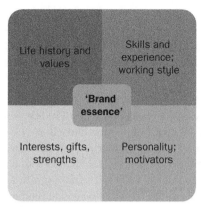

**Figure 5.1** The 'brand essence' jigsaw

You might represent this diagrammatically as a simple jigsaw for the client

I ask clients to write these sessions up as an aide-memoire, suggesting a length of no more than 400 words. Then they can use ideas from it in their CVs, as reminders before they go into a job interview or as the foundation of their 'elevator speech' (page 101) during the job-search phase.

*Freddie* is a manager in a not-for-profit organization. It has just announced a merger. Freddie is approaching his 60th birthday and sees the chance, in all the upheaval that will follow the merger, to rethink how he spends the next five years of his working life. Here is an extract from his 'Brand notes'.

### Brand Freddie

I see myself as a kind of outsider and shrewd observer with an insider's perspective. This means I can play the role of critical friend. I see myself as a competent manager though this is not a role I specially enjoy or want to carry on in the future. However, I can work with people who are seen as 'difficult' and I am also encouraging to those who don't necessarily appreciate their own skills – I can help them become more confident and effective. I seek consensus and tend to avoid conflict but this doesn't mean I can't make tough decisions. My seven years as a magistrate gave me the tools to make decisions based on what is known and unknown and where I also developed a high level of influencing skills. I write well and enjoy the policy side of my work. I enjoy training colleagues where my style is relaxed, participative and informal. I'm also a trained mediator where my motivation is to help others see that the solution to apparently intractable problems

> often lies with them. I believe strongly in equality, diversity, empathy and the value of personal development. Where an organization practises what it preaches here, it will get my wholesale loyalty and commitment.

As a result of this coaching it looks likely that Freddie will develop an enjoyable portfolio career where he might reposition himself as one of the in-house experts on creating the culture of the newly merged organization, possibly part time. In parallel with this, he plans to revive his familiarity with mediation so that he can work as a volunteer for a number of charities, along with some well-paid freelance interim work in the policy arena. This could include running training workshops. If in the longer term his job should disappear, he is well poised to step into a new life with minimal turbulence.

## You and your own brand as a coach

As a coach, exactly the same principles of branding apply to you as much as to your client. If you have not already done so, I recommend putting yourself through all the processes I set out in this chapter. Being clear about your brand is an essential part of helping the right clients to find you. It will enable you to stand out in a crowded marketplace of other coaches, to have confidence in your strengths, to clarify your pricing policy, to decide how personal image and your website should reflect your uniqueness and to craft your own 'brand promise'.

The work I describe in this chapter can easily absorb three or four hours, so for most coaches this will mean two whole sessions. It is the foundation of so much that will follow: job searching, preparing for the selection process, the even bigger question of 'life purpose', as well as how to construct a powerful CV, the subject of the next chapter.

# 6   The client in words: their CV/résumé

Once the client is clear about their personal brand they will need to know how to represent themselves on paper: the subject of this chapter.

> *Julian* has had a distinguished public sector career but his many promotions have all been achieved through personal recommendations and, as he puts it, 'a tap on the shoulder'. Now for the first time he is having to compete on an open basis for jobs that are being advertised. He is puzzled by his failure to get on shortlists, given that he believes himself to be well-known and highly respected in his sector. He brings his CV to his coach. It is a handsome document running to 25 pages, carefully bound and with a table of contents.

> *Pasha* has mild learning difficulties that affect her ability to process language. She gets an interview on the basis of her CV. The hiring manager quickly realizes that the CV must have been written by someone else and Pasha does not get the job.

> *Jessica* is 35 and has been a homemaker for 15 years. She is now ready to re-enter employment and knows that she needs professional help. She has never written a CV and describes herself as 'terrified'. 'I've looked on the internet', she says, 'and I can't see anything that seems like me. I haven't done paid work for so long. I don't know where to start!'

These three clients all need something different, but what might that be?

## Understanding what CVs/résumés are for

There is widespread confusion about the purpose of CVs. When people who have been unemployed for a long time talk about their disappointing experience, they will often indignantly describe sending out 'hundreds of CVs' and then having received not a single reply, let alone getting the offer of an interview. Even in the rarefied world of executive coaching where you might expect a more realistic view, I find that there are many clients who, deep-down, believe that the CV gets you the job.

## 78 COACHING FOR CAREERS

Start off the part of the coaching session where you have agreed to discuss the client's CV with some questions that will flush out any misunderstandings. For instance, if the client has been a recruiter themselves, ask them how they handled unsolicited CVs. If they have never personally recruited people, just ask a more general question:

What's your own view of what the CV is for?

Depending on the answer, discuss what clients need to know.

Overall: the CV is best seen as a piece of advertising copy where the 'product' is the client:

- The purpose of the CV is to get on the shortlist for interview.
- The CV is hardly ever read as carefully as it has been written.
- Unsolicited CVs are rarely read or retained, so promises that 'we will keep you on our system' do not mean much.
- The recruiter is looking for an instant match to the qualities and experience that the job needs, so any CV that does not reflect this is destined for the reject pile.
- It may be rude, but employers do not normally respond to unsolicited CVs or to people they reject for a shortlist.
- The CV is mostly read first by a busy HR person creating a 'long list', so is not a specialist in the discipline for which they are recruiting. Technical language will not impress them and they may have no idea of the candidate's reputation in their field.

### The 'safe pair of hands' trap

Most clients are aware that the CV is a formal document. It is a statement encapsulating your career. Somehow, a sense of unease can creep in, a feeling that you have to smooth out any jagged edges, present your best possible self and eschew risks. This can lead to *the safe pair of hands* trap where the client produces an unnecessarily bland and dull account of themselves. Employers do not want to appoint an unsafe pair of hands, but they will only appoint the candidate they categorize as 'a safe pair of hands' if this person is the least bad option – and who wants to be that?

Some years ago I was working with a 45-year-old client who was desperate to change careers. He had been jogging along in his role in a government agency until his partner had unexpectedly died. The ensuing crisis of grief and bewilderment led to a growing belief that life was too short to waste on work that had become tedious to him and it did not take long in our coaching programme for him to conclude that he would retrain as a teacher, applying to one of the schemes aiming to attract mature applicants. At that stage I asked to see his CV. I remember goggling

THE CLIENT IN WORDS: THEIR CV/RÉSUMÉ **79**

at it. The person I saw in front of me was a witty thinker full of lively anecdotes, a quirky dresser, talented organizer, keen self-improver, attentive listener, marathon runner and someone whose hobby was stand-up comedy. Nothing in the CV conveyed this. Instead it was full of management jargon about *strategic views, key performance indicators, government imperatives* and *policy development.* I remember dangling his CV in front of him and asking, 'Who is this person? Is he in this room?'

The client's reply was, 'That's the person I've been pretending to be at work. Let's shred him!' He dived forward to seize the document, tearing the pages dramatically into small pieces. His entirely new CV stressed the value of his dedicated public service experience while also giving full play to his interest in learning, his fearlessness as a performer with rowdy audiences, his empathy, listening skills and his intellectual accomplishments. He went on to a successful career as a teacher and then as head of a specialist unit for pupils who had been excluded from mainstream schools.

Clients who fall into the safe pair of hands trap believe that they must be super-cautious. They want to present themselves as a little bit good at everything. They expect the employer to be able to pick up hints about their 'real' talents. Such clients often cannot see what their true strengths are. Sometimes they feel they must disguise who they are through using the indigestible acronyms and meaningless jargon common in their organizations. By doing this they do not realize that their CV will join others on the reject pile because they have done nothing to differentiate themselves. There is all the difference in the world between coming across as dangerously eccentric at one extreme and dangerously dreary at the other. With your neutral perspective as their coach you will be able to help them judge exactly where the balance lies.

## Preparing the client for CV work

The less the client is experienced in the ways of the employment market, the more likely they are to talk about 'my CV', usually meaning an unchanging document that may not have been updated for some years. When it has been updated, the changes might have been added with recent haste, without much thought or effort. My first message to such clients is to brace themselves for hard work. If a client has never previously written a CV it may take them several hours to track down dates and precise names of qualifications, exact dates of entering and leaving jobs or checking actual job titles, all of which can be critical as a mistake here can mean that you fail the potential new employer's checking process or else appear to have mysterious blanks in your record that may be uncomfortably probed at interview. I recommend keeping a separate list of all these vital details, easily accessible on a computer file devoted to job search. This preliminary process can be time-consuming and that is before you take into account the effort needed to compose the actual CV.

**80** COACHING FOR CAREERS

It then comes as a shock to some clients to discover that there should be no such thing as 'my CV' because each CV will be composed as a unique pitch for a specific job. One of the main reasons that an employer rejects a candidate's application is that the CV appears to have been written without the slightest reference to the job description and person specification. This is also why it is far better for a client to aim their job search narrowly rather than just hopefully spraying out a general CV in all directions.

Ask the client to send you what they have in electronic form about the job. I then ask clients to come to the session we plan to have about the CV having done a decoding job on this information, highlighting key words. Many jobs sound impossibly nebulous and generic, using words like *senior, manager, leader, experienced* but if you look harder at the overall brief, the introduction about the organization, the person specification and then the job description, it is usually possible to discern something of what they really want by combing all the available information for the problems the organization faces and which the job holder would be expected to help solve. If a conscientious recruitment consultant is involved, they can often add more candid detail here verbally, for instance about why there is a vacancy at all. I do my own detective work on these documents and then compare my conclusions with the client's own.

*Bella* was applying for a role as a well-paid executive PA to a chief executive. At first glance the job seemed like any other senior PA role, but thanks to a more in-depth analysis these were her conclusions:

> I discovered from the recruiter that this chief executive was very disorganized and had a short temper. He had fired three previous holders of the job over an 18-month period and I also found out that there were two junior PAs sharing the same office space, to be managed by the chief exec's PA, and working for other members of the executive team. There were constant clashes over diaries and meetings. Taking notes at team meetings was an important part of the role but it would have been easy to overlook this in the job description. In my CV I stressed my calmness under pressure, my organization skills and ability to juggle diary commitments, my experience of managing other PAs and my extensive experience of minuting meetings. It must have worked because I was shortlisted and got the job!

## The importance of truth

No coach would wish to offend a client by accusing them of lying, but as part of the initial chat about CVs, I make a point of discussing where the line is between a little

THE CLIENT IN WORDS: THEIR CV/RÉSUMÉ  **81**

harmless self-flattery and actual distortion. Surveys and reports from qualification-checking agencies repeatedly show how common it for CVs to contain errors and omissions. While I was writing this chapter one such survey reported that four-fifths of checked CVs contained a discrepancy. A fifth of the candidates in the study had awarded themselves a more senior job title and more than a tenth had falsified the grades of their qualifications. The worst offenders were older people who felt that what they considered to be 'grade inflation' justified their decision to raise the status of their degrees. The proportion of people who make fraudulent claims seems to be rising despite so many high-profile examples of those who have been caught out making exaggerated claims about their experience and education, including two successive leaders of a UK political party, the Chair of an NHS trust and several candidates on the TV show *The Apprentice*.

You may feel that this is an uncomfortable topic to raise, but I have known desperate clients 'improve' their record in the belief that it will increase their chances of getting a job and I have only discovered this to be the case later when the client has been unmasked, for instance after having elevated their degree classification or claimed that they were at Big City University when they actually attended Big City Polytechnic. I will sometimes tell clients these brief stories that show that even minor exaggerations can be disastrous:

*James*, a 22-year-old graduate, claimed four weeks of internship at an oil company. When he turned up for his first day at a famous consultancy he was met by an HR person who gravely told him that he no longer had the job because checking had shown that his internship had been only two weeks. When James protested that this was a small difference, the reply was, 'If we can't trust you to be honest about this, how would we know that you have integrity on something bigger?'

*Eleanor* was so keen to obtain a job in publishing that she had changed the title of an early job from secretary to editorial assistant, foolishly giving her former employer as a referee. The former employer had pointed out that this was not the role she had been employed to do and the job offer was withdrawn.

I also tell clients that it is important to be specific about institutions and awarding bodies because most organizations do now check qualifications before confirming an appointment, along with job titles, length of employment and salary, even if, as is often the case, they no longer ask for detailed written references. The potential employer may be suspicious if the client does not provide these details.

**82** COACHING FOR CAREERS

## The different types and styles of CV

The standard chronological CV may not always serve the client best. There are different style and types of CV. Some are specific to particular professions. For some clients their choice will depend on their individual situations. Once the client focuses on a job that seems like a good fit, the next task is to choose the format that will give them the best chance of catching the employer's interest.

Check how much the client already knows about CV formats. Some clients are well informed, but many are only familiar with the chronological format where you work backwards from the present job to the much earlier ones. This is the format that HR people prefer because you can see the whole career at a glance:

> *Craig* is 42 and has worked in the finance sector throughout his career starting with two junior positions in retail banks then moving to a competitor bank in a more responsible role and then to an American-owned investment bank for his first managerial role and where he has had two further promotions. Now he feels what he describes as 'under-challenged'. He is realistic about the prospects of change in his present organization and he is starting the search for a better paid and more senior role in a different company in his sector. The standard chronological CV will work best for him as it will show his knowledge of the banking world and the smooth progression he has made from junior to more senior roles in four different companies.

When you have a clear understanding of the client's current situation, it may be obvious that the chronological CV format will disadvantage them: their first page is better devoted to a bulleted list of their skills with supporting evidence, with the second page giving a brief career history:

> *Jana* is 24 and an Olympic medal winner. She is still in the elite squad for her sport but is planning to retire from athletics when the next Olympic cycle ends. Such are the demands of her training schedule that she has very little experience of conventional employment although she does have considerable volunteer experience as well as developing her talent and confidence as a public speaker. She is now aiming for a career in sales management with a company that runs gyms and leisure centres or which manufactures sporting

goods. Jana and her coach agree that she will be best served by a skills-based CV where, after the profile paragraph, the whole of the first page is devoted to her transferable skills, all closely linked to what a potential employer has said they are looking for. For instance, one of her bullet points reads like this:

*Team membership*: member of GB [name of sport] squad, offering support with challenge under the stressful circumstances of preparing for and then competing in both Olympic and Commonwealth Games. Became known as 'go-to person' for resolving disputes between team members. Took over leadership of team when captain injured, maintaining morale in demanding circumstances

The whole of Jana's first page was devoted to these skills, making it easy for a potential employer to see that this was a confident, outgoing person with the considerable people-skills that are strongly connected with a successful role in sales.

The skills-based CV also works well for so-called 'job-hoppers', people whose stay in any one job has been limited. Its disadvantage is that it is not so easy for an employer to see the client's employment history at a glance although adding a section headed 'Career History' on the second page, with names of jobs, dates and organizations, can do much to meet this objection. It needs to be closely tailored to the skills the employer has identified as essential for the job and this can be harder to do successfully than it looks.

## Hybrid CVs

The chronological CV may not work so well for people who have been in one organization for a long time, even where they have moved upwards through a number of different jobs. When they want to change, the question in a recruiter's mind may be, 'What's kept this person stuck for so long?' Or, 'How flexible can they be?' In these circumstances a so-called 'hybrid' CV may be better. This blends skills and achievements with chronology. The CV starts with the normal personal details and profile paragraph. The next heading can be *Skills and Achievements*. The difference from chronological and skills-based CVs is that the focus is on achievements in the current job and then the previous job. Normally you would give the majority space to the current role, reducing it to five or six lines for the previous job and no further details other than titles and dates for any jobs before that on the

**84** COACHING FOR CAREERS

assumption that the employer is unlikely to be interested in what you did many years or even decades previously. The formula to use is this:

1  The challenge
2  What you did
3  Outcome, giving facts and figures wherever possible.

You link each bullet point or mini-paragraph with a named skill.

You may also want to introduce this formula to clients using other CV formats as the most common single mistake I see in client CVs is that their CV is merely a recitation of their job description. So they might write:

> Responsible for performance of team of eight working to the chief executive.
>
> Or
>
> Acted as Secretary to the Audit Committee.

The immediate response of any reader is likely to be, 'So what? You were just doing your job!' Good questions to ask when you are coaching a client whose current CV is written this way are:

> That's all very well, but what difference did you make?
>
> Where did you go over and above what was demanded of you?
>
> What did you increase, decrease or improve?
>
> What tangible results did you get?

This is an example from a client working in the performing arts sector who was looking to move to a bigger and better paid role and was able to spell out very clearly what difference he had made:

---

### Skills and achievements

*[date] – current*

*Artistic Director, Performing Arts Centre, [Name of city]*

*Artistic and commercial flair.* Initiated and led x years of artistic and commercial success in this major arts centre after inheriting situation where there had been many years of income decline. Increased income streams by 60 per cent through planned programmes of emphasis on new trends. Increased grant income by 30 per cent in highly competitive environment while simultaneously

THE CLIENT IN WORDS: THEIR CV/RÉSUMÉ **85**

increasing self-supporting commercially successful activities, reduced deficit to zero in Year 1 and created surplus of 15 per cent in Years 2 and 3.

*Team leadership.* Took over demoralized team. Rebuilt it through careful selection process, developing the current talented team of 6 specialists in dance, theatre, music and cinema through involvement, delegating budgets and responsibility.

*Partnership working.* Built mutually beneficial partnerships with Arts Council, primary and secondary schools, theatre and music schools, local government, other performance centres in region.

### Specialist CVs

Clients in some sectors and types of job need to conform to the standard formats used in that sector. So, for instance, people working in clinical professions will usually be well advised to start their CVs with their licensing and qualification details and then to give precise dates and titles of every job they have held. Any gaps need to be explained, for instance for maternity or sick leave. There is usually also a requirement to state whether they have ever been investigated or suspended for malpractice or are currently under investigation. Unlike other types of CV, applicants may also be encouraged to list all their publications and conference appearances as well as listing substantial training events that they have attended. The longer the career and the more senior the practitioner, the longer the CV will then become and could easily run to more than ten pages. The same is true of jobs in teaching, especially in higher education. Where a profession involves a license to practice, this may be the type of CV that an employer expects. Most clients in these sectors are well aware of the CV conventions that apply, but you might want to brief yourself by searching the internet for a range of examples so that you can give informed comment when the client asks you for feedback.

## Volunteer experience and personal interests

In one of the examples that I gave at the top of this chapter, a client who had been a homemaker for 15 years felt stuck about what to include on her CV, believing that she had nothing to record. Unpaid work is still work and depending on what it is, can offer the same opportunities for a client to pitch their skills and experience. For instance, being a reading-helper at a primary school demonstrates patience and interest in child development, serving in a busy charity shop gives

**86** COACHING FOR CAREERS

customer-handling experience. When people have been made redundant they often usefully fill the time between leaving one job and starting another with voluntary work. Apart from the specific skills that may be involved, for instance in running a local football coaching scheme or being the honorary treasurer for a club or serving in a soup kitchen, these roles demonstrate commitment to community need, something that many employers find attractive.

The final part of a CV is usually the brief section, no more than three lines, where the client describes their personal interests. I have been surprised to find some clients resistant to the idea of including these at all. Their reasons appear to have been their belief that their personal lives are no business of the employer or, a variant perhaps, that it looks 'unbusinesslike' to describe hobbies and interests. It is true that there are some employers, I think here of legal firms and high-powered consultancies, some of whom behave in practice as if their employees have no right to private lives. But naming your personal interests is yet another way of differentiating yourself. This could make it a powerful argument for inclusion.

However, there are effective and ineffective ways to write this part of the CV. The question is: *how can I describe my interests in a way that makes me stand out from the pack?* The way not to do it is to write something like this:

> Reading, walking, cooking, going to films.

These are interests that many people have. If the client insists that these really are their only interests, then ask,

> OK, well what kind of reading? Where do you walk, what sort of cooking, which kinds of films?

The list is then immediately more interesting if it is written like this:

> Reading books on 20th century history; long-distance walking around London; experimenting with Thai and Indian cookery; seeing popular blockbuster films, especially Sci-Fi.

A little humour can add further interest. Phrases that I have seen on client CVs and that made me smile have included: 'Hanging off fake rock faces in a Birmingham leisure centre'; 'Belonging to the UK Wolf Conservation Society and taking them for walks (supervised)'; 'membership of a squad of unfit 5-a-side 40-ish footballers' and 'making elaborate and ambitiously engineered birthday cakes for family and friends'.

## Length, grammar and word magic

As a coach you can make a major difference to a client's CV just by being able to offer feedback on the language. Here are some examples:

You tell the client that there is a special and possibly slightly strange phenomenon called 'CV language' where you avoid the first and third person, so for instance banishing *I* and *me* and also removing *the, a, an,* plus as many conjunctions (e.g. *so, thus, and, yet*) as possible. Just doing this can reduce the number of words dramatically.

You explain that any CV should be rigorously searched for long words, especially those of Latin-French origin, replacing them wherever possible with short words of Anglo-Saxon origin. This is because research repeatedly shows that short words are easier to understand and read. When text is easy to understand the reader attributes more intelligence to the writer, the reverse of what some clients may believe, thinking that long words show greater sophistication or seem more 'official'.

Examples:

| *Replace* | *With* |
|---|---|
| Commence | Start |
| Purchase | Buy |
| Terminate | End |
| Demonstrate | Show |
| Necessity | Need |
| Enquire | Ask |

In similar vein you suggest replacing feeble words such as *did* or *had* with more powerful words such as *led, delivered, improved, guided.*

---

Some clients will agonize about reducing the length of their CVs. 'But this is my LIFE!' protested one such client. In the end the choice of length is down to the client, as is every other aspect of the CV, but it is always worth discussing why shorter is usually better than longer. The first reader is likely to be an HR person entrusted with the initial scrutiny and who is unlikely to be familiar with technical content. Ask the client:

> Could your non-technical sibling/partner/friend read this and understand more or less every word?

Remind the client that although it may be unfair and sloppy, the HR person will give on average 30 seconds to this first reading. Shortlisted CVs will

## 88 COACHING FOR CAREERS

be read more carefully later. The client may want to list every single accomplishment and skill, but an overlong CV may give an impression of verbosity and self-importance.

The inexperienced CV writer lengthens their CV unnecessarily by including information in which the recruiter is uninterested. It is normally safe to remove all of these: references to training courses (the client could have attended and learnt nothing); school name and exam results if a graduate; photographs; date of birth, marital status and postal address; holding a driving licence; current or last salary; reason for leaving previous roles. Omit referee details as the employer will often specify what type of reference they need and from whom.

### Spelling and grammar

There is a whole generation of people who never had rigorous teaching on grammar and spelling. Some of them were told as schoolchildren that it was 'creativity' that counted and that dull stuff like grammar and spelling did not matter. Unfortunately that dull stuff does matter and the client's CV will probably be read by at least one self-identified pedant who may conclude that the client is 'illiterate' or 'uneducated' if the CV contains errors in grammar and spelling. If it is possible that your own knowledge here is less reliable than it could be, get yourself briefed by reading one of the many excellent books on the subject, for instance *The Economist Style Guide* (2018).

Read the client's CV with scrupulous care, watching for the most common mistakes: misplaced and misused apostrophes especially *it's* and *its*, noting that to write *its'* is always wrong; misspelt words like *accommodate* and *definite*; writing *could of* instead of *could have*; using *less* where *fewer* is the correct construction; writing *their* for *there*; incorrect use of commas and semi-colons.

# Looks matter

Fashions come and fashions go in graphic design and you will have your own tastes and prejudices here. A classic typeface such as Calibri, Gill Sans, Times New Roman or Arial is usually a safer choice than typefaces that imitate handwriting or chunky typefaces such as Garamond that take up a lot of space.

Whatever your knowledge of graphic design as such, trust your instinct. If the pages look cramped, then they probably are. If the typeface strikes you as having too many fussy bits, then it probably does. The main points to look out for if the pages strike a discordant note are these:

- Half the first page is taken up with contact details set out line by line.
- The client has a jokey email address at odds with being a serious contender for the job (real example: BuzzyBoo@-----).

THE CLIENT IN WORDS: THEIR CV/RÉSUMÉ **89**

- The client has cheated by narrowing the top, bottom and side margins: ask the client to select the whole document and then ask how many words it contains. 850 words is usually plenty: a busy reader is unlikely to have the patience to read more. The answer is to reduce the number of words not to narrow the margins.
- The typeface is far too small: 12pt is ideal, 11pt is acceptable, anything smaller is difficult to read.
- The client does not know how to use the paragraph option in Word and has simply made a double hit on the return button. Alternatively, or as well, the client has justified the lines on both left and right sides rather than only the left side. This will create odd-looking lumps of white space while making the rest looked overcrowded.
- Too many bullet points: eight on any one page is plenty.
- Combining underlining with bullets, boxes, tables and bold headings in a variety of sizes, colours and fonts will give an over-complex impression. Simplicity is better. Elaborate formatting may often disappear or change when the CV is opened on the recruiter's computer.

## That summary paragraph

The first page is the one that is always read more carefully than the rest and the summary paragraph is read more carefully than anything else on the first page. Its purpose is to grab the reader's attention and to be an introduction to the rest of the CV. I will sometimes spend anything from an hour to a whole two-hour session working 'live' with the client just on that paragraph. To do this, the client and I will go back to their notes from the session on their personal brand, highlighting the key words. Steer the client away from expressing opinions about how wonderful they are, for instance from writing, 'Outstanding thinker' or 'Excellent communicator'. Recruiters want facts: they will decide for themselves whether the client is an outstanding thinker or excellent communicator.

We then try innumerable phrases and sentences, drafting and redrafting, until we arrive at something that feels right.

### 'Banned' words

Remind the client that the CV must differentiate them. This is why I suggest banning all the words that so many profile paragraphs include, all of them clichés or wishy-washy claims:

> Self-motivated, enthusiastic, passionate, strategic thinker, professional, hard-working, go-getter, conscientious, proactive, creative, outstanding, team player.

**90** COACHING FOR CAREERS

Employers want to take all these qualities for granted. If you are not professional and enthusiastic, for instance, why would anyone employ you? Suggest that 40–100 words is about the right length. Anything less will be too short and anything longer gets into territory that the later part of the CV will set out. It can be helpful to offer the client a framework. This is the one that I find most useful:

> The name of the current job or role with the number of years of experience the client has had in it. This should be as near as possible to the role for which the client is bidding.
>
> The context in which the client has gained the experience.
>
> The typical problems the client has solved.
>
> Special skills, honours and awards; qualifications the client holds that the employer has named as essential.
>
> A flavour of how the client works.
>
> Any unusual and memorable additional information.

This client was a leadership trainer and facilitator who was looking to move into a managerial role in a learning and development department. This was her summary paragraph:

> Learning and development specialist, six years' experience delivering wide range of leadership programmes in [utilities and finance sectors, giving names of companies]. Dedicated to innovative course design with consistently positive feedback from participants; changed practice in current team from standard to bespoke events; provided consultancy and facilitation for executive team events. Commissioned external suppliers against rigorous quality controls. Linked all courses to business strategy of organization, increasing overall participant numbers by 30 per cent. Committed to coaching and mentoring as powerful ways of developing colleagues' confidence; have MSc in Coaching from Henley Business School. Former holder of fencing titles at UK national level.

## The covering letter/email

The covering letter or email is usually a simpler proposition than the CV, but it pays to remind clients that the letter has a different function from the CV. It is often read first and more carefully than the CV so the client will miss the opportunity to

THE CLIENT IN WORDS: THEIR CV/RÉSUMÉ **91**

impress the employer if all they write is 'Dear [name of recruiter]. I enclose my CV for the job of. . . Yours sincerely.'

Unless the employer has specifically asked the client to include a paragraph on why they want the job, the CV may not give the client this chance to claim interest in it, whereas the covering letter can do just that. The purpose of the covering letter is to complement not to repeat the CV and the best covering letters have a future focus, emphasizing what the client can bring to the job, whereas the CV has a past focus. Remind the client that it is vital to spell the name of the recipient and their company accurately and to avoid anything that seems too matey. Formal is better than informal when you have never met the person. However, the letter itself is best written in an informal though not over-colloquial style, depending on the sector, and one page is plenty. Advise the client to avoid bullet points and tables: they look stilted, and as in the CV itself, get the client to double-check grammar and spelling.

If your client is stumped about how to write the letter or email, this is a reliable framework:

---

Underneath the salutation: give all the reference details of the job

*First paragraph*: one sentence expressing admiration for the company and the essence of why you are interested in the job, summarizing your experience.

*Second paragraph*: why you endorse the company's or unit's mission and purpose; why its values and practices are a good match to your own; what attracts you to solving any of the problems that the job pack has said would await the successful candidate; what motivates you.

*Third paragraph*: why you think your skills and experience are a good fit for this job; what you think you would bring to it. Make specific links to the person specification here.

*Final paragraph*: any details about your availability for interview and underlining your interest in the role.

If it is an actual letter rather than an email, a handwritten salutation and sign off are usually better than typing because it looks more personal.

---

## The client does the work

In the volunteer work I do for the charity Smart Works (www.smartworks.org.uk) that aims to get unemployed women back into the workforce, something it does

**92** COACHING FOR CAREERS

with conspicuous success, I sometimes read CVs and covering letters that have obviously been written by well-meaning people at Job Centres or other agencies. On other occasions I read CVs that I recognize as originating from the internet. The immediate give away is that the client you see in front of you is nothing like the CV description. A version of this problem from the more mainstream world of work is the CV that, again, seems puzzlingly unlike the client you know. The client then confesses that they have paid a professional CV-writing agency to produce the CV for them. This does clients no favours. The client may sometimes get shortlisted on the basis of this CV but the interviewer will spot the discrepancy and the client is unlikely to get the job. The client's belief that they 'can't' write a CV is confirmed; their confidence is undermined.

It won't take long before you will have seen dozens and maybe, as in my own case, hundreds of CVs. You can get to the point where you believe you have magical CV-writing powers. It can be tempting to intervene and in effect to write the CV for the client, but please desist. The client must own what they write and if it is less elegant and less perfectly crafted than you might produce, so be it. Your aim, as in all coaching, is to increase the client's well-grounded skill and confidence. In future they will know how to write a powerful CV without needing to consult a coach. Make copious use of the Comment button in Word by all means when the client sends you their drafts and be generous with your feedback and suggestions face to face, but ultimately the client is the final judge of what is right for them and must do the work.

# 7   The search

Your client has raised their levels of self-awareness, identified their personal brand and totally rewritten their CV – all thanks to your hard work together. Now what? They still need that new job, so how do they find it?

When I train coaches on how to deliver career coaching, this is the area that I find most baffles them. It is also one of the most fast moving in terms of how technology is revolutionizing so many of the older ways of changing jobs. The messages that you might need to give them may also strike clients as uncomfortable and demanding because sometimes they want the search to be predictable, private, safe and orderly, based on jobs that are properly advertised and then competed for in the traditional way.

The traditional way isn't how it works any more, if it ever did. Even the vocabulary has changed. It used to be that people used mild words like *look* or *apply* for jobs. Now the language is notably more assertive: it's about *searching* or *hunting*. The bafflement of coaches can be matched by the bafflement of clients. Often, the failure to make any headway with finding a job is the very thing that leads people to seek out a career coach in the first place.

*Blake* lives in a sparsely populated rural area and has spent ten years with the only large employer in its one small city. The company has just announced that it is moving its operation to another country where costs are lower. Blake is stunned. His tentative explorations of the local job market suggest that there is limited demand for someone with his particular IT specialism. So far, his progress has been nil.

*Ailsa* is frustrated and overworked in her role as a junior buyer in retail. She spends every weekend hunched over her laptop searching job boards for something better. 'No one could say I'm not putting effort into it' she says mournfully, 'and I've probably sent out 30 applications and uploaded my CV all over the place, but I haven't even had a proper acknowledgement let alone been offered an interview!'

*Natalie's* management job in healthcare will end when her hospital is merged with its neighbour. Every week Natalie scrupulously scans the online journal

94   COACHING FOR CAREERS

> that is the recognized place to advertise similar roles. She has been through
> one interview but was not offered the job. Now she is panicking because the
> deadline terminating her employment is fast approaching.

People like Blake, Ailsa and Natalie are understandably anxious about their situations. Sometimes they are ready to compromise on needs that they had previously taken for granted as absolutes, for instance that they must find a job with an equivalent or higher salary and in the same geographical area. Many people have never had to consider how to look for a job: in the past they have been approached about job changes within their companies and these might have been offered to them without competition, or there has been a so-called 'slotting-in' process where there has been minimal turbulence to individuals. Sometimes their organization has assumed that people will be long-stayers and has a smooth process for promotions and secondments, so there has been no need to look farther.

## Common misunderstandings about job search

Start by asking the client what their job-search strategy is and base the work you do on this topic on whatever the answer is.

So many articles in newspapers, magazines and online make the same point: that the great majority of jobs are found through the *invisible* market of personal contact not through the visible market of advertisements aimed at individuals or through agencies. The given percentage varies. Most commonly it's described as 70 per cent though I have never seen evidence from any well-conducted study to prove it one way or the other, but my personal and professional experience certainly supports the idea. When I was in the hiring role myself, it was an exception to appoint anyone through an advertisement or an agency. But what is familiar to me and to the journalists who write the magazine articles seems to come as a total surprise to many clients. They express shock and disbelief. Often they don't want it to be true; it seems scary, alien, weird. Even when their own current or most recent jobs have been found through a personal network, clients will often imply that this was mere chance, a blip.

Offer clients the theory that 'most' jobs are found through personal contact, acknowledging that this might be less true than often asserted, or untrue for their own sector, but pointing out that 'personal contact' embraces internal advertisements and appointments that are made where the hiring manager may have advertised the job but already knows some of the candidates, including the one who is eventually chosen.

### Job-search strategies that don't work

For your own benefit and to pass on to clients at your discretion these are some popular job-search tactics that don't usually work well:

| | |
|---|---|
| *Sending a standard CV at random to employers* | The employer doesn't see anything in it that expresses interest in their company or the types of job they offer |
| *Uploading a CV on to many job boards* | It joins thousands of others |
| *Applying for dozens or even hundreds of jobs in response to online advertisements* | Unlikely that you would have time to tailor the application to the job so the CV goes straight onto the discard pile; alternatively there is a brutally short questionnaire to complete, leading to instant rejection |
| *Too little effort* | Once every three weeks to write a new version of a CV or to investigate targeted companies is not enough |
| *Too slow in responding to a recruiter* | They work at speed and if you don't you will be dismissed as 'not serious' |
| *Too blinkered in your thinking: trying to find the 'perfect' job, e.g. salary; location; level of seniority; title; permanence* | Flexibility is better than rigidity. Many temporary jobs turn into permanent ones |
| *Aiming exclusively at large organizations* | There are many more small and medium-sized enterprises; by and large they are more flexible and less bureaucratic than big companies |
| *Lack of the right key words in a CV e.g. on LinkedIn* | Specific is better than vague, tailored is better than generic |
| *Not realizing that you are working in a dying sector or geographical area and continuing to search in it* | Dismaying – and may suggest unwelcome upheaval, but it's possible to waste a lot of time here on a fruitless search |
| *Prejudiced views about networking; not knowing how to do it; lacking social skills* | It's all about who you know and how you approach them |
| *Over-relying on one strategy, e.g. expecting an agency or head-hunter to do all the work for you* | A multi-channel approach is always better |

## 96 COACHING FOR CAREERS

# The poor quality of so many job ads

One reason that none of the above processes is likely to yield a satisfying job is that when companies do place advertisements, the copy can be full of the kind of puffery and fluffery that encourages hundreds of people to believe that it might be worth applying. The smallest amount of research into the world of job advertising will yield all the following descriptions of the ideal candidate:

- Excellent communicator
- Self-motivated and disciplined
- Creative problem-solver
- Professional
- Passion for customer service
- Team player.

These are characteristics of any well-motivated employee, they are not skills. Most of us, for instance would imagine that we are 'persuasive', another popular word that appears in these ads. Sometimes this imprecise stuff is followed by ludicrously detailed descriptions of the qualifications and experience that the company wants, usually closely based on the career of the person whose job is now vacant. Companies seems surprisingly unaware that this is historical data and that the future may not be like the past. When you put these two factors together, the ridiculously imprecise with the ridiculously specific, maybe it is not surprising that so many applicants do not fit the bill.

### How employers think

The way employers think is the exact opposite of the way candidates would like them to think. The job seeker wants the employer to reach out to them, to cast the search net as widely as possible, to be open-minded, to be influenced by an outstanding CV, guided by impressive-sounding qualifications and to set up a transparently fair and objective screening process. In reality employers don't want to do any of this. They believe it's too risky, too expensive and too time-consuming. They prefer people who are personally known to them, ideally because they are on the staff already or have been working in interim or temporary posts. Next in preference would be people recommended by other staff in the organization, peers in professional associations or a trusted recruiter, especially if they have good track record in suggesting people who have proved to be excellent employees. It is only when all these tactics have failed that employers turn to the perils of hiring unknowns. When they do turn to the unknowns, the employer's drive is to *eliminate* people, not to include them, which may be why the initial sifting is so often done carelessly.

All of this is why as a career coach one of the most helpful things you can do is to encourage your client to think like an employer, not like a job seeker. For this reason, I will frequently sprinkle into the dialogue questions like:

> If you've hired staff yourself, how have you set about it?
>
> If you were the employer here, what would impress you?
>
> Put yourself into the employer's shoes for a moment: what would you be looking for?
>
> If you were them, what questions would you be asking?

## The vital importance of networking

Some clients will wrinkle their noses in distaste when you talk about networking. They will tell you that networking is an egotistical activity, a self-serving attempt to ingratiate yourself with people you don't really like. They assume that it is therefore humiliating, something that is only done by shameless narcissists or the desperate. None of this is what networking really is. While it is true that some networking can be shallow, manipulative and pointless, I see it as essentially a generous activity, as much concerned with giving as with taking. A lively network of friends, family, colleagues and associates means that you stay in touch with trends, you get challenge to your fixed ideas, you can be nudged out of your immediate assumptions and prejudices, you have people you can ask for help when you need it, you will offer help in return and you will have connections that you can make available to others. In the search for a job, a large working network is one of the prime elements in what will make it successful.

Earlier sessions may already have revealed a reluctance to socialize and could mean that the client's network is too small. It will always be worth exploring what might explain it and how ready the client is to acknowledge it as a problem that needs some work:

> *Celia* grew up as the only child of older parents who rarely went out and had few friends. She says, 'My parents implied that you couldn't trust people and that it was best to close your doors tightly. I see now that they probably shared a social phobia but unfortunately this has left me without role models for mixing easily and I know I am gauche.' When her coach administers and debriefs the FIRO-B (page 63) with Celia, her scores on Inclusion are extremely low and they agree that she is at risk of having too few people

## 98  COACHING FOR CAREERS

in her life. Together they look at some of the safe ways in which she could practise and improve her networking skills.

*Billy* spent his early childhood in care homes. Attentive foster parents spotted his intelligence. They encouraged him to work hard at school where he eventually excelled. But he is chronically diffident socially, telling his coach that he knows this is about his long-lasting fear of abandonment. He understands the principles of networking but is reluctant to put them into effect. Billy and his coach spend time exploring how much of a barrier this might be before agreeing that Billy will start his explorations with networking through social media first.

*Steve*: every psychometric that Steve has taken shows his unequivocal preference for introversion. He and his coach discuss the need for privacy and thinking time that lies behind this preference. The coach comments that Steve typically speaks slowly and sparingly, sometimes avoiding eye contact, and that this could be mistaken for aloofness or lack of confidence when meeting people he doesn't know. Together they practise a quicker and livelier style of talking that can be brought into play when active networking is what is needed.

### Drawing the client's network

The client's network may prove bigger than they first realize. Take a large sheet of paper and ask the client to draw it as an ever-widening set of circles splaying out from their own name at the centre. This works on the familiar principle of 'mind-mapping', usefully mimicking the way the human brain works where one connection sparks off another, rather than just making a dull old list. Identify the possible clumps of names first, for instance:

| Close friends | Family | Current colleagues |
|---|---|---|
| Former colleagues | Professional associations | Service providers |
| Personal interest groups: hobbies, religious organizations | Clients/customers | School, university staff |
| Social clubs such as Rotarians | Fellow participants on training courses | Former classmates |

Run this as a high-energy brainstorming exercise that just starts the client off on the process of identifying names – they can complete it and add to it in their own time later. Then suggest that they highlight names that look like interesting people to contact for advice and information. The questions to ask here are:

> Who always seems to know a lot of people – their own network seems extensive?
>
> Who works in a profession allied to yours and whose contacts and information might therefore be a useful way of broadening your understanding?
>
> Who works in a company that has always interested you?
>
> Who is influential in their world?
>
> Who has actually offered to help?

The essence of this phase in the search process is open-mindedness. Discourage clients from clinging to any of the defensive beliefs that will keep them stuck, for instance, *I must know the answer NOW to where my next job will be; These people will be too busy to see me; It's no good talking to X because they only know about Y and what I'm interested in is Z.*

## Research interviews/conversations

Richard Nelson Bolles' influential book *What Color is Your Parachute?* (2019) is a must for career coaches and career-changers alike. It is a comprehensive compendium of ideas and advice, updated annually, and now has a number of spin-off cousin-volumes. It was here, more than ten years ago, that I first encountered the idea of *research interviews* (called *Informational Interviews* in the book). It made immediate sense to me and I have now explained my own version of it to hundreds of clients, seeing it pay off over and over again. The word *conversation* is probably a better one to use in making the contact rather than the word *interview*, which may suggest journalism or academic research.

The idea is that it ingeniously combines market research with broadening a network and with making the kinds of personal contact that could eventually lead to a job. It most emphatically is not a way of asking people for a job where any sense of neediness creates anxiety, embarrassment and resistance in the person who is being asked for help. None of this applies when you are merely asking for information and advice. This takes much of the potential awkwardness out of the process on either side. How it works is that the client approaches someone in their network by phone or email emphasizing that what they are doing is looking to understand the organization, the sector and its typical careers. If they already know the target person well then it is likely that they will get an immediate positive response. If they don't know them personally then the mention of a mutual friend or acquaintance will usually

**100** COACHING FOR CAREERS

ensure that the email is read or the phone call accepted. The email or phone call is to ask for a 30-minute conversation, ideally face to face but by phone is probably easier to arrange, about the other person's job, their career path, their organization, the kinds of people their organization might be hiring and what sorts of background and experience such people have. The emphasis is on information. The conversation ends with asking for other suggested people to contact, thus broadening the client's network, and seeking permission for their name to be mentioned.

Having described how research conversations work, ask the client how it strikes them. If they seem enthusiastic, discuss how they might approach it. A structured plan is best, ideally a spreadsheet set up with boxes for notes made after meetings, records of follow-up thank-you emails or requests for a CV and prompts for further contacts if appropriate:

*Lily* set herself a small budget for entertaining and then kept a detailed record of meetings over coffee, lunch and dinner. She continued to meet head-hunters during this time. Three of her contacts asked for her CV. One recipient forwarded it to a colleague who asked Lily to 'drop in for an informal meeting'. Many such 'informal' meetings later, Lily was offered a job specially crafted for her.

*Jon* worked as a team leader at a thriving chain of coffee shops. He was sent by his employer to a leadership training event. He was captivated by what the trainers did. First he contacted the trainer who had run one of the events asking for a research interview, ending it by asking for an introduction to one of the company's directors, knowing that a request from someone representing a client company was unlikely to be refused. Jon followed up by offering to work free as a 'runner' on one of the courses he had himself attended, persuading his own company to pay for a month-long secondment to the training company. Jon then went back to his previous role but eight months later the training company had a vacancy. Jon was invited to apply and got the job.

## Why it works

Jon's experience is a perfect example of why this process works. The job seeker is taking the initiative, including reaching out for help, rather than just suffering their misery or boredom silently and hoping that something will turn up. The search is highly targeted. Jon positioned himself as an inquirer not as a desperate person grasping at anything.

These conversations are a way of finding out whether the client's beliefs about the possible new career path are borne out by reality and they may find out that this is not the career for them. If so, this is a bonus as they will waste no more time on it. If it does seem promising then they can tailor their CV, bidding for any vacancy in the well-informed way that is likely to appeal to the employer. From the employer's perspective, the client has already demonstrated commendable interest in their business. Through meeting the client in person they have data about who they are and how they work. There may not be an immediate vacancy but when there is, the client is already at an advantage.

## Direct approaches

All companies have websites and if, thanks to your work together, the client knows what kind of organization and what kind of job they need to find, it can be worth making regular checks on the 'work for us' tab on the websites. Even if there are no specific jobs on offer there will often be helpful information and a named person to contact when the same research interview methodology will apply.

The research interview approach is not for every client. Sometimes, depending on their levels of confidence and maturity, it is just too much. The mother of a young graduate contacted me to say that her daughter was 'desperate' to get into TV. She had heard that I had a background in TV myself as well as now being a coach, so could I help? I worked with this gentle, modest young woman for two initial sessions. We discussed how research conversations might help, especially in a sector where everything is about who you know. I had already seen that although theoretically attracted to work in the media, she was entirely without the obsessive interest and buoyant self-assurance that typically drives media researchers and producers, but I gave her three names in my own network. At the next session she told me straightaway that she had contacted none. 'I couldn't do it' she said, then burst out, 'and I realized that if I couldn't even do that, there is no way I could be a TV researcher because that's what they do all day isn't it – call strangers?' Indeed it is. This conversation was not wasted, however, as it led to a more honest and open discussion about what she really wanted to do, which was to train to become a children's services social worker, a career she has since followed with distinction.

## The 'elevator speech'

Most clients have heard the phrase 'elevator speech' but few actually have one at the ready. The idea is simple: if you are in a lift (elevator) and a fellow passenger asks you, 'What do you do?' you have just a few seconds to answer the question, so what you say needs to be pithy and interesting. Remind clients that they will be asked the question repeatedly, for instance by recruiters or by the people they meet doing research interviews where a variant might be, 'So what are you actually looking for?' It's a completely predictable question and the way not to answer

**102** COACHING FOR CAREERS

it is with the mumbled answer and downcast look that shows that you have been taken by surprise.

This is where the work you will already have done with the client on their personal brand will pay off. Go back to the summary paragraph they created for their CV/résumé. It can probably be easily adapted as the basis of the elevator speech. I give clients a copy of a simple handout that we fill in together:

> I'm a [describe name of current role, possibly adding years of experience if this is impressive].
>
> Working in [name of current or most recent organization].
>
> Typically the problems that really interest me are/have been [describe them].
>
> And the solutions, for instance, include [describe them, depending on how much time is available maybe miniature stories, no more than a sentence each].
>
> What I'm looking for now is [a capsule version of their perfect job].

Where the client is conducting a research conversation, more often than not the person being interviewed will say, 'What about you?' This is the perfect intro to a version of the elevator speech and could end with, 'So this is me', ending with, 'But what advice would you give me?'

It is well worth rehearsing this little speech and developing a number of variants of it so that the client can produce it at will, using their own words and in their own unique style. Rehearsal will give you the opportunity to offer them feedback on how spontaneous it sounds and how enthusiastic they seem. The formula works regardless of the age, seniority or situation of the client. As examples, here are two from opposite ends of the privilege spectrum:

---

**Saeed**

I'm a 50-year-old doctor and I've been a general practitioner for 21 years working in an area of chronic deprivation in London where every day we see patients traumatized by their experienced as refugees and asylum seekers, often having escaped from civil wars and living impoverished lives. We're dealing as frequently with their social as with their medical problems. I'm of Middle Eastern heritage myself and realize how lucky I've been to have had a stable background, brilliant education and a good salary. I want to retrain as a teacher where I believe I can make a different kind of impact on the lives of so many children who are living in difficult circumstances like these and where education could be their way out of poverty.

> **Jackie**
>
> I'm on licence from [name of women's prison] because I committed a very serious crime three years ago [she describes it]. Prison has given me a second chance and I've just completed my NVQ Level 3 in hospitality and catering. Cooking is my passion, I specially love baking and I'm determined to become a chef-pâtissier in a high-end restaurant. I'm looking for a placement where I could learn from an expert. By the way, I'm a quick learner!

Jackie is a good example of how such startling frankness can pay off when faced with what might seem like an intractable barrier to employment. It would have been impossible for her to hide her custodial sentence anyway, but she and I were convinced that it was better to describe it in direct and dramatic terms straightaway. It certainly claimed people's attention and she found her placement easily.

## Recruitment agencies

Recruitment agencies act as facilitator between potential employer and potential employee. They pitch themselves to employers as taking the hard work out of recruitment by finding and then screening applicants. For job seekers they offer a way of refining and short-circuiting the labyrinthine task of finding employment. That's the theory. In practice standards vary hugely. At the upper end of the job market I have known dozens of clients well served by skilled, patient recruitment consultants who have taken the trouble to interrogate the employer's brief thoroughly, getting to the essence of what is needed and then to do the same with the job seeker. I have also heard many tales of recruitment consultants whose approach has been slapdash and lacking in the essential finesse that will keep everyone happy.

Encourage clients to use the same scrupulous research here as they might deploy in making direct contact with employers and to see recruitment agencies as just one possible route to a new job. You will want to help clients distinguish between the two different ends of the recruitment consultancy spectrum. At the high-street end are the agencies that deal in jobs where there is a continual flow of relatively low-paid or middle-level roles with similar characteristics, for instance jobs in catering, construction, administration or junior roles in finance.

These businesses make their money from volume. Increasingly their work is online-based so it may be hard to make a personal relationship when you want to be a walk-in client, but it's worth a try. Agencies expect quick responses and an

# 104 COACHING FOR CAREERS

immediately obvious fit to the jobs they are trying to fill, so by and large they are not the places to look for help if the client is trying to change careers. They need a steady supply of strong candidates; that is why they put a friendly face on their PR. They work for the employer not for the individual so the amount of tailored work they are willing to do for any one person is usually limited. Clients will get best treatment out of them when they present the impressive CV that you and they will already have worked on, the CV contains the key words in a specific job ad, clients are clear what they are looking for, honest about any career blips, are scrupulously accurate with dates and qualifications – and realistic about salary expectations.

At the other end of the spectrum are the executive search consultants, *head-hunters* in popular language, hired to find candidates for senior roles. Far from the cheerful informality of the high-street shops, these are companies that emphasize their exclusivity with premises in expensive postcodes, with plush carpets, nicely spoken receptionists and the guarantee of an intensely confidential and personalized service. The higher the salary on offer, the more handsome the head-hunter's fee from the employer: they calculate this fee as a generous percentage of the new employee's salary.

This market, like every other, has become sharply differentiated, specializing by sector, by role and by hierarchical level. Senior clients may never have worked with a recruitment consultant before and may need guidance on how to find the right one and then on how to work with them, for instance by taking their calls out of work time, responding swiftly, listening carefully and being prepared to invest energy in the relationship. Encourage them to see all meetings as rehearsals for job interviews, even where it seems unlikely that the job on offer will be a good fit. Where a client is never contacted by head-hunters and yet is in a senior role, it may be worth looking at why. Often the reason is that they are not visible enough in their field of operation, for instance that they never speak at conferences, blog, write articles or host webinars. Where you have the luxury of working with a client over a long period of time, how to raise their public profile might be something to mention and discuss.

Executive search consultants work entirely on the networking principles that you will already have explored with the client. Their contacts could be in any or all of three roles: referrer, client, commissioner, so once again it's all about who you know and who you can recommend or be recommended to:

> *Lesley* started her search for a new job by specifically devoting time to finding the right head-hunter before she did anything else. She looked for three so that she was not reliant on any one person or firm. She described the search as 'triangulating', meaning that she asked colleagues for recommendations then discreetly enquired into which firms and people the HR professionals in her current organization were using, then internet research through LinkedIn.

> *Conor* has been 'placed' by the same head-hunter over four increasingly senior jobs in a 15-year period. There is a high level of liking between them and they keep in frequent touch informally. Conor sees the consultant as a trusted career advisor who has rightly steered him away from some jobs as well as pointing him in the direction of others that have turned out to suit him much better.

When it works, just like coaching, it's a mutually rewarding personal relationship. The best recruitment consultants will work, in effect, alongside you with the client. They can offer many of the same services, for instance, help with CVs and interview prep. A client who has already worked with you on what they really want, on their CV and on their personal presentation will get better work out of a recruitment consultant than one who hasn't. Unlike you, the recruitment consultant will be able to convey feedback from the employer at every stage, including failed and successful bids for jobs so for this reason alone can be enormously helpful.

## Still worth a try

Since a multiple approach is always better than relying on a single source, it is still worth encouraging clients to scan newspaper and journal websites noted for their job ads in particular sectors. At the least this will reveal trends in types of job and salaries. Asking for the job pack is a useful first pass at deciding whether this job is an even moderately good fit with what the client needs and can offer. Often the ad will suggest making contact for 'more information' giving a named person who will do this. Remind clients that all such contacts are part of the recruitment and selection process even when they are described as 'informal'. They are best conducted as a courteous search for data about the organization and what it is looking for rather than as a selling conversation.

## Social media

As part of your own preparation for this session, use your browser to search for the client's name. What kind of internet presence do they have? If you knew nothing about them, what would you conclude? Then ask clients how they currently use social media. Some may give you scornful replies, telling you, 'it's for kids' or as one client told me firmly, 'it's for people who are addicted to shouting over the internet'. Be that as it may, once a client has aroused the interest of an employer, perhaps through their skilfully conducted research interview, the first thing the employer will do is to check them out on the internet.

**106** COACHING FOR CAREERS

No presence? *Could this person be a technophobe or else chronically behind the times?* Indiscreet photographs on Facebook of the client drunkenly cavorting on New Year's Eve? *Not our kind of person!* Long rants on Twitter about politicians? *Should keep immoderate opinions to themselves!* You may already have had this conversation as part of the personal brand discussion on the basis that everything about the client should be a seamless whole, so you and the client will probably have concluded that any unwise tweets or embarrassing Facebook posts should be ruthlessly and permanently deleted, noting that this is a lot more difficult to do than it first appears. If clients protest that only friends and family can see this material, you will be doing the client a favour to point out the flimsiness of privacy controls on most platforms.

In general I encourage clients to see social media as a way of reinforcing and adding texture to their personal brand. Retweeting interesting articles in their area of interest can show community-minded spirit; following the thought leaders in the client's sector will keep them in touch with the latest ideas; being a thought leader themselves is even better; writing well considered blogs on a personal website or hosting a group on LinkedIn will serve the same purpose. It is worth putting a Twitter handle on a standard CV so that a hiring manager can find the client easily. A LinkedIn CV needs to be updated in the form of a shorter version consistent with the client's longer CV, making sure that it has a snappy headline and includes the key words used in their sector. Unless the client is actually unemployed, when it will be no secret that they are looking for work, the profile should omit anything about 'now looking for. . .'

It could be the case that social media eventually replaces every other medium for alerting people to jobs and facilitating introductions, but this does not seem to be situation at the moment. It is true that many people identify potential jobs as a direct result of being approached or making an approach via LinkedIn or through tweets. But mostly social media appear to be a supporting act, not the main attraction. They make employers and job seekers more visible and more speedily accessible to each other but face-to-face contact is still far more important when it comes to making the match.

## Allowing time for experiment and learning

This phase of the coaching programme can be lengthy. It takes time to connect with people, await their replies, have the conversations, experience some ignorings, refusals and disappointments, to ponder and to follow-up. Rigid coaching programmes that allegedly must follow a preordained path at set intervals don't allow for the reality of this stage where flexibility is essential. I suggest keeping in close touch by email or text and arranging the next face-to-face session for a comprehensive review when there is enough material to justify it.

# 8 Coaching for interviews

Most coaches will have been candidates at job interviews at some point in their earlier careers and many of us have sat on the other side of the table as the hiring manager or as an advisor. There is nothing like the experience of being on a selection panel to fine-tune your understanding of the mistakes that so many candidates make and of what needs to happen to impress. Without thinking of yourself as a specialist in career coaching, you may well feel confident of your ability to give substantial help to clients on this aspect of the task. If this is the case for you, see this chapter as a quick reminder of what you already know, plus some examples of high-impact coaching interventions with which I find many coaches are less familiar.

## The bad old days

For many years, the job interview was scorned as the lazy organization's way of hiring. It was not hard to find examples of ludicrously bad practice: selectors who asked impertinent questions or who ran their interviews with just one person in the chair – themselves. It was common for interviewers to discriminate against women and people of colour, to ask questions that sought opinions rather than evidence and to talk too much. Then there were the interviewers who asked daft questions: hard to choose the silliest here but I will go for these, both recounted to me by candidates who didn't know whether to laugh or cry when describing their interview experience:

> Luke Skywalker or Darth Vader, if you had to choose, which would you be?

> If a giant crane suddenly scooped you out of this room, how would you get out?

Interviewers tended to be untrained and yet often credited themselves with extraordinary powers of intuition. I was consultant to one such boss who told me unblushingly that he could tell within seconds whether a candidate was 'a 20 watt or a 200 watt person'. He had not made the connection between these allegedly miraculous powers of insight and the revolving door of people who came into his department and then left just as rapidly. There are still many pockets of poor

**108** COACHING FOR CAREERS

practice, particularly in those small- and medium-sized firms that cannot afford a professional HR person to steer them away from their prejudices and lack of knowledge of the law relating to discrimination in selection. But by and large things have improved.

Interviewers are more likely to have been trained, they will ask competency-based questions which begin, 'Give us an example of a time when you. . .' and it is more common to add at least one other way of obtaining data about a candidate than relying on the interview alone, even if this falls short of being a full-scale assessment centre. Employers know that they could be taken to a tribunal if a candidate believes there has been unfairness so it becomes important to have criteria that are openly available to candidates, scoring sheets for the panel and consistency in how questions are asked. All of this has made it more objective, easier to prepare for and also more searching, so a different type of prep is needed.

Despite these welcome improvements, all of which make it more equitable and transparent, job selection remains as it has always been, a fundamentally flawed and irrational process and our role as coaches is to be straightforward with clients about what this means. There are a number of myths about job interviews, the most pervasive of which is that it is a test of analytical thinking, qualifications and background knowledge. Candidates who believe these myths can waste hours on pointless homework and miss out the kind of preparation that really does make a difference.

The most important single message we can give to our clients is this: of course it matters to have the right kind of experience and if you get on the shortlist it will be because your CV has demonstrated that you do, but at the interview *at least half of it is about your social skills*. The panel will be asking themselves, not necessarily at a conscious level, *Do I like them? Is this our kind of person? Will they fit in? What would it be like working with them?* The panel will base their answers on how they experience these social skills at the actual interview. We all decide our answers to these questions in seconds and despite the safeguards that a well-run panel puts in place, this is probably still the dominant way that candidates get chosen or rejected.

Many years ago I was head-hunted for a job that I was extremely keen to get. I knew that I was a strong candidate, and as I thought, a perfect match to the experience that the organization sought. The head-hunter shocked me by telling me with tremendous niceness and directness, 'Jenny, you lack interview presence'. What on earth did this mean? In my innocence, I had no idea! Of course he was absolutely right. I did get the job, but without his coaching it is entirely possible that it could have gone to someone else. This is why one of the most valuable types of prep you can do with a client is to observe and then give them feedback on that whole issue of *presence*, which means that you will be concentrating as much on *how* they answer the questions as on their content.

## Getting clear what the client needs from you

Some clients may feel that they have no problem with interviews because they have consistently been offered all the jobs they have competed for. Even if the session is a one-off, specifically focused on the interview, it is worth asking what the client needs because the answers may surprise you. The failsafe question here is:

> There's a lot we could do potentially on this subject, but what do you need from me?

> Or

> Let's imagine you're leaving here today with all your questions on job interviews answered, what would have changed for you?

Common answers are, 'I get paralyzed with nerves', 'I never know how to plan for the questions, they always take me by surprise', 'I don't know what I'm doing wrong but it must be something because I get as far as the interview and every time I get turned down'. Always ask what feedback people have had from previous interviews, including those where they have been successful. Mostly the quality of this feedback will be flimsy because organizations have no interest in those they reject and rarely bother to say what it is that a successful candidate has done to impress them. Often people will have been told straight lies about 'coming second' or given vague platitudes such as that 'the other candidate had more experience', but there may be a few scraps of data for instance, about not giving convincing detail in answers. Just occasionally the client may have met a conscientious panel member who has been kind enough to give thoughtful feedback. It all helps to fill out the picture.

Experience has taught me to be mildly sceptical about the quality of advice that clients have already had. For instance, in my role as a volunteer interview coach at the charity I support, I find that many clients sent by Job Centres seem to have been taught and then learnt a gabbly all-purpose answer to the first question, regardless of what it is. This answer goes something like, 'I'm a self-motivated, enthusiastic, hard-working, conscientious person who is a good team player, bla, bla'. This is not a tactic likely to impress selectors because its artifice is obvious. It will just tell them that someone has drilled the client into answering a question that has probably not been asked.

You may also meet a degree of over-confidence, for instance in the client who assures you that they have already planned their answers to every possible question and then produces a bulging sheaf of notes. When this happens I might say, 'Well let's just try out a few of the questions that I would want to ask if I were one of the panel'. This client can then get flustered because they are trying to match my version of one of the obvious and predictable questions with their own over-rigid guess and its matching ideal answer. Of course it is desirable to prepare carefully

**110** COACHING FOR CAREERS

for an interview, but learning a 'script' is never the solution because energy goes into remembering the script rather than into listening properly to the question.

## Image

Some clients will say defiantly, 'People should take me as I am'. They hate the idea of having to do what they see as playing some kind of embarrassing charade where they *dress up* as someone they are not. They will tell you that it feels *inauthentic* and *uncomfortable*. Some clients are honest enough to confess that this is a thin excuse to cover a deep dread of looking as if you are trying too hard, then of getting it wrong and of exposing yourself as ignorant or ridiculous. The comparison with a charade is in some ways an accurate one because an interview is indeed a kind of performance that starts with the impression you make from the moment the interviewers meet you for the first time, though the performance is to be the best possible version of yourself, not some fake version who is nothing like you. The usual metaphor to describe this process is instructive: *you have to look the part.*

Some coaches will feel unsettled by the whole idea of offering people opinions on how they look. It can seem as if you are preoccupied with the trivial and superficial or with 'fashion', even though it is not trivial and nothing to do with fashion. It can feel too personal. Male coaches may feel especially uneasy if they are working with women clients and women with male clients because an unwelcome sexual dynamic may seem to intrude. When you offer another adult an opinion on their appearance it puts a premium on how well you deal with your own image: you need to feel confident that your own choices will stand up to scrutiny. Then on top of that you have to be able to base your judgement on facts not whim. I solved this conundrum myself by getting trained as a style and colour consultant and frequently do a whole session just on this topic but I'm aware that this would not be an appealing route for more than a minority of other coaches.

Remind clients that we all make snap judgements on the basis of the weak data that is available. A sagging hem may suggest someone who is sloppy about their work; an outfit that looks dated may lead an employer to conclude that the candidate's thinking is equally behind the times; inappropriately sexy or sporty clothing may hint at general lack of self-awareness. This may be unfair but it is the reality.

### A safe way to discuss image

Start by inviting the client to express their views on the whole subject. How important do they believe personal image is for the interview? It is impossible not to have an image so what do they believe theirs is? The majority will agree that it matters. Then ask how confident they are about their proposed choices of clothing and how much research they have done into dress codes in the organization they wish to join. This is not necessarily as simple as it may seem, as it may be the case

COACHING FOR INTERVIEWS  **111**

that everyday informality in the organization is replaced by a more formal style for interviews. Since you will be encouraging the client to research the organization and its culture, make a point of suggesting that they get advice on what it is customary for interviewers to wear and to match this with their own choices. You can usually predict that a more formal style will prevail since a job interview is a serious process, but always check because sometimes it is worse to be too formally dressed – yet another way that a candidate can seem 'not like us'.

### General principles of good dressing

What you do next will depend on the levels of confidence you feel in this area but you can follow some general principles of good dressing, though note that these may vary depending on country and climate. *Dressing for relaxed authority* is a reliable mantra, so darker rather than lighter colours, structured or semi-structured clothing such as a jacket rather than anything too loose. Good quality pays off. Both sexes are well advised to hide tattoos and to remove piercings. All-black or all-beige is not a flattering look and is often about dressing to disappear. The aim should be a polished, contemporary, well-groomed impression in a style that is a pleasing match with the client's 'brand'.

| For women | For men |
|---|---|
| Minimize visible bare skin: legs, toes, shoulders, cleavage, arms; avoid very short skirts as they may ride up when sitting in a low chair | Wear a good quality shirt. It is uncommon to wear a tie now, but if this is de rigueur in the hiring organization then a plain or discreetly patterned silk tie will work best |
| Go for clean lines and simplicity avoiding ruffles or anything sparkly. Wearing a traditional suit has become unusual but a toning jacket with dress, skirt or trousers can work well | Choose a dark or darkish outfit. Avoid suits that have become shiny from over-wear. If the advice is to go informal, opt for smart-casual trousers and a toning jacket |
| Choose tidy hair rather than a wild child or no-style look. Long hair may be better worn up | Make sure shoes are polished; no sandals or anything that looks too sporty |
| No dangling or jangling jewellery | Well-cut hair; bearded clients might benefit from a professional shave |
| Avoid anything that looks girlish: e.g. pastels, flowery dresses | Good-quality accessories in good condition – e.g. briefcase or document case, cuff links |

**112** COACHING FOR CAREERS

You should feel able to comment on any of these topics as they are widely accepted as sensible advice and you do not need to be any kind of style expert to offer feedback on them. Your feedback will often represent what everyone thinks about a client but no one says and if this is the case then you cannot allow yourself to fall into the same trap. I observed a session recently where a trainee coach handled this with aplomb. Her client was a middle manager applying for promotion and was wearing the outfit he had planned for the interview. She had already established that formality was the custom in the organization. I had noticed his somewhat dishevelled appearance and wondered how she would deal with it. With great warmth and straightforwardness she asked permission to give him feedback, then used phrases like:

> I noticed that the back of your suit jacket and trousers and also the elbows look very shiny and this suggests to me that they've had a lot of wear. The impact on me is that I'm finding that a bit distracting because it doesn't look to me like the sort of suit that a senior chap would wear. I wonder if you think the panel will notice and at some level mark you down on that?

Then, a few moments later

> Those look like really good-quality shoes, I like the formal lace-up style and black is a good choice, but it looks like it's been a long time since they had a polish. There's always someone on a panel who notices this kind of thing and it may suggest that if you neglect your grooming you may neglect other things as well – I know that's ridiculous, but that's how the human brain works!

The client confessed to not having noticed any of the points she raised, accepted all her comments with cheerful grace, addressed them all before his interview – and got the job.

I ask people to come to the interview coaching session wearing the outfit that they plan to wear for the event itself, or failing that to bring me some photographs taken from several angles of how it looks when they put it on. I double check on what the client knows about dress code for the interview and then ask, 'What kind of image are you hoping to project?'

Reading this I imagine many coaches will shudder with horror, thinking that they could not envisage themselves making such intimate comments to a client. I do it because I have confidence in my own judgement, but if you don't, then get some training or outsource this task to an expert. The thing not to do is to ignore it out of timidity.

### *Make-up*
Around 75 per cent of British and American women wear make-up. The minority who do not divide roughly into two. Some women believe that make-up is a

betrayal of feminist principles, it is pandering to female insecurity and is linked with craving the approval of men, a variant of the 'people should take me as I am' philosophy that I described above. Other avoiders will say that they dislike a heavily made-up look and when probed, will usually express a fear of looking clownish if they try it and it turns out badly. I will usually mention to such clients the evidence that women who wear make-up get promoted a lot more often than women who don't, although this may or may not be anything to do with the make-up, and that make-up can even out skin tones and increase attractiveness. It also tends to make people look healthier, a different thing from looking attractive and probably another of those pieces of unconscious bias that is at play in job interviews.

Many non-make-up wearers lack information about contemporary cosmetics and are unaware of the large range of subtle options available to enhance skin tone and appearance. I will sometimes suggest that a nervous non-make-up wearer might try a low-risk experiment by going to the make-up counter in those stores where free lessons are always available, asking for 'a light day make-up', taking with them a large pack of wipes that would enable them to scrub it all off instantly if they hate the results.

## The handshake

Shaking hands will most likely be the only time any actual touch takes place during the interview and it is astonishing how much information it can convey. It is more often an issue for women than for men. You will experience the handshake yourself for real, so note how it comes across to you. Problem handshakes that convey lack of assertion and confidence include the little mouse's paw that is offered as a feather-light touch where only the fingertips are involved, a limp and fleeting clutch, a full grasp but one that has no power. These handshakes will often be accompanied by lack of eye contact, failure to say their name and the absence of a smile.

Give your feedback straightforwardly:

> That didn't work for me: it was too soft, it seemed to be telling me that you were feeling frightened and you never even looked at me, let alone smiled!

At the other end of the scale is the overenthusiastic power-grip or the overfamiliar two-hander that is held a fraction too long:

> It felt very confident but a two-handed shake is something that should be kept for close friends or family. It lasted a few seconds too long for me and I felt for a moment that you might even be going to hug me, but if we've only just met that could feel threatening!

**114** COACHING FOR CAREERS

Discuss why handshakes matter: most clients will already know why they do but will rarely have had any feedback on their own handshake. Show them how a proper handshake works: web-to-web with the right hand, a firm but not bone-crunching grip with one pump being plenty along with good eye contact and a confident smile while saying your name. When I was a coach in a firm that had an outer office full of good-natured people who were used to my eccentricities, I commonly paraded clients around the room getting them to introduce themselves to whoever was there, with immediate feedback from the other person. The improvement was always instant. Today I just ruthlessly drill the client until they and I are happy.

## Dealing with nervousness

Most employers understand that candidates are likely to be at least a little bit nervous and some tension is probably a positive way to feel alert and engaged. But I have worked with many clients whose terror has got well out of control. They describe gulping and gasping for breath, sweating, damp hands, flushed necks – and then feeling humiliated that their anxiety has been so visible. Often this is the number one item on a client's list of what they want to get out of an interview coaching session: *how can I manage my nervousness?*

One way to tackle it is to ask the client how they describe the interview to themselves. Common answers are to use words that suggest pain and powerlessness: *torture, exams, interrogation, third degree, trial* or *inquisition.* I challenge these metaphors, suggesting that they are unhelpful because the words we use, either out loud or to ourselves, have a direct impact on our attitudes and behaviour. Instead of 'nerves' I suggest that 'excitement' is a much better way of thinking about it. You do want excitement because it suggests alertness and being at your best. Being too relaxed may suggest indifference or complacency.

The truth is that the interview is always a two-way process and a wise organization understands this well. The candidate is choosing the organization as much as the organization is choosing the candidate. Where there are skills shortages, as there are in many sectors, the panel may in their desperation be more nervous than the strong candidate whom they are so keen to impress. A much better metaphor is to offer clients the idea that the interview is best seen as a social event. The panel are the hosts and you are the guest. The host role is to be warm and welcoming, to put you at your ease; the guest role is to play your part through willingness to join in on the host's terms and to be engaging. When the host fails in this role, they may lose an outstanding candidate because it is probably a reliable guide to how they treat their staff, as vividly recounted to me by this client:

> They changed the day, time and venue of the interview twice without apology, then on the day kept me waiting for an hour and a half. The receptionist was rude. The man who would have been my boss started by singing a

COACHING FOR INTERVIEWS **115**

hymn of praise to himself for about eight minutes. One of the interviewers yawned openly several times, another got up abruptly and left without explanation. After 30 minutes I'd had enough. I pushed my chair back, stood up and said, 'OK guys, thanks, but this isn't for me', shook hands briskly with each one of them and left smartly while their mouths were still open.

It is essential to normalize nervousness, offering proof that there is nothing 'weird' or 'silly' about it, so I show clients the excellent free app *The 3-D Brain* with its well-presented diagrams and use it to explain that nervousness has a biological as well as a psychological element, that the amygdala in our brains works out of our conscious awareness to protect us from perceived danger by preparing our muscles for fight or flight and shutting down higher-level thinking. Fight or flight are the very things that we can't do in a job interview, leading to that unpleasant sensation of 'freezing'. I then teach clients how just naming the anxiety, ('I'm feeling anxious') paradoxically helps to reduce it because it brings the rational part of the brain into play. After that there is a range of well-known techniques that will work. It may be worth mentioning that this is how sports psychologists prepare sportspeople for major competitions. They encourage these elite athletes to learn the techniques as reliable routines that can be put into practice at will, whatever the drama of the event:

- Visualizing success: the client imagines they are seeing a stage-by-stage video of themselves handling the interview well
- '7–11 breathing': breathing in slowly through your nose to a count of 7, breathing out gently at the same rate through your mouth to a count of 11, repeated at least a dozen times. Do it with the client until they have got the hang of it and can see for themselves how steadying it is and how easy it will be to do this to good effect on the day and immediately before the interview
- Conscious relaxation: progressively releasing tension in muscles, especially shoulders, chest and hands.

Nervousness will also betray itself in body language. You will have done your best to create a calming environment but despite this, it is likely that the session will evoke some version of the feelings of fright that the client could display at the real event. The most common way this may show itself is in hunched posture – the client is trying to protect themselves by making themselves smaller. Here I introduce the idea of high-status and low-status sitting and ask the client to show me how a high-status person sits. Everyone can do this, though sometimes the shoulders are still held too rigidly and too high at first. After discussion, practice and feedback, I then say:

OK, give me your phone with the camera on. Show me again!

116 COACHING FOR CAREERS

I snap them looking confident and then hand the phone back saying,

> So this is what a high-status person looks like. Would you give him/her the job? Look at this as often as possible before you go in to the interview.

Other common manifestations of nervousness include: plucking at invisible fluff on clothing; hair twirling; touching spectacles, pushing back stray strands of hair; throat-clearing; mouth-covering and face-touching. Selectors will notice all of these immediately and they are highly distracting. Offer the client straightforward feedback:

> I notice that while we've been talking, you've covered your mouth with your hand a number of times. The impact on me is that first of all I found it very distracting, I couldn't concentrate properly on what you were saying and then I started to doubt whether you believed what you're saying. I'm wondering whether you're aware that you've been doing it?

The point about these behaviours is that mostly we are unaware of them. Their purpose is self-soothing and it is highly likely that the client habitually uses them in their everyday life with little idea of how much others notice or can get irritated by them. Keep reminding the client if they repeat the gestures. Where women clients have the sort of long, wispy hair that provokes blinks because it constantly gets in their eyes or needs pushing away because it falls across their faces, discuss how their hairdressers may be able to help, either with a different style or with a product that will reliably tame the wisps.

## How is the client doing their research?

There are two common problems about how clients do their research. There is the client who rates their chances of getting the job so low that they don't bother to do any, thereby most probably creating the self-fulfilling prophecy that dooms their bid for the job. Then there is the client who takes it seriously but does too much of the unproductive investigating that will not help at all in the interview. Unless the client is bidding for a chief executive role or a senior job in finance or strategy, there is little point in obsessive scrutiny of business plans, accounts, strategy documents and committee papers and even less in perusing government documents such as White Papers that may or may not affect the whole sector. If there is a document that the organization considers it important for candidates to read, it will normally be included in the job pack.

Clients can see their research as a one-way process: how to impress the panel with what they understand about the organization. This is important, but equally important is that it will help decide whether they want to proceed with their

COACHING FOR INTERVIEWS **117**

application. The research that makes a difference is the kind that investigates what it is like to work in the hiring organization. What is its culture? What gets rewarded, what gets punished? What is the biggest single problem that it faces, now and in the near future? What is the reputation of the potential boss – do they retain the loyalty of direct reports or is there a constant churn as people arrive and leave quickly? I encourage clients to see this as an investigative project that they approach as a journalist might. The internet and social media have made it all much easier than it used to be: what Twitter and LinkedIn accounts do people in the organization have? What stories have there been in the press about it? What does the website say about the company? Are its fine-sounding values the ones that people seem to act on in practice? Is there feedback on Glassdoor about what it is like to work there? Which people does the client know who work there and who might be discreetly interviewed?

## The question of questions

Virtually every client will have some concerns about questions and how they should be answered. This is another area ripe for favourite myths, for instance that the panel will deliberately try to torment you with trick questions or that questions are unpredictable and that therefore there is no point in trying to prepare for them. Poor quality and silly questions are more a sign of an untrained interviewer than one who is out to trap you and the typical arc of a panel interview is entirely predictable, though of course the actual wording of the questions is not. A good employer is at pains to take as much of the mystery out of the interview as possible by setting out in their job packs exactly which areas will be explored at the interview and which will be assessed in other ways.

At some point in an interview coaching session I find it is helpful to de-mystify the question of questions. I often give clients a handout to take away with them as a reminder of what we have covered in the session. This shows that almost all job interviews will follow a similar pattern and suggests tips for avoiding common mistakes and replacing them with powerful answers. This table provides a summary.

| | Typical questions in order | Don't do this | Do this |
|---|---|---|---|
| 1 | **What are you currently doing?** Intention: settle candidate down; check match with job on offer | Talk interminably about the day-to-day detail of your current role | Pick the elements from current or last role that are closest match to job on offer |

**118** COACHING FOR CAREERS

| | Typical questions in order | Don't do this | Do this |
|---|---|---|---|
| 2 | **Why do you want this job?** Intention: check intrinsic motivation; see how much research candidate has done into job | Talk about why the job is good for YOU e.g. you're 'ready for a new challenge' | Describe what you admire about the organization and its match to your own skills and values |
| 3 | **Competency-based questions** linked to the person specification and job description. Expect this to form the bulk of the interview<br><br>Intention: match candidate's experience to the role on offer | Give opinions; talk about 'we' rather than 'I'; go on too long; be too brief | Use sharply focused story-based and lively accounts of your experience, each lasting 2–3 minutes |
| 4 | **Strengths and weaknesses** Intention: explore self-awareness<br><br>Alternative: ask for examples of what candidate most and least proud of in last year | Smirk, look embarrassed; refuse to answer; give examples of weaknesses that could wreck the organization | Give examples of feedback from others on strengths; give one example only of a well-managed weakness |
| 5 | **Optional: exploration of problems and issues in the organization/job** (Unlikely if you have been asked to do a presentation on this topic) | Let rip with all the problems you have uncovered in your research, by implication blaming the interviewers for their stupidity | Be judicious, tactful, putting an emphasis on solutions not problems |
| 6 | **Personal situation**, e.g. availability, travel to and from work<br><br>Intention: would candidate accept job if offered? Would they stay? | Talk about child or elder care, seem over-eager or remote, get offended by a clumsy question about childcare | Answer briefly; reassure panel re: ease of travel |
| 7 | **(Uncommon) Tell us about your personal interests** Intention: understand more about the private person | Go on too long about hobbies or your family | Brief enthusiastic account of some leisure pursuits |

## COACHING FOR INTERVIEWS 119

| | Typical questions in order | Don't do this | Do this |
|---|---|---|---|
| 8 | **What questions do you have for us?** Intention: see where candidate's hesitations about the job might lie | Launch into a long list of questions where you try to interview them | One well-chosen question is enough, e.g. about training and development or about how much autonomy the successful candidate would have |

### The most critical question

One potential question stands out as a contender for the most important single question in the interview. It's the one about why you want the job. It is normally asked early in the interview. Prepare clients for the plethora of ways in which the question can be asked, for instance as a challenge, 'You've already got a wonderful job at [name of current organization] so why on earth would you want to join us?' Job interviews have well-charted weaknesses in terms of their ability to predict success in the actual job, but their strength is that they really can be a good measure of motivation. A badly pitched answer to this question can mean that in effect the candidate is written off for the rest of the interview.

As a panel member myself I have seen countless examples of people who threw away their chances by the way they answered this question. Flirting with the questioner by saying in effect, 'Go on, you sell me the job!' will exasperate, as will the reply that says, 'I really don't know, I'm still trying to make up my mind'. If the client is still essentially undecided then probably they have not done enough research. Desperation is unappealing, seen in the sort of reply that conveys, 'I've been unemployed for six months and I'm ready to take anything even this rubbish job that you're offering'. I tell clients what is but the truth, that the employer has no interest whatsoever in solving their career problems, so to say, 'I'm bored with my present job and I want a new challenge' fails on two counts: it seems disloyal to the current employer, raising the probability that the candidate could be equally disloyal to any new employer, and it suggests self-centredness.

Rationally, all panels know that of course the candidate is concerned for themselves, but irrationally they want to be flattered, to feel that this person is keen to join them because of what they admire about the organization, what they want to give rather than what they want to take. I offer clients this four-stage way of answering the question, linking it to the research that they will have done into the organization:

1 What they admire about the organization, weaving in references to its culture, values and achievements.

**120** COACHING FOR CAREERS

2   Why the organization's values are a good fit with the candidate's own.
3   Why the overall skills and experience that the organization wants are a good fit with the candidate's skills and experience.
4   Why the job is a good fit with the candidate's personal career aspirations.

This is the opposite way around from how most people instinctively answer the question. The reply needs to be given with enthusiasm, a cheerful face and good eye contact. I will often spend at least ten minutes of the session practising variants of this framework with the client, keeping going until we are both happy with the result. Where the practice answer still sounds equivocal and unconvincing, this sometimes means that the exercise has revealed deep doubts about the desirability of the job. If you suspect that this is what is going on, raise it and delve into the pluses and minuses of the application all over again. It is sometimes better to withdraw an application before the interview than to go through an interview for a job that you know you do not want.

### A reliable framework for answering the competency questions

A well-trained interviewer bases the bulk of the interview on probing for evidence of the candidate's previous experience, pegging the questions to an analysis of what the job ideally needs the holder to be able to do, that is, the competencies that are involved. This is a radical step forward from old-style questions that either asked unanswerable and unfair hypothetical questions ('What would you do if. . .') or asked candidates for an opinion. Describing experience gives interviewers an insight into how the candidate actually works. Remind clients that these questions are entirely foreseeable because the competencies will be listed in the job pack.

Many clients will already be familiar with useful acronyms like STAR:

**S**ituation: what was going on, the background

**T**ask: what needed to be done

**A**ction: what I did; this forms the major part of the answer

**R**esult: what happened, giving tangible evidence as far as possible in numbers

SPAR is my own version where the **T** of STAR is replace by **P** for Problem – maybe a little easier to remember.

Although this is a solid basis for an answer, I find that it only goes so far. Instead, I build on it by teaching clients to think of their answers as stories. Stories work because the human brain loves narrative. We really can't help ourselves, we want to know *what happened next?* Interview panels get tired, hungry and bored just like the rest of us, so they may need something to keep them alert and to

COACHING FOR INTERVIEWS **121**

entertain them. Storytelling is a good way to do this and fits perfectly with the idea of job interviews as essentially social events.

I start by asking the client what films or TV series they have seen recently then say, 'so tell me the plot in outline'. Everyone can do this. Often, since I am an avid filmgoer, I will have seen the film they name. Then I point out how the story has conformed to the structure of every story in the world, whether fairy tale, fable, religious narrative, novel, TV, film. I usually say that the longer the story, for instance a two-hour feature film, the more cycles of this framework there will be, nesting inside the overall tale:

1  Things are going along as usual
2  Then everything is disrupted by a crisis: we want to know, 'What terrible things will happen if no one intervenes? What will the protagonist do?'
3  What the protagonist does to solve the crisis, the skills and mental toughness that were needed
4  How it ends

It may help the client to scribble down this framework for reference while they practise. Then I will say, 'So choose one competency at random and tell me your most dramatic story, one which illustrates how you were the hero/heroine of the day'. I have never known a client unable to do this. Then we refine it. Here is how to do it:

> Ask the client to time it using the stopwatch on their phone: under two minutes is too short and will force the panel to ask a follow-up question; over three minutes is too long. This is because in a typical job interview there will be six or seven competencies to explore so with the average interview being 45 minutes long, this part of the interview needs to take up no more than 25 minutes, about 3–4 minutes for each question and answer
>
> Make sure the client emphasizes their own part in the saga by saying 'I' and not 'we'; saying 'we' will force the panel to ask, 'But what was your personal role in this?'
>
> The most common weakness is omitting to describe the dire consequences of the crisis to the organization; prompt the client to include it on their next attempt
>
> The 'what I did' section should be the longest – minimally 90 seconds
> Encourage them to add tangibility to the final phase – 'and so we saved two million pounds in that financial year. . .' or 'the customer left the shop really happy, saying she would come back'.

Once the client has learnt the framework, work on adding some drama, for instance simple dialogue, short descriptions of the characters involved, pauses,

## 122 COACHING FOR CAREERS

changes in tone and pace. Most people have read stories to children – remind them of how much more effective it probably was when they added such touches.

Some clients are naturally brilliant storytellers and I have many times found myself in awe of their immediate ability to create a compelling yarn in such a short time. Others may need encouragement, feedback and practice. Be that as it may, I get feedback all the time from clients who have been successful at interview on how, when they have been offered the job, they have had specific praise on how well they handled this part of the interview. The beauty of it is that as a technique it will work for almost any question – and the same incident, flexed appropriately, could potentially form the answer to several questions:

> *Maya* has been unemployed for several months but has now been shortlisted for a job as a customer service assistant in a call centre. She has no call centre experience but her previous jobs have included stints as a waitress, shelf-stacker and care worker. She is apprehensive about the interview but she has a fund of examples involving upset or angry customers, of working well under pressure and of finding sensible solutions using her own initiative, all of these being skills that are needed in call centre work. Her most vivid story will work equally well as the answer either to 'give us an example of a time when you had to work to a tight deadline' or to 'give us an example of a time when you had to deal with a customer who was angry'.

Some coaches get good results from role-playing a complete interview, saving their feedback to the end. I find that it works better for me and my clients to concentrate on learning storytelling technique and then on practising getting this delivered with impact by working on a few examples. The client can then work up their anecdotes in the time between the coaching session and the interview.

### Other dangers

Preparation also helps with the problem of verbal fillers, those *ums, errs, sort-ofs, kindofs, you knows, like.*.. that we can all use when we are nervous or need thinking time. Clients who use a lot of verbal fillers are usually unaware that this has become a habit that suggests uncertainty and lack of confidence. At an interview, like any other mannerism, it can annoy and distract so you will need to offer feedback. The more comfortable clients are with their general preparation, the less likely they are to use verbal fillers.

It may be worth alerting clients to the dangers of appearing to criticize and blame their current or last employer even in the mildest way. However justified, it

COACHING FOR INTERVIEWS **123**

will sound whiney and narcissistic – not attractive qualities. This is an especial danger in relation to a question about why the client is unemployed or wants to leave their current job. Any sense that the candidate is running away will create alarm in the panel's minds. It is usually relatively easy to reposition an unwise answer by encouraging the client to express responsibility for their own career rather than appearing to make the employer responsible:

| Client is tempted to say | Safer answer |
| --- | --- |
| They've taken away all the most interesting parts of my job and I'm bored | What my current job needs seems to be changing and I'm ready for more responsibility |
| I don't get on with my boss, he's a bully | I've learnt a lot in this job about handling challenging people |
| I'm fed up with having to work all hours, I want better balance in my life | I'm attracted to the clarity around responsibilities that you are offering with this job |
| It's a toxic culture, I can't wait to get away | Your values as an organization seem to be a really good fit with mine and I'm very drawn to that |

## 'What questions do you have for us?'

Clients sometimes worry about the final part of the interview where the employer invites questions from the candidate. Tell them that it is definitely better to have at least one question than none but two questions are plenty because the panel will be getting ready to see the next candidate and more often than not will be running behind time. Some people see this part of the process as, 'Good! Now it's time for MY questions!' and hurl themselves into a cross-examination of the interviewers: this is not a good idea. The questions not to ask are the 'me' questions about salary, holidays, working from home and quirky topics such as whether or not you can wear shorts in hot weather or bring your dog to work (I promise you that these are real examples). These are subjects for negotiation after a job offer has been made. It is also best to avoid questions that the client could answer for themselves, for instance by looking at the organization's website or reading the job pack. Encourage clients to have at least one possible question up their sleeves and the more genuine their interest in the answer, the better. Possible questions might be:

**124** COACHING FOR CAREERS

What are the next stages in your decision about this job?

How will you judge the successful candidate's performance after their first six months?

How much autonomy do you expect the job holder to have?

What kind of training and induction will be on offer?

## A note on 'stress interviews'

The 'stress interview' is a hangover, now fortunately rare, from the bad old days of naïve interviewing. The idea is that the interviewer tries to frighten, bemuse and insult the interviewee, allegedly giving the hiring company an insight into how the candidate would behave under pressure. Techniques include deliberately keeping the candidate waiting, asking inappropriately personal questions, shouting, telling the candidate that their body language is annoying or making sexist and racist comments. This approach is rare in companies that have an HR person who can point out the self-defeating nature of such interviews, the most obvious of which is that if offered the job, most candidates will wisely turn it down and will probably shame the company on Twitter into the bargain. But there are still small organizations whose boss has got foolishly seduced by the kind of reality TV show whose hosts and judges routinely use bullying tactics. Where you are working with a client whom you believe might just encounter such an interviewer, discuss the best ways of handling it. My own belief is that the best thing to do is to calmly terminate the conversation and to leave with dignity.

For some types of job, the client will be asked to do more than just go through an interview. These methods of assessment are the subject of the next chapter.

# 9 Not just an interview: more scrutiny for the client

From the middle of the 20th century, the limitations of the traditional panel interview became more and more obvious. There were some high-profile employment tribunals where big name organizations were forced to admit that they had got it embarrassingly wrong. Research showed repeatedly how poorly the interview performed as a predictor of success in the job. In the UK, there was a dramatic expansion in higher education, creating many thousands more young graduates ready for employment, but when there is so little in the way of work experience, it is hard to judge how one candidate be may better than another. It was clear that a straightforward interview, or just relying on degree classification, would not be enough and the cost of making a mistake at selection became glaringly apparent. The more there is at stake, the more critical it becomes to choose the right people. Assessment centres offer solutions to these problems by gathering more data about candidates, typically through setting tasks that resemble the work that the successful candidate would be expected to do and through psychometric assessments. Assessment centres do not guarantee that an organization makes a perfect selection decision but they do minimize the chances of making a poor one.

Full-scale assessment centres are expensive to run. It takes skilled and experienced people to design them; observers have to give up time from their normal work and they have to be trained; spacious venues have to be found. An elaborate centre may run over two or even three days though one day is more usual. This is why they are more common for entry-level jobs where there is a continual flow of recruits to the same type of job, or, sometimes, for one-off senior roles where the cost can be justified by the strategic importance of the job and the high salary that will be paid. However, assessment-centre philosophy has permeated general thinking about selection. Many organizations pick its low-cost aspects, for instance, giving a presentation, completing psychometric assessments and meeting informally assembled groups of staff. This chapter is about how to prepare clients for any of the variants that they may encounter.

## Presentations

The more senior the job, the more likely it is that the client will be asked to give a presentation. The topic rarely varies: it will be some kind of analysis of the organization's

**126** COACHING FOR CAREERS

or unit's problems. It may be phrased in any number of ways, for instance, 'what would you hope to have achieved in your first six months?' or 'what are the main problems facing. . .?' The client may or may not want your help on this but always check. The answer might vary from, 'Let me run through the whole thing where I give you the complete performance' to, 'Could you just take a look at my slides?'

The most serious misunderstanding about presentations at job interviews or during assessment centres is that they are a test of analytical thinking. While a base-line ability in analytical thinking is necessary, the presentation is actually a test of communication skill and persuasiveness. The panel will be asking, 'if this were a presentation to our staff, how well would it go down?' Just introducing this question to clients will often be enough to create a thoughtful pause. 'Ah!' said one client recently, 'so it's not about showing how amazingly smart I am but it is about how well I can win hearts and minds, especially hearts!' Exactly.

## PowerPoint

Start with the issue of whether or not to use PowerPoint. On balance the answer is probably to avoid it. From being a brilliant asset to nervous presenters, PowerPoint has become a pesky intruder, a groan-inducing nightmare where the presenter becomes entranced by their own slides, shoves an enormous number of words and numbers into each one and then reads off everything while turning to look at the screen. I worked with one client who prided herself on her skills as a presenter. She was a talented woman, a strong candidate for the job. She failed to get it. I was baffled until she confessed that she had used 25 slides in a ten-minute presentation and that she had read out every word in each one. The head-hunter's feedback, rather measured, I thought, in the circumstances was, 'The panel felt that this was not very appropriate since the job was as director of communications. . .'

An outstanding communicator makes constant eye contact, adjusts to tiny signals of interest or lack of it from the audience and more often than not does not use slides at all. A compromise might be a severe reduction in the number of slides – perhaps to five at the most and to limit the characters on each slide to 40 or fewer, presented in a large typeface. An alternative is to print the slides or make a handout for the panel but not to show the slides in the presentation. If the client needs reassurance about 'drying', suggest the old-style solution of simple cards, each of which has a few key words on it in big letters.

## The content: storytelling with passion

Where the content is concerned, less is usually more in terms of the numbers of points that can be made with impact. No more than one point for every two minutes is a rough rule of thumb so in a ten-minute job interview presentation this means four to five points. This can be dismaying to people who want to cram in everything they have discovered in their pre-interview research.

Discuss how the principles of storytelling could apply as they do in the interview (page 120). I will offer the client the view that it is still important to do the analysis but to keep it light while telling compelling human-interest stories around each point. Some clients may feel this is too risky and will prefer to stick to something more conventional. I had this email from a client who had used storytelling with aplomb as part of his bid for a senior job in government:

> After our session I junked my dull old trad presentation. Instead I painted a verbal picture of 'my' department a year into the future and told the story of a typical day from morning to late afternoon, describing evidence, with little human anecdotes, of how things had changed and improved each one pegged to my diagnosis of the problems. I really enjoyed doing it and I could see I'd made them smile and gained their interest. This got me off to a terrific start and I'm sure it's a big part of why they've offered me the job.

It is always going to be more captivating for the hearers when the presentation seems personal rather than impersonal and has human interest rather than being some apparently objective evaluation heavily freighted with facts and figures. I ask clients what their favourite TED talk is. We then find it and play five minutes of it, looking together at how the presenter has compelled attention. I have yet to view an example that is a dry, factual analysis. This especially applies to the opening sentences where a gripping personal anecdote is the norm. For clients who are interested in the TED 'secrets' you might direct them to Carmine Gallo's entertaining book *Talk Like TED* (2014). What also makes the difference, and is readily observable in all the most popular TED talks, is *passion*. If passion is missing, any presentation will lack impact. Ask the client:

> What do you really care about here?

> What is the link with your personal values?

> How can you convey this in what you say and how you say it?

### Seeming too critical

When the client has done a fine job of research into the role and the organization it can be tempting for them to think that they now know all about its problems and that it is their bounden duty to inform the panel about what these are. The difficulty is that however thorough the research, it will inevitably be superficial compared with how the same problems will look to those on the inside. Remind the client that the panel is likely to include at least some of the very people who have created the problems. It is easy to offend. Raise this and discuss how to get around it. Usually the answer will be to focus on the solutions that already seem to be emerging and then to offer ideas about how to build on them. Another

**128** COACHING FOR CAREERS

tactic that works is to emphasize the impressionistic and tentative nature of the diagnosis.

Clients may ask you to be their audience for a practice run of the whole presentation. Many people have already had training and feedback here: ask if they have and if so, what they have learnt about their own strengths and weaknesses or from feedback on real-life presentations. If they have not had such training and feedback then ask what they have observed from being audience members themselves. What is the best and what is the worst presentation they have attended? Usually the answers will be that the most effective presenters use the 'lighthouse effect' (slowly making constant eye contact around the room) occupy the space effortlessly, stand confidently, speak slowly, keep the volume up, move a little but not too much and have mannerisms (such as winding one leg around the other, leaning on one leg or addressing only one side of the room) under control. Use these criteria for your feedback to the client on their efforts, starting with asking what their feedback to themselves is on how well they did. Video provides solid evidence: record it on the client's phone, play it back as the basis for discussion and then re-run the whole thing, videoing it again so that the client has a permanent record of the improvements they have made and can review it at their leisure.

Whether the client rehearses the whole thing with you or not, encourage them to rehearse it somehow, if only in order to time it. Panels hate it when a candidate exceeds the limit they have been set. I once saw a notoriously impatient chief executive leap to his feet while making a throat-cutting hand gesture to a candidate who looked set to go on – and on.

### Learning to slow down

Nervousness can mean that we slow down our speech, but a more common problem is the reverse: speaking much too quickly. When a client has got into the habit of ultra-fast talking generally, they can speed up even more when giving a presentation without understanding how difficult this can make it to follow them or how it robs them of gravitas. As an experiment I might hand clients a piece of text where I have already calculated the number of words. My favourite is to choose one section from Roald Dahl's amusing take on folk tales, *Revolting Rhymes* because the poems are funny and subversive and lend themselves to being read aloud. I time the reading on my phone. It would not be uncommon for this kind of client to read at 250 words a minute or more. Then I find the most recent news bulletin on the BBC iPlayer and ask the client to guess at what speed the newsreader is speaking. The correct answer is 150 words per minute, or for solemn news, 130. We discuss the impact of speaking so quickly: I might read part of the same piece myself at the client's speed and ask them how it comes across. We will usually agree that what it does is create the impression that the speaker is uninterested in the responses of the listener or else is super-anxious – or both. Radical slowing down is the solution.

NOT JUST AN INTERVIEW **129**

You could design a variant on the same exercise aimed at people who speak too quietly, where the challenge is to raise their volume.

### Accents and pronunciation

Giving a practice presentation may also throw up sensitive issues such as mispronouncing words, for instance people who say *ex-specially*, or *nuc-u-lar* instead of new-clee-ar or *mis-chee-vee-us* instead of mis-chuv-us. This can be tricky where it is linked with social class, so in London there are many people with humble origins who pronounce the word *something* as *some-think* or who use constructions that are considered ungrammatical by those who pride themselves on being well-educated. Examples: confusing the words *lend* and *borrow* or using a phrase like *more better*. My experience has been that clients with these speech patterns have all been totally unaware of them. I had one very senior client who had an even more idiosyncratic way of saying the word *something*: she pronounced it *son-thin* along with *pitcher* for picture and *undoubtably* for *undoubtedly*. I did comment on it. She was astonished and said that all her life she had 'heard' the words this way, then felt mortified, wondering if people had had private jokes at her expense and instantly decided to correct herself for good.

People whose speech includes these deviations from the norm most probably learnt them from a parent. Often, for one reason or another, they have missed out on the kind of rigorous education where a teacher might have corrected them. Although others will have noticed, no one has risked pointing it out. You will have to judge how much you think it matters in relation to the job on offer and how ready and able the client might be to change. If you believe it could matter and that the client could self-correct if they wish, then raise it, using feedback principles. Having asked permission to offer the feedback you might say:

> I notice that when you say *something*, *nothing* or *everything* you pronounce them as if they end with a k.

Pause here to see how the client responds, then

> How aware are you that this is what you do?

Then

> It's up to you, of course, but the 'received pronunciation' here is to end these words with –i n g not – i n k. What do you think?

Then you coach in the usual way around whatever emerges.

Class prejudice is like any other kind and in this case might be secretly justified as I once heard it from a fellow panel member, 'We can't have someone who

**130** COACHING FOR CAREERS

talks with a Cockney accent dealing with our customers. It's vulgar. It's wrong for our brand'. For this reason alone it is worth risking the client's embarrassment at having something so personal pointed out. It might make all the difference between getting the job and getting turned down.

A few years ago I was one of the faculty on a project to train senior doctors in how to use coaching in their work. I vividly remember one such group where Dr L, originally from Sri Lanka, was unable to make himself understood, either to me or to the rest of the group. Every time he spoke, the group would lean forward with puzzled expressions while I and my co-tutor would ask him to repeat himself, still uncertain of the points he was making. Eventually I took him to one side. He expressed his frustration with his career, saying that he had got stuck at a 'special' grade, a euphemism for someone who was never likely to be fully promoted, and that, sadly, he believed racism was behind it. Dr L's ability to read and write English was impeccable but he was applying the pronunciation, intonation, rhythms and general speech patterns of his native Tamil to spoken English. He was literally unintelligible to me and to the group a lot of the time; in fact it didn't sound as if he was speaking English at all, and this was probably enough to explain why he had not been promoted but no one had been straightforward with him about the reasons. I recommended that Dr L ask his employer to pay for accent modification sessions from a specialist speech therapist known to me as one of the leading experts in the field. This path is not for the faint hearted as it involves learning different ways of using tongue, lips and palate and over a long period of time. The aim is to increase intelligibility, not to lose the accent completely. Dr L succeeded in getting funding for this help and I have to hope that it worked well enough to break the logjam in his career.

## 'Meet the staff' sessions

'Meet the staff' sessions are another cheap and favourite way for organizations to get more data about candidates. Staff may be randomly assembled or there may be some attempt to make them representative of particular groups. Feedback may be gathered later verbally and impressionistically or through a simple questionnaire while making it clear to these audiences that they do not have voting rights. The stated point of the sessions is to expose the candidate to the kinds of people who would be colleagues and opinion formers if they got the job but the actual point is again the intangible question of 'presence', then to see how well the candidate communicates through skilled, patient listening, persuasive answers and through handling challenge. The sessions might be 30–40 minutes, chaired by one of the group. The candidate will be asked to introduce themselves for a few minutes first – in effect this is a miniature version of the 'who I am and why I want this job' topic, then it will be up to the group to ask questions.

Ask clients how they like to deal with Q&A sessions after a 'normal' presentation, as the same principles apply. If they seem uncertain about what counts as good practice here, discuss how they have seen such sessions well handled by others and then offer them some additional hints and tips if necessary:

- Repeat the question to make sure you have understood it
- Keep the answer brief – it's not the right time for another mini-presentation
- If you don't know the answer, say so
- Where the question seems to be a statement, ask the speaker to say more, then summarize
- Check how answers have been received by saying, 'Have I answered your question?'
- Where the questioner seems abrasive, say, 'I can see that this is a real concern for you, would you like to say more about it?'
- Don't get into ping-pong dialogue with any one person. If you are tempted, say, 'Maybe we could continue this after the session?'
- Solicit questions from those who have been silent so far by saying, 'Some people haven't spoken. Is there a question you'd like to put?'
- Where there seem to be themes emerging, say what you believe they are, e.g. 'It seems that there is lot of concern about topic X – is that right?'
- Expect hypothetical questions that reflect ongoing worries and issues, for instance, 'What would you do about X?' The best answer will probably be, 'I'd investigate it and take advice from as broad a range of people as possible. . .'

In the final 5 minutes of such sessions it can be disarming to ask, 'If I get this job, what would your advice be to me about the one big problem that's waiting to be solved?'

## Psychometrics as part of assessment

Psychometric assessments get mixed reports on their usefulness for selection. There are hundreds available, many – possibly the majority – of indifferent quality, either feeble copycats of their gold standard betters or weirdly off-kilter attempts to measure the unmeasurable. The best of them are invaluable for career coaching and Chapter 5 has more information on this topic. For selection purposes, organizations may deploy them because it makes it look as if they are doing more than just interviewing, and the cost is minimal. Where personality questionnaires are concerned, a cynical occupational psychologist friend once told me that he believed their only true value in selection (as opposed to development, of which he was a fan) was 'to rule out the obvious crazies' and there could be some truth in

# 132 COACHING FOR CAREERS

that, given the superficial nature of the computer-generated reports that the organization may choose rather than going to the expense of having a qualified person produce a much more subtle and in-depth interpretation. It is relatively common to administer psychometrics that genuinely are 'tests' on verbal reasoning and numeracy and which have right/wrong answers, unlike personality questionnaires that are not 'tests' in the true sense of the word.

Some clients worry a lot of about this topic. Personality questionnaires are not usually timed, but ability/aptitude tests are. For clients who, for instance, believe they are 'hopeless' at maths or secretly believe themselves to be 'dim', this can create anxiety.

## Personality questionnaires

There is a limited amount of help that you may feel able to give to clients here other than discussion to uncover their worries and to offer reassurance. Where personality assessments are concerned the best advice is to answer honestly and without too much pondering. It may help to tell clients that some questionnaires have 'lie-detector' questions. These are items that might be phrased, 'I always tell the truth – true/false'. A candidate who clicks 'true' is probably lying because almost all of us will lie in some circumstances. This is known in the trade as 'faking good'. There is also 'faking bad' where a respondent may exaggerate what they believe to be a less desirable trait. In either case these answers would be noted and may change the overall profile. Where there are many 'faking good' responses, this may throw doubt on to the truthfulness and reliability of all of the answers. Clients sometimes ask whether you should take a guess at the kind of person the organization needs and answer as if you were that person. This is a very bad idea. The speculation about the 'kind of person' is likely to be wrong. Then, the best personality questionnaires are constructed so expertly that it is impossible to identify the factors that any one item is assessing.

## Ability tests

With ability tests, the organization may send a sample test. If so, encourage the client to complete it and to discuss with you how it went.

The best advice you can give a client may be just the same as the advice you received yourself when facing an exam, or use to steady your children:

- Get a good night's sleep before the day
- Use your best calming techniques several times in the period before taking the test
- Look at how much time you have available and at how many questions there are; divide the time by the number of questions, so for instance, if there are 40 questions and the test must be finished within 40 minutes, you

have less than 1 minute per question after you have allowed for time to read and take in the instructions
- In most timed tests you do not get credit for working accurately but slowly so it is important to keep the pace up
- Read the instructions carefully
- Read each question carefully: in a multiple-choice questionnaire one of the answers is right; consider which one is justified by the evidence
- Don't make assumptions: previous knowledge of the topic is not helpful
- Answer the easy questions first; go back to the harder ones later
- It would be rare for a selection decision to be made on the basis of results from these questionnaires. If your score falls below the level expected for someone in the targeted job, this will most likely be discussed with you at the final interview.

### Verbal reasoning tests

Clients sometimes ask whether you can improve your score with special tutoring to prepare for tough verbal reasoning tests. There are online sites and courses that claim to be able to do this, but I am dubious about whether it is possible, especially in a short period of time. The Watson-Glaser, the benchmark test, is fiendishly clever in its design, the secrets of its scoring are closely guarded and it is as near to a perfect test of logical thinking as it seems possible to devise.

### Numeracy tests

Many people had hang-ups about maths at school and the prospect of a numerical reasoning test may fill them with dread. Again, sample tests sent in advance by the employer will give an idea of the level and type of question – usually for a straight-forward managerial job this will be no more than GCSE (high school) arithmetic, for instance, calculating percentage increases and decreases. Hoping for the best is not a sensible strategy, but practice and specialist coaching can make a big difference with numerical reasoning. It can increase the client's confidence and their mathematical performance, for instance pinpointing areas for improvement. There are books and online courses that can be an effective first line of preparation and if the client is so inclined it might be worth their exploring how these might help. For instance, the BBC website is a free source of high-quality mathematical explanation and tests (bbc.co.uk). One simple piece of advice for the day itself is that if calculators are allowed, bring your own and get thoroughly familiar in advance with how it works.

# Full-scale assessment centres

Clients who have not met the term 'assessment centre' previously will benefit from having its purpose explained, for instance that it is a process and not a place.

**134** COACHING FOR CAREERS

Reassure them that running an assessment centre is a sign of a healthy organization because its purpose is to create as much data as possible about shortlisted candidates, increasing fairness and transparency, telling them that assessment centres have an impressive record of predicting closeness of fit between the candidate and what the job needs. From the candidate's perspective they convey some flavour of what the work would actually involve, another way for clients to decide whether this really is the job for them.

Good organizational practice on running assessment centres includes: straightforward briefing on what will be expected; several well trained 'raters'; a variety of tasks with clear criteria on what counts as success; close simulation of the skills the job needs and a well-run process at the end when the raters share their observations. If briefing information is not available then prepare the client on the typical activities and what they will probably measure. For instance they could include a selection from any of the tasks in this table:

| Typical task | Purpose |
| --- | --- |
| Creating something as a group with simple materials, e.g. Lego, paper, pens, scissors | Looking at leadership and followership style or preferred roles in a group |
| Leaderless discussion | How you behave in a group, e.g. how often you contribute, build on what others say, offer solutions, deal with conflict |
| Performing a task central to the job role, for instance selling a product, handling a difficult phone call, having a performance conversation with a member of staff. This is often done using a professional actor | Assessing how you deploy the skills needed for the job, e.g. listening, persuading, explaining |
| Giving a presentation | Persuasion and verbal communication |
| Meeting groups of staff | How you handle challenging questions; how composed and confident you are in front of a group of colleagues |
| In-tray exercise: a collection of documents or emails simulating a typical set of demands. Used for managerial jobs | How well you prioritize |
| Case study: usually requires a written response | Can be designed as a test of strategic thinking or as a test of written communication |

| Typical task | Purpose |
|---|---|
| *Psychometric assessments: could be ability and/or personality instruments* | Ability tests have right/wrong answers and are commonly about verbal reasoning (logic) and numeracy

Personality tests assess personality traits, often on a ten-point scale comparing your results with those of a similar group of other people |
| *A second interview for selected candidates* | To include feedback and questions created by the assessment centre |

## Development centres

You may work with clients who will go through or have gone through *development centres*. These are essentially the same kinds of activities but their purpose is development rather than yes/no, in/out selection. Instead of a selection decision they will end with a report written by a psychologist who will give feedback to each individual. Sometimes these events are a blend of development with selection, for instance, identifying a cohort of people believed to have talent important for the future of the organization and who will then be offered further development and training opportunities.

## Advice to clients on assessment centres

The point about assessment centres is that you can't really prepare for them because the purpose of a well-designed centre is to reflect your normal behaviour, assumptions, skills and personality. The longer the centre runs, the more difficult it becomes to stay on your absolutely best behaviour. However, there are a few hints and tips you can pass on to clients, probably most needed for young people rather than for seasoned professionals who may have been through assessment centres previously:

- Get there in plenty of time
- Remember you are on display from the moment you come into the building until the moment you leave
- Make a point of being courteous to any staff you meet – they may well be asked for feedback on you later
- If there is a lunch involving staff from the organization, see it as an opportunity to find out more about the job and the company; be discreet about your opinions and your reasons for wanting the job

**136** COACHING FOR CAREERS

- Introduce yourself confidently to everyone you meet, be friendly, engaged and helpful to the other candidates as this shows a willingness to be a team player; turn your phone off and put it away for the day as constantly checking it could create an impression of indifference
- If you don't understand the instructions for an exercise, ask for guidance
- Role-played exercises with an actor: there is often a hidden 'backstory' waiting to be uncovered in the actor's brief; listen out for this. Sometimes it will work to say, 'I think there may be something more that needs to be discussed – could you tell me what's really worrying you here?'
- Group exercises: don't dominate, don't stay silent. Make facilitative interventions such as offering to be the timekeeper or chair, summarizing what others have said, offering new solutions. Most groups hare straight off into the task without discussing the best ways of setting about it. A candidate who raises this and facilitates the ensuing discussion will meet with considerable approval from raters
- Don't be dismayed if one exercise appears to go badly; it's the overall impression that counts.

Clients often enjoy assessment centres more than they had expected. Even when they don't get the job they can feel that they have been given a fair chance to show what they can do and may have gained valuable clarity about what kind of job will suit them better in the future. If it does go well it is worth capturing the essence of what worked so that the client has a good base for future assessment adventures.

# 10 What's the point of it all? Working with clients on life purpose

'Does everybody die? Will you die?' Then, a long, tremulous pause, 'Will I die?' Samuel, my youngest grandchild was just 4 years old, when, exactly as predicted by developmental theory, he realized for the first time that life was finite. How else could his parents answer other than to say 'yes' followed by hugs and kisses to soothe his heartbreaking sobs?

We and our coaching clients have had many more years to get used to the idea, at least in principle, but my own belief is that this 'existential crisis' is behind the question that a substantial minority of people bring to their coaches. When you have no comforting belief in a life after death, when individual human existence can seem meaningless because it is so brief, what are you to do? This chapter is about how to work with clients on finding some kind of answer. I will say right now that if there is a quick fix, some set of ideas, tools and techniques that will magically supply a eureka moment, I have yet to find it. More commonly the work feels maddeningly incomplete or fragmentary, though I also relish it as possibly the most satisfying and challenging work that I do:

*William* is in his late 40s, successful enough as an entrepreneur to appear on a list of the richest people in the UK. He has more money than he could ever spend, a house that has appeared innumerable times in design magazines, a beautiful wife and two delightful children. He says, 'My life feels empty. I'm bored silly with my work. I don't see the point of anything. What now?'

*Zoe* is an early-years teacher deeply dismayed to find that so much of her life feels 'disappointing'. She is 38, single, consistently gets praise for her work, is clear that she has no wish to progress in the teaching hierarchy and is finding her work repetitive and dull. To her colleagues and friends Zoe presents a bright and cheerful face yet she says to me, 'I see a life of meaninglessness stretching ahead of me. Is this all there is?' In our third

# 138 COACHING FOR CAREERS

> session, Zoe confesses to acute health anxiety, meaning that she frequently visits her doctor with minor symptoms, believing them, wrongly, to be a sign of life-threatening illness.

Some years ago when I first began to recognize that clients were presenting with this issue of life purpose, I eagerly searched the coaching and academic literature. I found a mass of familiar material on why we need a sense of purpose with innumerable pyramids, triangles, box-and-arrow diagrams, theories and 'models'. Every philosopher of note has addressed the question. But I was shocked to find that there was virtually nothing that answered my questions about practical applications for coaching and as far as I have been able to establish, this is still the case. Our books, courses and researchers are mostly silent on the topic or at the most offer a few short paragraphs of advice. There are some inspiring self-help books, for instance the enjoyable *Designing Your Life* (2016) by Bill Burnett and Dave Evans and there is John Lees' best-seller *How to Get a Job You Love: 2019–20 Edition*. These can provide some suggestions to coaches searching for usable ideas. Books written by people with strong religious faith advocate surrendering to God or to some 'higher power', but this is unlikely to appeal to clients and coaches who have no such beliefs themselves.

I found that there was very little more in the vast canon of psychotherapy with the noble exceptions of Viktor Frankl with his extraordinary book *Man's Search for Meaning* originally published in 1946 as a reflection on his survival at Auschwitz, and Irvin Yalom whose work has long been an inspiration to me. His scholarly masterwork, *Existential Psychotherapy* (1980) tackles the subject head-on and I have drawn on his wisdom throughout this chapter.

I use the terms *purpose* and *meaning* as synonyms here, though aware that they may have slightly different meanings. Finding purpose is also not necessarily the same as the idea of *changing career*, though in practice the need to find a sense of purpose is often behind the feeling that you need to change career and vice versa.

## Themes in films and books

The world of the arts has been more diligent in exploring these themes – film, long-form television and novels especially. Many of the world's great novels have been preoccupied with it. In Charles Dickens' *Great Expectations*, the hero, Pip, has to confront his dismay at discovering that his life-long striving to deny his origins and to be a 'gentleman' has been based on a sham. Perhaps the finest film example is Harold Ramis' *Groundhog Day*, made in 1993. Ramis says that his question in

WORKING WITH CLIENTS ON LIFE PURPOSE **139**

writing the screenplay was, *What if we could live forever, how would we change?* In the film, the character played by Bill Murray is forced to repeat the same day until he learns how to put the needs of others before his own. The film has been praised by Buddhists who see their own philosophy of rebirth and of living in the moment through selflessness reflected in it, by Jews who see their tradition of *mitzvahs* (good deeds) and by Christians who see salvation through good works.

## Why now? Getting an historical perspective

In working with clients in those countries in Europe, Australasia and North America that are increasingly secular in their outlook with fewer and fewer people claiming religious affiliation, we need to remember that globally we are a minority. Religious belief is in fact growing with roughly 85 per cent of the world's population identifying with one of its main religions. So, for instance, the Judeo-Christian view of the world offers a well-synthesized set of principles based on the belief that human life is part of God's plan for us and that living a good life means reward in an afterlife. The way that 'a good life' is defined will depend on which branch of belief you follow, so it might endorse finding meaning in work, in the vividness of your faith, in your sense of personal salvation or in the purity of your dedication to a literal emulation of what has been laid down in the Bible.

This world and life view dominated Western society until the Enlightenment, the blossoming of scientific, political and philosophical thinking and experiment in early 18th-century Europe. During the Enlightenment, gifted thinkers challenged traditional beliefs and instead sought evidence, for instance from physics, biology, geology and physiology, to explain the puzzles of life. The motto *sapere aude*, 'dare to know', meant defying authority of all sorts through rational debate. It was also part of the inspiration behind the French and American revolutions and led ultimately to Charles Darwin's discoveries in the mid-19th century, at the time controversial and astonishing: humans had evolved as a dominant species from other animals and through the ruthless rules of natural selection rather than through the design of God. After that there was no going back, though even today there is a small but vociferous minority of Christians and Muslims who believe in 'Creationism', denying the comprehensive evidence that Earth is billions of years old and that we evolved from other primates.

When you ask yourself, 'Why is this an issue for so many people now?' the answer must surely lie in our increasing prosperity and longevity. We have the money and the better health; we have the luxury of being able to worry about it. In previous generations, the harder you had to work to survive, the less likely you probably were to be troubled by questions of meaning. Today it is typically a question for the second half of life and for people affluent enough to have the energy to consider it. In past centuries, work itself was more connected with the land, with the rhythm of the seasons and perhaps with the satisfaction of tending livestock

**140** COACHING FOR CAREERS

and plants and seeing your children survive hunger and illness. Restrictive though such a life must have been, there may have been a stronger sense of belonging to your family, your spiritual community, your tribe and your country than there is in many Western societies today.

## It's not trivial

It may seem like a statement of the ridiculously obvious to say that this is a serious topic. But my guess is that we are only really at the beginning of understanding just how serious. The currency of life purpose as an issue may have been debased by the popular hunger for simple recipes that will apparently guarantee happiness and for the many tyrannical claims made for 'positive thinking' by people who may be more interested in selling courses, videos and apps than they are in assessing whether their nostrums actually work.

Unfortunately some kinds of coaching have also been contaminated by this over-optimistic thinking. The US journalist Barbara Ehrenreich has whacked some much needed cynicism at the farther reaches of these claims in her book *Smile or Die* (2009) whose subtitle tells you exactly what her thesis is: *How Positive Thinking Fooled America and the World*. She points out that positive thinking cannot cure cancer nor can it turn a failing business into a successful one. However, there is an increasingly impressive body of academic research telling us that happiness, meaning and purposefulness have to be taken seriously in the context of health and well-being. For a comprehensive summary of the argument you could read Andrew Steptoe's article (2019). Professor Steptoe heads up a large longitudinal project on ageing at University College London. The project involves over 7000 English people over 50. It seems from his findings that having meaning and purpose in your life, in other words, seeing what you do as worthwhile, reduces markers such as inflammation, depression, cognitive decline and raised blood pressure among many others. Which is cause and which is effect in such a complex subject is tricky to disentangle, along with the exact biological processes involved, but that the link is present, there can be little doubt.

## What kind of client brings life purpose questions?

When you ask what kind of client brings the question of life purpose, the true answer is that it could be anyone. However, in practice there are certain types of client that you are more likely to see asking these questions.

### Life stage challenges

Human life presents stages where each has its developmental challenge. Infancy and early childhood are about learning to trust, to belong, to grasp the rules, to

WORKING WITH CLIENTS ON LIFE PURPOSE **141**

acquire basic skills. Adolescence means developing your own identity and separating from your parents. In young adult life you grow the skills that will earn you a living and you find a sexual partner, you develop more confidence and may begin a family of your own. You learn to balance dependency with freedom, and intimacy with understanding that you are essentially responsible for yourself. It would be unusual for clients at the early mid-life stages to bring you questions about 'purpose': they are simply too wrapped up in the daily challenges of being a young parent or of striving for success at work.

Many thinkers have addressed the question of the challenge that each life stage presents. The German-American writer Erik Erikson suggested in his book *The Life Cycle Completed: Extended Version* (1998) that it is in the years from 35 to 65 that we become concerned with questions of purpose and legacy. He described the challenge as one of 'generativity v stagnation' where there is a wish to make a wider contribution to society along with raising the next generation. Then in older age comes the more purely existential question: *what has my life been about? Is it OK to have been me?* Erikson's wife and collaborator, Joan Erikson, touchingly added a final stage, written when she herself was in her 90s, about learning to cope with inevitable bodily deterioration in old age when versions of the early stages of life reappear in reverse, for instance learning how to surrender to your body or how to overcome a sense of stagnation. I have found that it is useful to spend a little time describing these theories to clients: it normalizes their quest.

## Pointless jobs

Working as a coach you will always ask clients in conventional employment what their work involves. In 2018 the anthropologist David Graeber published a book called *Bullshit Jobs,* an amusing and somewhat melodramatic romp through this territory. He defines a bullshit job as one that is pointless, usually feeding other unnecessary jobs up and down the system. He identifies five types of bullshit job: flunkies (helpers to people who consider themselves too grand to do simple tasks), goons (bullies and aggressive lawyers or those he considers to be professional liars such as PR people), duct tapers (patchers-up of things that should never have broken in the first place), box tickers (collectors and fillers in of data that no one will use except other box tickers) and taskmasters (managers of people who don't need managing). Working in apparently 'creative' sectors seems no different and reading the book I thought of my client Anna who had this to say about her job at a museum-gallery:

> A big part of my work is that I research and write pitches for exhibitions and events, the fancier the title the better. No one says it out loud, but few of these ideas will ever see the light of day. However, there is a lot of wise murmuring, sympathetic listening, pseudo-debate, encouragement, that 'maybe this or

## 142 COACHING FOR CAREERS

> that proposal needs more development/come back to the next meeting with some further ideas'. Sometimes my boss takes the idea to the next level up, when it is subjected to the same process with even longer 'papers' and with even more senior people present but invariably comes back to me with suggestions for 'more development'. The truth is that decisions are actually made by a tiny group of powerful curators – and in secret – but we have to keep up the charade of 'involvement'.

### Something is missing

Our first task as coaches is to name what is going on, raising it explicitly as a question. People do not need to have 'bullshit jobs' in order to feel that something is wrong or missing. I have worked with many clients who have founded businesses, made a lot of money and proved wrong the spiteful or unthinking teachers who told them that they would never amount to anything. In their 40s or 50s they are asking themselves about the price they have paid in terms of the relationships that matter or of work that makes a difference to someone or something else. They have sometimes distracted themselves with over-work, sex, drugs, alcohol, luxury goods and sometimes with fame – but now their lives feel empty. Sometimes success seems to have come too easily and for a product or purpose that seems valueless, despite the business world having put a high actual price on it. I think here of a client who had developed a simple product in the world of fast-moving consumer goods. The product took off. Still only his early 40s, he sold his company for an astonishingly high sum while telling me that he felt secretly 'guilty and ashamed' that something he thought was 'trashy' and that he had only developed originally for the fun of seeing if he could, had earned him many, so many, millions of pounds.

Some clients are playing leading parts in other people's businesses or may be earning staggeringly high salaries, yet still feel that something is awry:

> *Ashley* has made a steady rise in a series of roles in PR companies. She has been feted as a successful woman in a sector dominated by men, is known for her flexible, kind but firm leadership style and for earning the owners of the current business a lot of money. For this she has been rewarded with shares and a generous salary. Initially she came to coaching to discuss performance issues in her team but we quickly got to the nub for her: 'Why am I working so hard to make yet more money for shareholders who already have too much and in a business that's all froth?'

WORKING WITH CLIENTS ON LIFE PURPOSE **143**

You may work with clients who are approaching retirement or who have been made redundant from organizations where they have worked for many years. Sometimes they have over-identified with their jobs and with the organization: it has apparently provided all the purpose they needed, they have loved and respected it and now it can feel as if their whole self has been stripped away. These clients can be challenging: what some of them really want is to wake up and find that the loss of their jobs has been a bad dream. A small minority is never able to move on from their feelings of anger, hurt and rejection. I was once shown around the home of an acquaintance who had been fired in his early 50s, and with a generous pay-off, from a job he had prized. His bitterness was unquenchable and he proudly pointed to a small brass plate in the new extension to his house. This read, 'The [name of organization] Wing. Paid for in blood money'. He had never worked, in either a paid or volunteer role, since leaving his job ten years earlier, despite constantly declaring that this was his wish.

## The trigger points

The client raises the question of purpose and meaning, most commonly by saying, 'I don't know where my life is going'. It will usually pay dividends to ask:

What makes this an issue now?

In fiction, there is usually a well-defined crisis point that drives the plot: an unexpected loss, an unexpected gain, an illness, an unfair accusation, a divorce, a marriage. In real life it is much more likely that any 'revelation' will emerge slowly. However, it is true that sudden life events can bring submerged feelings to the surface. These events trigger the realization that something needs to change and that the underlying question is a profound one about meaning and purpose.

Among recent clients I think of one whose parents had died within a few weeks of each other. They had been in wrenchingly poor health so their deaths, although occasions for sadness, were neither unexpected nor unwelcome. This client had opened her mother's wardrobe and had found many dresses inside with their tags intact. The client said, 'I was stunned when I saw them. They symbolized all my mother's self-imposed restrictions and fears, her sense that bad times were always around the corner and that you could not indulge yourself, ever. Yet she had bought this clothing. It represented life unlived and unfulfilled and I knew I had to get a grip on my own life and its purpose.'

These dramatic turning points seem to be less common than apparently small and mundane events that nonetheless represent a point of no return, even if the client rarely acts on them immediately. I have heard versions of this story repeatedly from clients, for instance the marketing executive who was giving a presentation to Korean clients, the final leg of a tiring journey through several countries. He

**144** COACHING FOR CAREERS

said, 'I saw myself with these polite people who were nodding and possibly not fully understanding what I was saying since there was no interpreter and I found myself thinking, "the ratio of effort to reward is all wrong here, I can't do this anymore, it's costing me too much and I don't really care about the product".'

Some clients have been exceptional in their achievements. They have done what so many 'life coaches' advocate and have ruthlessly defined their goals. Where this has been at the expense of everything else in their lives, the achievement can seem hollow. As soon as it has been reached it feels valueless whether it is a PhD that has taken years to complete or a promotion that will mean a fancy title and an office with two sets of windows. A very senior civil servant had just failed to get an even more senior job. He told me that he would be able to do what he called 'feeling better about myself' if he were offered a knighthood as some kind of compensation for his disappointment. I remember staring at him in amazement and privately forecasting that if this were indeed to happen (it never did), it was most unlikely that he would feel 'better' for long. These achievements are *extrinsic* – they depend on the praise, rewards and judgements of others rather than on the *intrinsic* satisfaction that comes from knowing that you have done something that you yourself prize. The question to ask clients here is:

> Would you do this [whatever the activity is] if there were no external reward such as money, an important-sounding title, the praise of others?

## The quest and its principles

In working with clients over the years on the issue of finding meaning and purpose, I believe there are a number of principles that it helps to keep in mind and to share with clients.

*Self-transcendence.* The essence of the quest for meaning and purpose is that it is about self-transcendence. It is not about being self-preoccupied, self-absorbed or 'self-actualized' and it is not even about that popular coaching concept, 'achieving your potential'. It is about giving, not taking.

*The quest is slippery and elusive:* there is no one right answer sitting there somewhere waiting to be uncovered. There are no moments of epiphany. When we ask, 'What is my purpose?' we are asking about something that is aimed outside ourselves and that will do some lasting good to a cause, a community, a group or an individual. The paradox, and this is why it is so tricky to do this work as a coach, is that the more you hunt for a 'purpose', the less likely you are to be successful. There is a comparison here with 'trying to be happy' where the more you try, the less happy you are likely to be.

Working many years ago on a leadership programme in the USA with a distinguished American professor he told me to expect that in the opening icebreaker people would give predictable answers to the question, 'If you were independently

WORKING WITH CLIENTS ON LIFE PURPOSE **145**

wealthy, how would you be living your life?' His forecasts were subtly sabotaged by several of the group, most of whom were resentful about having to be at the event at all, sourly announcing that they were already 'independently wealthy'. Nonetheless, their answers did fall into exactly the patterns he had foretold: living on an island, running a B&B, breeding cats or dogs, starting a children's charity, sailing around the world. To these I would add a favourite of British men: becoming a postman, where as one client said with a grin, 'You can wear shorts all the year round and you go home at one o'clock'. The light-hearted way clients propose these notions will usually show you that they are not ideas to be taken seriously. A moment's exploration will show you that they are escapist fantasies and don't represent what the client truly wants, though I did have one client, formerly a chief executive of a large non-profit organization who really did leave to run a B&B with his wife. He sent me a photograph of himself a year later captioned, 'This is me in my pinny, serving breakfast', but he was a special case and I noticed soon afterwards that he had become a non-executive director for a number of organizations in his sector. The real life of a writer, an animal breeder or a B&B owner is one of relentlessly hard graft and little money, not the carefree existence that the overworked executive breezily imagines.

Other clients will describe a wish to write a novel or memoir, act, sculpt, paint pictures, make films or explore some other type of creative expression. These can be worthy and fulfilling projects but it would be rare for them to form the basis of the new career that some clients say they want. When a middle aged or older person achieves unexpected commercial success in these fields, the backstory will invariably show that they have literally spent a lifetime obsessively practising their craft. The only change is that they have at last gained recognition for it. Your client may be the exception to these 'rules' and a good coach will assume that this might be the case while still encouraging realism and research: *What are the current trends in painting/film/fiction? How do people get noticed? How might you test out your ideas? What might be a good first step here?*

*This is not a straight-line process* where the client ponders with you, finds the single solution, concocts a neat plan and then flawlessly implements the plan, all within a few weeks or months. I have never known it happen like that. In Herminia Ibarra's book *Working Identity* (2003) she gives 39 fascinating examples of people who have made life-changing transformations, the most radical of which is the man who gave up a successful career as a psychiatrist in order to become a Buddhist monk. All her subjects took their time and the bigger the transformation, the more time they took. Their routes were zig-zags and included innumerable blind alleys, working part time in a new role while continuing the old one, volunteering, training, pilot projects and cautious steps into the unknown. This is one of the aspects that makes it challenging for a coach: unless you have the privilege of working steadily and over a long period of time, by which I mean years, with a client (even if this is off and on), you are unlikely to see the change through from start to finish but you will certainly be able to add significant value at whichever point the client engages you.

## 146 COACHING FOR CAREERS

*Clients do not find their life purpose by mixing with the same old crowd.* Encourage them to expand their networks, for instance through exploring the connections suggested by LinkedIn, asking for personal introductions, talking formally and informally to people in areas that interest them but that still seem relatively unknown. If their networking skills need attention (page 97) then work with them on improvement. The shift can seem small but it may make a big difference. A doctor client with a belief in patient advocacy had an inspirational idea for an app and asked a friend in IT for advice. The friend suggested another friend who worked in the medical technology relevant to my client's idea. This led to an introduction to a US insurance company looking for new ways to put patients in charge of their own health data that led to a role as consultant to the company that led to a satisfying freelance career as speaker, blogger, campaigner and writer, strongly aligned with a sense of doing something that really mattered. This took many meetings, much thought and experiment over an 18-month period, willingness to push on through apparent indifference and to do a lot of hard work. It was not accomplished in a trice.

*Finding mentors.* There will be little point in clients looking for support from their existing networks as the chances are that most of the people currently in their lives will have a stake in keeping the client exactly where they are. Ideally clients need an informal board of advisors, people who can be objective, challenging and supportive. You will be one of them, but it will pay to find others.

*Knowing you are on your way: finding your tribe.* In *The Element* (Robinson and Aronica 2009) Sir Ken Robinson talks about the importance of finding your 'tribe', a combination of the field they are in and the kind of people who inhabit it. I agree that this is important and helping clients specifically look for and recognize that this is what is happening can be a valuable milestone. When Bob Nelson, my then boss at the BBC sent me to Columbia University to attend a course on what was described as 'organizational development', for the first time I met my tribe: 39 other people who thought like me, were interested in what interested me and were eager to share their insights and concerns. I felt instantly at home even though I was one of only three British people on the course. It was also the first time I had met people who were calling themselves 'coaches' and I made some long-lasting friendships there. It was an exhilarating experience and a turning point in my decision to change career.

The feeling that you do not belong to your current tribe is a symptom that something is wrong, a phenomenon I have heard clients describe innumerable times: the stockbroker who could not share his colleagues' excitement about a profitable trade, the hotelier who walked out of a conference because she was bored silly by talk of sales targets, the estate agent who found his colleagues' chatter about houses unbearable. It goes without saying that to find the new place where you feel comfortable you need to step away from your usual networks because you won't find your tribe there. The right tribe provides synergy, buzz, challenge; it becomes an environment where people achieve far more together than they could ever do as individuals. For examples, I think of the Cavendish Laboratory in 1930s Cambridge, with its starring role in the development of nuclear physics, the production team on *Breaking Bad*, possibly the greatest TV series yet made, or the feverish innovation in the early years of Silicon Valley where playfulness met extraordinary technical ability.

*To transcend yourself you first have to understand yourself.* This seems at first to be a paradox, but it is a vital initial step and it is why work on life purpose needs to be preceded by doing all the work on personal brand that I described in Chapter 5. Knowing your strengths and weaknesses, understanding your impact on others, being able to manage the weaknesses and exploit the strengths, being able to identify your values in explicit terms – all of this is essential to moving on to the next phase.

*Finding 'purpose' may in itself be a false quest.* I have several clients, each of them a Westerner brought up in the Christian tradition, who have become Buddhists. They find peace in the idea that the quest for life purpose is a cultural artefact, created by the Calvinist theology which insists that goals are intrinsically valuable, striving towards an 'end' which is just a preparation for some other 'end', a future which is always just out of reach or a ladder of achievement which must be climbed. These clients see their task as 'being', not 'doing': life purpose is not a puzzle to be solved, life must just be lived a day at a time in all its puzzling complexity.

*Exclude depression as a cause.* It has not been my experience that clients who ask these questions are suffering from depression, but it is always possible. Familiarizing yourself with the symptoms of depression and being prepared to have a frank conversation with clients is the solution here, with your coaching aimed at how to find professional help, starting with their general practitioner.

*Finding purpose is always about giving something up as well as moving to something new.* This work is invigorating for a coach because clients can easily get stuck between their intense desire to lead a new life and their intense fear of the unknown. This is why pilot projects and taking one step at a time, accepting some failures and disappointments are all part of what will eventually make it work.

## Making small steps first; improving the present

Perhaps it is no surprise that as coaches we avoid this topic. When a client presents the question in its baldest terms, as some clients do, 'My life has no purpose. Help!' it will instantly remind us of our own vulnerability, of the likelihood that our own quest is imperfect, unfinished or troubling. It rattles us. 'Parallel process' will kick in, that is, in this case the intrinsic insolubility of the client's problem reminds us of the insolubility of our own and we will feel trapped and incompetent, leading either to sidestepping the question altogether or rushing to cliché: 'Oh everyone

**148** COACHING FOR CAREERS

feels that, don't worry!' Or even diagnosing and then telling the client what their purpose is or should be.

Since finding meaning and purpose is not about making radical, sudden changes, it makes sense to start by reframing the question and to work with clients on how their current situation might be improved. How could the present become more satisfying? Often there is work to be done on improving other aspects of the client's life. Once these have been addressed, the question of 'purpose' may fall into place:

---

*Dominic* became a father while he was still a teenager and was fiercely determined to earn enough to sustain his new family. After many setbacks and with some modest help from his and his partner's parents, he started a business and saved enough for a deposit on a house. The business has thrived but Dominic cannot let go of his need to work obsessively hard, despite telling me that he is 'exhausted and stale'. Still only 40, with his two children now at university and the mortgage paid off, Dominic feels he needs to find a new purpose in life. Rather than tackle the question of purpose head-on, I suggested we first look at how to introduce more calm and enjoyment into his current life, commenting that when we feel the degree of frenzy he described, we are in no fit state to consider broader questions. It was soon obvious that, like many entrepreneurs, Dominic was finding it hard to relinquish hands-on control and that his business could grow again if he were to create a new structure, learn some mentoring skills and to delegate day-to-day management to the staff who were eager to take it on. If he did this, then it would be possible to sell the business in a year or so, if that was his wish, while simultaneously working on the question of 'what next?'.

---

## Some other ideas for 'exercises'

Most of the time, ordinary talking will be enough. But there is a case for using something more structured from time to time. These suggestions represent shortcuts that will work when it seems that discussion alone is not working.

### Getting to 'self-concept'

'Self-concept' means the sum total of how we see ourselves: our values, beliefs, skills. When people are considering making a major change in career or seeking more meaning in their lives, this is a starting place. Needless to say, it would provoke incredulity, silence or mockery if you were to say to a client, 'So what's your self-concept?' You have to come at it sideways. This way of doing it draws on the idea of role models, alter-egos and heroic figures:

> Who do you admire wholeheartedly, living, dead, real or fictional? What do you admire them for?
>
> If you were not doing your current job and could choose absolutely anything, no constraints, what would it be?
>
> What would appeal to you about that?
>
> When you were growing up, what books, tv shows, plays, films did you seek out and enjoy?
>
> What was it that appealed to you about them?
>
> What one favourite story stands out?
>
> If you could have a dinner party where you can invite anyone living or dead to attend, who would be there?
>
> What is it about those people that intrigues, excites, interests you?

The discussion is then about what the choice of role models says to the client about what matters to them, including enthusiasms and needs that they may have been ignoring. This apparently simple exercise can throw up some interesting insights. One client, then a middle-senior manager in a retail bank, feeling stuck and frustrated, described his role model as the British World War 2 fighter pilot and double amputee, Douglas Bader. The real-life Bader was not at all like the modest, pleasant, collaborative chap depicted by Kenneth More in the 1957 bio-pic *Reach for the Sky* and the client knew this. But as a person with a facial disfigurement this client found inspiration in Bader's courage and in his work as an early champion of disability rights. The client's own change of career began with founding a support group for people with disabilities in his organization followed by speaking and running workshops in other organizations. Then, finding this exciting and fulfilling, he negotiated a year-long secondment to a pressure group from which he was offered a permanent job as its strategy director.

### 'In flow' moments

Although it is inevitable that you and the client will spend some time poring over their dissatisfaction in their current role, it is unwise to stay in this negative mode for too long. There are a number of versions of 'in flow' exercises inspired by the work of the Hungarian-American psychologist Mihaly Csikszentmihalyi (page 67) who put a name and a description to a familiar human experience. 'Being in flow' means those moments where time passes seamlessly, you are confident, no self-doubt is present, you feel exhilarated because you know you are using all your skills, you know you will be successful. Identifying 'flow' moments

**150** COACHING FOR CAREERS

means the client taps into what really matters to them; it reveals core values, skills and needs.

Here are two ways of doing it. Clients with a preference for introversion may prefer the first. Clients who like talking may prefer the second:

---

## Method 1

The client keeps a journal recording main activities and the level of energy and enjoyment each generated. Ask the client to keep it for a week – to include the weekend.

| Day/date, activity | 1–10 scale | |
|---|---|---|
| | **Energy needed** | **Enjoyment** |
| | | |
| | | |
| | | |
| | | |
| | | |
| | | |
| | | |

This can reveal some startling discrepancies, for instance that there are activities that involve maximum energy but minimal enjoyment. There may be routine activities that involve neither energy nor enjoyment. You are looking for the positives: where were the high scores for enjoyment and energy?

## Method 2

Explain the idea of 'flow' and ask the client to spend a moment or two thinking about times in their life when they have experienced it. Look for at least four examples, possibly more, encouraging the client to think of personal and work life examples as well as from different decades of their lives. As they talk, write down all their key words, ideally on a flip chart. Then hand them a pen and ask them to highlight what leaps out for them, listing the words as they speak.

---

WORKING WITH CLIENTS ON LIFE PURPOSE **151**

**For both methods**

The discussion is now about what was going on in these moments that made them special. Ask why these events stand out, who was there, what role the client was playing, what learning there was, what emotions were involved, what needs the client was fulfilling. Your role is to synthesize the results. You are creating a list of criteria: the skills that were being used, the conditions that were in place. It may be useful to have a flip chart available:

*Paolo* and I did the second of these two exercises. At the time he was running a large department in a university and described himself as 'a dismal bureaucrat who's lost his mojo'. His examples of 'in flow' moments included all of these: the thrill he got from performing in an amateur string quartet; his violin lessons and love of learning; hearing Daniel Barenboim play the complete cycle of Beethoven sonatas; resolving conflicts between staff; family holidays and mentoring young staff. There was little or nothing in his accounts that linked to his daily life as a busy departmental manager. He gazed at the flip chart thoughtfully. 'I can't go on like this'. Paolo stepped down from his many committees and established a series of initiatives with the music department in his own university, aimed at nourishing young musicians. This became a thriving operation and after he left his job, Paolo took over as director of what had become a half-time job and part of a portfolio of other activities including enrolment for a music degree himself.

## A message from the future

There are many variants of this exercise but they all involve thinking yourself into the future and asking, 'For what do I want to be remembered?' One simple version might be called 'No Regrets': here you ask the client to imagine themselves some self-chosen number of years into the future. You ask, 'In what ways would you be able to say at that point in your life that you had no regrets?' then depending on the answer, 'What does this suggest about what you need to change or start doing right now?' Another variant asks the client to write themselves a postcard from their future self, maybe set two years ahead. The postcard describes their life and gives the present-day client advice about what they should do in order to get there.

**152** COACHING FOR CAREERS

## Engagement as the answer

Irvin Yalom (page 138) makes the point that what he calls *engagement* is key to the answer of how to work with clients who have taken up a 'galactic' stance – that is, that when viewed from a cosmic perspective, our lives can seem foolish and trivial. He says:

> The first step in dealing with the question of meaninglessness is to analyse and refine the question. Much that is subsumed under the aegis of 'meaninglessness' belongs elsewhere and must be treated accordingly. 'Pure' meaninglessness is best approached obliquely through engagement which vitiates the galactic perspective.
>
> (Yalom, *Existential Psychotherapy,* page 483)

He advocates identifying and then removing the obstacles that prevent people from enjoying life in the here and now, for instance from creating satisfying relationships, relishing their work or exploiting their creative potential. I find this to be true and think here of one of the first clients who ever presented this issue to me, Sylvie, a 33-year-old senior nurse, a single woman uninterested in having children, in theory already doing a satisfying job, but in practice exasperated and frustrated by the limitations of the role and complaining of lack of purpose in her life. Sylvie was torn between her inner belief that she was the intellectual equal of the doctors she worked with and her fears that this might not be true. In coaching we tackled the fears and proved them groundless. I still get Christmas cards from Sylvie updating me on her work as a consultant chest physician.

In identifying and removing such obstacles, Irvin Yalom emphasizes, as he does throughout his remarkable body of work, that as the practitioner you are your own main tool. By relating deeply and authentically to your client, because this is the heart of your own mission and purpose, you become a model of what purpose means in practice.

# 11 Decision time

Your client gets the job offer. Or seems set on starting their own business. Or decides to take voluntary redundancy. Or decides to resign rather than continue with a job they hate. Great – or is it?

When you have the privilege of working at length with a client, you may be witness to these decisions and to the wobbles that often accompany them. This chapter is about how you may be able to add value here as you do in the earlier phases of career coaching.

## The flawed nature of human decision-making

We flatter ourselves as a species when we apply the label *homo sapiens* – wise man – to describe ourselves. Although we can certainly do 'wise' thinking and it is true that the quality and quantity of this thinking is what distinguishes us from our near relatives in the primate chain, we are nothing like as wise as we like to imagine. The distinguished writer, behavioural economist and Nobel prizewinner, Daniel Kahnemann, identifies the processes in his brilliant book, *Thinking, Fast and Slow* (2011). Fast thinking is what he calls *System 1*, the rapid, intuitive decision-making that we do automatically. We do it when we are speaking our native language, driving down a safe, empty road, reading newspaper headlines, doing simple arithmetical calculations. We rely on System 1, and we are right to do so, because there is too little time to think through the implications of every single daily challenge. *System 2* is slow thinking and what he calls the *Lazy Controller*. It requires self-awareness, energy and concentration. It needs more glucose than System 1 and can easily become depleted if we are distracted, have had too much alcohol or too little sleep. Among many other examples, he quotes one study involving parole judges whose decisions were most definitely affected by hunger and tiredness. The further away they were from a break, the more likely they were to refuse parole.

Kahnemann points out that we are often guilty of *delusional optimism*: we can read that smokers die a decade earlier than non-smokers but believe, if we are smokers, that this will not apply to us, or that even though some high percentage of small businesses fails, ours will be the one to succeed. We can make a budget to build a new kitchen and then find that the un-thought-through extras will cost as much again as our original plans. Because we want the optimistic scenario to be true, we believe that it will be. Delusional optimism and System 1 thinking apply as much to large corporations and governments as they do to individuals and explain

**154** COACHING FOR CAREERS

why lotteries make so much money, why it is more or less unheard of for an IT project to be completed on time or on budget and why politicians start wars. What he calls the *Planning Fallacy* means that although information is available to weigh risks and benefits, this is rarely done coherently; benefits are over-estimated and costs underestimated. Kahnemann says that just knowing all of this does not mean that we can avoid falling into the traps and in relation to one personal project he disarmingly describes himself as 'chief dunce and inept leader'.

## Applications to career coaching

Decisions are intrinsic to career coaching. At some point the client will be deciding. Should they stay in a job that is safe but dull? Should they make the bold decision and move from the rural charm of North Yorkshire, where the chances of finding the right job are minimal, to the cityscape of London with its endless possible jobs but with prohibitively high rents and property prices? Should they accept a job as an unpaid intern in order to make the connections that might be so valuable later? Should they invest their retirement pay-off into buying a business?

System 1 may well predominate in the client's thinking. It is enormously valuable to be able to consider the decision with a coach, someone unattached to any one outcome and who can help the client to do System 2 thinking. Just to be clear: being unattached does not imply indifference or detachment. Your role is to work closely and warmly with the client to make the prudent decision that is the best possible one for them.

This does mean setting aside your own System 1 thinking on the topic and avoiding any inclination to offer whatever you personally think might be good for the client, even when they specifically ask you for an opinion:

> *Ivan* has confessed to his career coach that his marriage has been unhappy for a long time and that he is having an affair with a much younger woman. The relationship is in the early stage of giddy infatuation and it coincides with the offer of a well-paid job in Dubai. Ivan is strongly tempted to leave his wife and to take off to Dubai with his lover. Although the coach has worked with Ivan on his preparation for the job interview and is pleased that this work seems to have been successful, she is horrified by the thought of Ivan leaving his wife of 20 years and does not believe for a moment that the new relationship can last. She knows that it is not her role to be a moral arbiter or marital counsellor. She is silent as he describes the dilemma and then he asks, 'Come on, tell me, what do you think? Should I take this last chance of happiness?'

DECISION TIME **155**

> *Sophie* is a young graduate with a first class degree from a respected university and has been hoping for a job with McKinsey or similar consultancy. Instead she has been offered what she considers to be an 'inferior' job with a 'boutique' firm. She is inclined to turn it down even though there is no other job in prospect and she is tired of living with her parents. Sophie's coach has adult children of the same age and finds himself annoyed at her sense of entitlement. His own children have moved out and are self-supporting.

All coaches will meet situations where you are tempted to tell the client what they should do, often because you are reading your own situation into theirs. You will already know that the short answer is 'don't'. Remind yourself that you can never truly understand the client's world, however much of it they have disclosed to you. You don't know what is good for them and never could.

## Establishing criteria

We can have been bitterly unhappy or just restless in a current role but then when the prospect of moving becomes real, can get paralyzed with indecision. Reassure clients that this is a normal reaction, in fact it is healthier when the 'push' and 'pull' elements are roughly in balance. A perfect solution is rare and change always involves some loss, even when it is a change that you have yearned for, have worked hard to achieve and seems to have everything going for it. When we are consumed with discontent we are inclined to seize anything that looks like escape, regardless of whether this is likely to have long-term benefit. But then at the decision-point, suddenly all the hidden pluses of the current role come into focus: the pleasant colleagues, the subsidized restaurant, the easy journey to work, all the so-called 'hygiene' aspects, the well-known theory first developed by the American clinical psychologist Frederick Herzberg (1969). This proposed that while the job equivalent of good hygiene (salary, pleasant offices, security) prevents a degree of discontent, these elements cannot on their own create happiness. At times of making difficult job choices, the hygiene factors may assume a lot more importance. However nasty some aspects of a job are, at least these are known, whereas the new situation is by its essence largely unknown. The hidden question is, 'How well will I cope?'

Go back to the work you will have done on what matters to this client, for instance through the 'in flow' or similar exercise (page 149). If you have not done an exercise like this then just ask what the client's criteria are. Prompt them if necessary with headings such as:

- Practicality
- Financial costs and benefits
- Fit with personal values

**156** COACHING FOR CAREERS

- Moral duty
- The amount of autonomy and control that the job would offer
- Status
- Opportunity to use and develop skills
- Fairness
- Stability
- Effect on important relationships in the client's life

How does the decision stack up against these criteria?

It may also help to remind the client of the realities of the VUCA world – volatile, uncertain, chaotic and ambiguous (page 14) and the mythical status of the Perfect Job. You might ask the client to prioritize their criteria in order of most and least important to them and then discuss how well the proposed course of action stacks up against them:

> *Jez* is 39 and has been working in the pharmaceutical sector. He has been offered a one-year interim role job in a small start-up pharmaceutical company. He has been unemployed for six months after a somewhat bumpy career that involved being fired from two previous roles. He badly needs a new job. The salary is 30 per cent less than he earnt in his previous role, the title does not include the word 'senior' and he is inclined to reject it. He sounds agitated and angry while he describes the job offer. He believes he deserves something better but the truth is that his market value has been damaged by the upheavals in his earlier career. Jez and his coach revisit the criteria they listed in earlier sessions, number one of which is 'learning and challenge'. Jez is being offered a role that could potentially give him exactly the learning and challenge he craves, with personal support from a boss for whom he has enormous respect. What is his hesitation? It comes down to the emotional arena of pride and status: can he see himself telling friends that he works for this small company? Will he tell them that he is earning less than in his previous job? The coach stays with this calmly and patiently, saying little. There is a long pause before Jez says, 'I think I may be falling into that perfect-job trap. I think I'm being swayed by emotion. It's the best offer I'm likely to get at the moment. I think I'm being childish. I think I should say yes'.

## What's at stake?

Two good questions in these circumstances are:

> What's at stake for you here?
>
> What will happen if you do nothing and stay with the status quo?

Sometimes the answer is a shrug: nothing terrible will happen, in which case the status quo might be a viable option. Or the answer may reveal that the price to be paid by staying put will be too high. It also helps to consider where the problem is on the spectrum of complicated–simple. A simple problem will be one that has a relatively straightforward answer with a low chance of unwelcome negative consequences.

Discussion of any decision needs to be preceded by framing as clearly as possible the essential question that the client is asking themselves:

> Should I resign in order to give myself enough time to concentrate on a part-time degree course?
>
> Is it viable to start a consulting business?
>
> My company wants me to relocate to LA for a year, but is this possible given my family commitments?

It is unlikely that the client will not already have given the topic a lot of thought, so precede any further coaching by saying:

> Talk me through your thinking so far.

Don't forget to double check what the client's goal is for the coaching conversation itself because the answer may be different from the one you anticipate. Ask:

> What help do you need from me on this question?

It will only rarely be that the client wants to make the decision then and there. The most common answer is, 'I want to get more clarity about the whole thing'.

## Simple decision-making tools

There are two approaches that you might like to try for decisions that fall into the category of being relatively simple. One is to toss a coin, saying, 'Heads it's yes, tails it's no'. You then toss the coin and announce the 'result'. The point is not that you are actually encouraging the client to make a decision on the basis of chance but that regardless of how the coin falls, you ask, 'Let's assume you're going to live with that decision. How does it feel?' The answer will reveal the client's emotional landscape in relation to the decision and their instinctive wishes. Typically the first words might be, 'relieved', 'disappointed', 'thrilled'. This may or may not be the right path to take but it will stimulate a useful discussion.

A more elaborate version of the same approach is to say, 'Let's imagine it's a year from now and you are in that new job. Tell me what you'd be doing. How does it feel?'

158  COACHING FOR CAREERS

> Try as he might, Laurie falters as he imagines returning to university to complete his degree after a breakdown. 'I think it would send me right back to all the things I hated before. Yes, I would cope with them better, but do I really want to do it? Would there really be any advantage to me? Just more debt and for what?'

## More complex decision-making tools

There are hundreds of possible decision-making tools and they all have the same aim: to encourage System 2 thinking. I return to a few favourites that have proved their value time and again. You will want to consider how you present these to a client. Some clients loathe the idea of having a 'technique' practised on them, in which case relying purely on a verbal description will work well. Some like a visual approach so if you have a flip chart and some big coloured pens available they might enjoy using these to stimulate their thinking. People who prefer taking their time with private pondering may appreciate having a form sent to them in advance. There is no one right way; vary your choice and approach to suit you and your client.

### Six Thinking Hats

This framework was developed by Edward de Bono. The story has it that Dr de Bono wrote the first draft of the original book, *Six Thinking Hats* (1985) on a long plane journey and it is certainly short enough and simple enough for this to be possible. 'Putting on your thinking hat' was the inspiration for the framework, the idea being that where decision-making and problem-solving are concerned, we are prone to one style of thinking and frequently that we confuse facts with emotion. By mentally putting on different thinking hats, we broaden the way we consider any problem.

| 1. White hat: FACTS | What is known for certain? What important facts are missing? |
|---|---|
| 2. Red hat: EMOTION | What are the feelings around this decision? How intense are they? How much are they affecting my thinking? How far are these feelings based on evidence rather than just on assumption? |
| 3. Yellow hat: OPTIMISM | If everything went well, what would be happening? What would be the benefits? Who would benefit? |

| | |
|---|---|
| 4. Black hat: PESSIMISM | Playing devil's advocate: what is the worst possible outcome here? Who and what would be affected? If this were to happen, how would I cope? |
| 5. Green hat: CREATIVITY | What might be possible? Am I looking at this too narrowly? What other ideas might be lurking here? |
| 6. Blue hat: THINKING ABOUT THINKING | Given the thinking stimulated by 'wearing' all the other hats, what does this suggest? What gaps does it reveal, e.g. in information or in who else needs to be involved? |

De Bono's book has been criticized for its extravagant claims, for instance that it represents 'the most important change in human thinking for the past twenty-three hundred years' – something which seems unlikely. Equally unlikely is the idea that this method alone has transformed organizational performance. Others have found the idea of different coloured hats intrinsically 'silly'. If your client shows signs of sharing this opinion, then maybe it is not the method to use with them. What I like about this framework is that it often exposes our tendency under pressure to narrow our thinking. The focus tightens to black/white, yes/no, on/off and we can box ourselves in unnecessarily as a result:

> *Serena* is a senior research scientist with a talent for operational management. Her company has now asked her if she will compete for a promotion where she would in effect have to leave her research career behind. In considering this issue, the most interesting area for Serena is the green hat. She realizes that it's not either/or, given that she is in a strong position to get the job if she does compete for it. She could happily leave most of her research role behind but she enjoys some aspects of it too much to surrender it completely. She decides to base her bid for the job on the understanding that she would have one day a week to continue her research.

### Decision matrices

There are many four-box matrices that can help with decision-making. For instance, SWOT is a venerable decision-making tool with obscure origins that

**160** COACHING FOR CAREERS

date back at least 60 years. It is largely used in a team context but it can work just as well for individuals. By looking at Strengths, Weaknesses, Opportunities and Threats, it balances any tendency to be blinkered by what we would like to believe might happen. The Opportunities and Threats boxes have a future focus that can be useful. I use my own variant with clients who are wrestling with career decisions:

|  | *Pluses* | *Minuses* |
|---|---|---|
| *Short term* | *Benefits*<br>What are the immediate positives of this proposed course of action?<br><br>How much do they matter? | *Disadvantages*<br>What are its immediate downsides?<br><br>How much do they matter? |
| *Longer term* | *Possibilities*<br>What possibilities might this create for me in the medium to longer term?<br><br>How likely are these to happen? | *Risks*<br>In what ways might this be a risky path in the medium or longer term?<br><br>How likely are these to be real risks? |

*Joel* is wondering whether he is making the right decision. He is 24 and has been doing an admin job well below his capabilities in his uncle's property company. He likes and admires his uncle who has promised that there could be a more interesting and better paid job in prospect, possibly even taking over the business eventually. Joel finds the whole matter of collecting rents and arranging repairs extremely dull. Making a lot of money does not motivate him. He wants to spend a year travelling and doing volunteer work before considering his next move. The decision matrix enables him to stand back and consider the decision a different way. He concludes that he has been over-influenced by the minuses, especially the potential loss of his uncle's goodwill and affection. He is certain that whatever happens he does not want to make his future in the property business. Joel realizes that rehearsing with his coach how to have the conversation with his uncle in a positive and respectful way will probably solve the problem.

### DECISION TIME  **161**

### Revisiting the life scan

If you did some type of life-scan exercise in the first session (page 49) you might usefully revisit this, perhaps in this adapted version. The non-work elements can be more important than the work elements to many clients and this gives an opportunity to reflect on how much these matter and may need to influence the decision:

| The question is [whether to . . . ] | | | |
|---|---|---|---|
| What might be the impact on | Positive | Neutral | Negative |
| Important relationships<br>    Partner?<br>    Parents and other family?<br>    Children?<br>    Friends? | | | |
| Physical health? | | | |
| Mental health? | | | |
| Leisure? | | | |
| Money? | | | |
| Your home? | | | |
| Personal development? | | | |
| Spiritual life? | | | |
| Career? | | | |
| Community activities? | | | |
| Overall work–life balance? | | | |

Discussion will frequently reveal gaping holes in information or untested assumptions about what key people in the client's circle feel and think. Consider it a successful session if the client leaves telling you that they feel much clearer about the whole issue, that they need to think, sometimes to do more research and often to re-open conversations with family members before making their final decision.

## Negotiating the deal

The client has been offered the job and is strongly inclined to say yes. Or the client has been offered a redundancy package and wants the whole business to be over

**162** COACHING FOR CAREERS

quickly so is eager to agree it. But I find that many people feel uninformed and sometimes even a little helpless when it comes to negotiating the deal. As their coach you may be able to offer significant support and advice at this stage. For instance, some clients may not even realize that negotiation is possible, assuming that an employer's offer is take-it-or-leave-it. When you discover that this is the client's belief, that in itself is worth discussing because most employers, though not all, will expect and be willing to negotiate, even if only a little. The context and the sector is important, but even in the public sector where grades and salary scales may look rigid, there is often more room for manoeuvre than there may seem, for instance to appoint someone at the top rather than in the middle of a salary scale.

Clients may also feel timid about how to conduct themselves, telling themselves that they are bound to come off worse or to damage the relationship with the employer before it has even started. Self-doubt kicks in – *who am I to ask for more?* You might want to remind them of that well-known story about the farmer who wants to borrow a plough from a richer neighbour. He sets off feeling humiliated, angry and miserable because he has to ask, thinking that it will be difficult and as he gets nearer and nearer the neighbour's house he believes more and more strongly that he will get a rejection. As the neighbour mildly opens the door, the farmer shouts, 'Keep your plough! I don't want it anyway!' The moral of the story is that if you assume rejection then you will make it happen. I will sometimes say to clients, 'So you don't want to ask because you think you will be told no. OK. And how prepared are you to live with the resentment and self-scolding that you will feel because you never asked?'

### In advance

It pays off if the client has already done some thorough 'due diligence' on salary and conditions as it will probably be too late to do this at the point where the employer makes an offer. The questions here are:

> What are other people in comparable jobs earning in this organization?
>
> If it's a redundancy offer what is the statutory minimum? What kinds of deals have other people been able to secure?
>
> What are people in this kind of job earning in competitor organizations?
>
> What is the employer's record on equal rights where pay is concerned? Is there some sense that women or people of colour come off worse than standard issue white men despite the organization's stated code of values?
>
> Are bonuses paid and if so how much are they typically worth?
>
> How much latitude is there over the working day, holidays, freedom to work from home, ability to barter healthcare or other perks for something else?
>
> What is the employment market like for this kind of job in this location?

DECISION TIME **163**

This preparation is all about realism. I worked a while ago with a client who wanted his potential employer to pay for four transatlantic trips home a year. After discussion in one of his sessions with me, he realized that although there was no harm in asking, as a charity under intense and hostile scrutiny for the quality of their financial management, it was most unlikely that they would agree – and they did not. However, they did increase the level of re-location expenses they were willing to pay. Or to take another example, if the client is much like other talented young graduates in a sector where there is a lot of competition for jobs, then their power to negotiate might be relatively small. On the other hand if the client is a scarce commodity in a sector where there are a lot of vacancies then their power will be much greater. While I was writing this section I read a news story about a small village in France whose mayor had tried in vain to fill the vacancy for a family doctor. The desperate mayor was offering free Michelin restaurant meals and trips on his own yacht as an incentive for a doctor who was willing to accept the post.

It is useful, too, to discuss how emotion can get in the way of realism. We can all get unfeasibly preoccupied with symbolic goals. After tax it will make little difference whether someone is earning £45,000 or £44,000. People outside the organization will be unlikely to understand the difference between vice president, procurement and senior executive, procurement. Where a client has become fixed on the idea that they 'must' earn a particular sum or 'must' have a particular kind of title, this is likely to get in the way of their securing the job at the negotiating stage. It is better to discuss all of this in advance than when the negotiations have already begun.

Remind the client that the job offer will often be made by phone, usually on the evening of the final interview and that it may be made by the HR person who chaired the panel. This is unlikely to be the decision-maker. Depending on the circumstances, alert the client to the danger of being overcome by the pleasant flattery at getting the offer and of blurting out a 'yes'. After you have said 'yes' the negotiating window is effectively closed. It is virtually always better to say, 'Thank you, that's wonderful. What are you offering exactly?' Then on hearing the reply to say, 'I need a little time to think it over, can I get back to you within 24 hours to fix a time to discuss it?'

## The principles that make a difference

Ask clients what their assumptions are about negotiating. They may reply by using phrases like 'win–win' or 'the bottom line'. Other ideas about negotiation include what are essentially manipulative tactics. I don't find these ideas effective. Sometimes it is impossible to achieve 'win–win' and identifying a 'bottom line' nearly always leads to disappointment and unhelpful rigidity. Manipulative tactics backfire, threats get you nowhere. Honesty, openness and flexibility are much better.

**164** COACHING FOR CAREERS

I offer clients a different set of principles that I describe below. None is peculiar, unknown, difficult to do or anything less than obvious, but I find that in practice they are often ignored:

1 *Get your goal clear*: is it to get a better salary, to change the essential conditions of the job for instance from full time to part time, to report to a different boss?

Just clarifying the goal for the negotiation can in itself transform the chances of a successful outcome. Clients may tell you that 'something' about the offer does not feel right, but what, exactly? What do they want to achieve from the discussion?

2 *See it from the employer's perspective*: what are their needs, constraints, the room to manoeuvre that they actually have? What are their standards and stated values? How might these play into the negotiation? Do a lot more listening than talking because it matters to find out what is in their minds.

This is probably the biggest shift in emphasis that we all need to make in a negotiation. We are thinking about ourselves, our needs, our status, our pride. Emotion gets in the way. This is not how to succeed. Brilliant negotiators ask penetrating questions in the spirit of seeking to understand the other party's views. They listen, they smile, they respectfully ask for more information, they summarize what they have heard. Once you have this information and have shown willingness to listen, you are so much better equipped to negotiate skilfully.

It will help the client to ask straightforwardly about how much freedom the employer has and to state upfront that they don't want to play games. I have known many clients get excellent results from saying something like, 'I'd really like to understand how much latitude you have here. I'd rather be frank with you about what I'm hoping for and for you to be frank with me about anything you see standing in the way'. This degree of courtesy, patience and willingness to make yourself vulnerable – but with dignity – can often unblock an impasse.

3 *Who is the decision-maker?* It's no good negotiating with the HR person if the real decision-maker is the boss's boss.

Encourage the client to find out who actually has the power here. If the line manager him or herself is making the offer call then it is simple, but always check. 'May I ask? Are you the person with the power to agree the terms for this job?'

4 *It's about the relationship* and relationships are emotional and irrational. Persuading through logic alone will never work.

DECISION TIME **165**

In effect the negotiation will continue the excellent platform created by the interview, where mutual liking will have been established. If it hasn't then the client would have to question whether this is the right job. Empathy matters, so starting the negotiation with some genuinely warm words, saying that you feel sure you will be able to reach agreement, staying authentic – they will all help. So for instance, it will be better to say, 'I must say I'm disappointed with this salary offer as I'd hoped it would be higher' is far better than snapping, 'This offer is insulting for someone of my experience'.

5  *Be prepared to trade things that the employer can give away easily* rather than getting stuck on salary alone.

Sometimes there really is little that the employer can do to increase a salary. They may be bound by agreements made with tough trade unions, or they know that to give a newcomer a higher salary than people already in the job would create widespread resentment, however much of a short-term problem it would seem to solve. This is why it is so important to find out at the start what the negotiator's constraints and freedoms actually are. It may be much easier for an employer to agree to one day a week at home than to create a one-off bonus payment.

6  *Small steps and small asks are more likely to be successful.* Making strident demands will back the client into a corner from which it is difficult to escape. So it is easier to agree to a slightly smaller starting salary than they wanted on the condition that it will be reviewed in six months' time. It is easier to compromise on a neutral-sounding job title than to stick to a request for a title that is alien to the employer.

I have seen many clients do well at the negotiating stage. They achieve much better deals in their redundancy packages, for instance by getting the employer to agree to pay for re-training. They increase the salary offer, sometimes by significant amounts. I think here of my young client Lorna whose heritage is African–Caribbean. She found out that she was being offered what seemed to be slightly less than the going rate for her role. She was keen to negotiate and politely mentioned at the outset of the negotiation that the company had a widely quoted policy of helping young black and minority ethnic people into fully professional roles. She said, 'One of the things that really attracted me to this company was that I can see this isn't just words and to prep for this post I talked to some of your BAME staff and they were really positive'. The boss beamed and agreed enthusiastically that this was true. 'So,' said Lorna, smiling, 'I think I could be another beacon for you but I'd really like it if you could offer me another 10 per cent'. This little prompt about the company's values and standards made the boss roar with laughter. 'Touché!' he cried. 'Of course we can.'

Despite the client's skill as a negotiator, it is not always possible for there to be a happy ending. One client entering this phase was appalled to discover that

**166** COACHING FOR CAREERS

the salary on offer was suddenly 10 per cent less than had been advertised and that what appeared to be spurious reasons were given to explain it. Others have reported being treated rudely, a dismaying piece of evidence about the company's culture to add to the experience of being interviewed, which had also been unpleasant. Another client entered the negotiation with an open mind about the proposed reporting arrangements but discovered that the autonomy promised in the job description and interview had somehow evaporated in a restructure and that she would have been reporting to someone for whom she had little respect. These clients turned the jobs down and felt nothing but relief at their decisions.

## Disappointment

Coaching hugely elevates the client's chances of getting what they want but no coach can promise that it will always work. When clients don't get the job despite their hours of preparation, they can feel crushed. I always ask clients to text me with the outcome of an interview. If it's rejection I suggest they call me or arrange a face-to-face session. If they want to discharge some anger, I encourage a few moments of it while suggesting that while a little rage can be cathartic, too much can fix you unhealthily in a victim state.

There might be learning in the rejection. We will explore how to press for feedback by picking the panel member who seemed most alert and sympathetic and asking for advice, where the question is, 'What specifically would have made my bid for this job stronger?' This feedback can be constructive, for instance saying that the client needs to boost their experience in particular ways or could improve their presentation skills. Sometimes the answer is that there was nothing that the client could have done. When clients tell me that they suspect a set-up, I know that this is not just understandable paranoia but could be true, though usually there is no way of finding out whether the suspicion is justified.

It can be helpful to discuss how the client should tell people that they have not got the job, keeping it brief and positive. If the job was an internal appointment then it will be worth talking through how to behave with the successful candidate. Your main value is to listen and to reassure the client that they are employable and to get them to think through their options, which may take you into the whole cycle again, for instance encouraging them to re-contact agencies, head-hunters and the key people they interviewed as part of their preparation. It is always a good idea to send a brief, friendly email to the person who would have been the boss, thanking them for the chance to bid for the job.

## The exit

It is easier to leave an organization when it's entirely your own choice, harder when it isn't. Some clients will have chosen redundancy as part of a scheme asking for volunteers. Depending on the degree of attachment people have to the organization and to their job (two separate but connected elements) the parting might be upsetting.

## Clients who have been fired or made redundant

The news that they will have to leave may come as a shock or it may have been stealing up on the client for a long time. Organizations do not always handle the process well, despite good intentions. It can be a painful transition to make.

You may have been in a longstanding coaching relationship with the client when they discover that this is what will happen or they may be coming to you for the first time because it has already happened. You will listen to their story, responding with a judicious blend of empathy and objectivity, being aware all the time that unless these are uniquely special circumstances it will not help the client for them to spend the entire session in the grip of the kind of helpless emotion where thinking becomes impossible.

## Legal processes

Some clients are angry enough to consider taking the organization to a tribunal because they consider that they have been unfairly treated. They may describe what they believe is discrimination. They may say that the redundancy has been triggered by their pregnancy or some other form of unfair dismissal. They may want to discuss this decision with you. My default here is to urge clients who feel like this, depending on their financial circumstances, to get independent legal advice from an employment law specialist or free from a mediation service, as the first question to be answered is whether there is any legal basis for a tribunal and if there is, what the chances of success might be. A lawyer can also take over the negotiating role for the client if this is what they wish and can afford.

As coaches, we have a duty of care here, the essence of which is offering perspective. It will most probably be the first time the client has been in this situation but you may have seen it many times. Ask what they see as the pluses and minuses of pursuing a legal case. Just raising this question may be enough to help the client gain a sense of proportion. The pluses that the client describes are usually entirely about emotion. The wish to punish the organization may be intense but may be presented to you as a principle involving fairness: 'it's important to stop them behaving like this and to deter them from doing it to others'. The client may believe that they could be awarded a large amount of money to compensate for losing their job. They may tell you that organizations so dread the bad publicity surrounding a tribunal that they settle before the case ever gets to court – and there is some truth in that. Sometimes the organization will make an offer of financial compensation without admitting fault, but the client will turn it down, saying doggedly that in effect they want an apology and their 'day in court'.

**168** COACHING FOR CAREERS

The minuses, and they are enormous, start with the evidence that people pursuing employment cases can become obsessed and often depressed. Cases may take months to be heard and the decision may not go the client's way, including the possibility of awarding costs against them. Depending on the type of issue, winning a case may involve a relatively small amount of money. The complainant's anger grows; psychologically they cannot move on. It is much harder to find another job because, however unfairly, future employers apply the label 'troublemaker'. If the client does not raise these points themselves, though most do, then I will.

Sometimes there may be a case for plain speaking. I remember my client Ryan, whose lawyer had told him that his case was flimsy, but who still seemed determined to pursue it. I said, 'So, Ryan, your lawyer has told you that you are unlikely to win, you've been unemployed for nine months with no time to look for another job because of all the energy that this is taking up. Your case won't be heard for another two months. You've refused the offer of mediation. Our own sessions have been dominated by it. Do you really want to pay the price, real and psychological, for carrying on with it?' I was aware in asking this question that it fell into the category of a closed, leading and rhetorical question – though I did ask it with a smile – the kind of question that I sternly warn beginner coaches against asking. But in this case it seemed like one of the rare occasions when this was precisely the kind of challenge that was needed.

At some point in the process of leaving, it may be beneficial to work with the client to consider what, if anything, they contributed to an unwelcome decision that has forced them out of their job. If they have been guilty of gross misconduct then it will be obvious enough, but most cases are not so clear-cut. The answer may be that the client has brushed aside hints about all those annoying aspects of their behaviour, not realizing that these are not merely the baseless comments of idiots but widely held views about their performance. Or it may be something altogether subtler, just not facing up to the probability that the organization was failing and that job losses were inevitable. Asking the question, 'What learning is there in this whole experience?' may be one way of encouraging a healthy sense of responsibility that walks the path between complacency, feeling like a victim or indulging in lavish self-blame.

## Leaving well

The decision has been made, the client is leaving their job. You and the client could profitably spend a whole session on how to do this, regardless of whether it is entirely the client's idea and they are going to something better, or whether they are leaving reluctantly as a result of being made redundant. A good place to start is by establishing the principles involved in how to do it well. When the client has witnessed other people leaving, what have they observed about what works and what doesn't? What are their own wishes? Depending on circumstances this is my own mental list:

- Reputation is everything: preserving good reputation will always be at the top of my own suggestions about what matters. Good reputation helps with finding another job and with self-esteem
- Recovering equilibrium; feeling positive about the change, maintaining good mental health
- Avoiding falling into the traps of blaming bosses, sulking, hiding, taking up a martyr posture: the only person who truly suffers here is the person leaving because it suggests that their departure is justified by their immature behaviour
- Negotiating a quick departure, for instance not being made to work out a long notice period; if 'gardening leave' is possible then it should be taken. As soon as colleagues know someone is leaving they stop coming to them for decisions or inviting them to meetings; the person becomes invisible and going into work becomes pointless and unpleasant
- Maintaining good relationships with the people who matter, especially the ones where there has been genuine friendship
- Being merciful with people who are staying: they may well secretly envy the client or be worrying about their own futures
- Taking control because this is what creates psychological health; owning the decision as far as possible, even when it was not originally the client's choice
- Doing everything they can to accept that this is an ending and that it needs to be celebrated as such. Clients often say that they want to slip away without fuss, but virtually every leaver is grateful after the event that they have marked their departure with a party of some sort.

## The 'leaving script'

Having this discussion usually makes it clear what the client should do, but there is one extra that adds value. This is to work with the client to create their 'leaving script'. News about a departure travels fast and rumours proliferate. The more the client takes charge of the rumours, the better it will be for them because this will be one of the best ways of protecting their reputation. Regardless of whether this is a forced or a voluntary departure, the client needs to be ready to convey the most upbeat possible reason for the change and to make it clear that they own it. Whining about unfairness may create apparent sympathy but what people are really thinking is, 'No smoke without fire'. Clients need to accept that people love gossip and that the juicier the story the more reputational damage it could do. The aim here is to equip the client with something that says they are in control and that there is no need for anyone to feel sorrow, anger or envy on their part. They need

**170** COACHING FOR CAREERS

to convey politely and cheerfully that there is no hidden story (even if the truth is that there is indeed a hidden story) and that they have no wish to discuss it in more detail. The script will be totally consistent with whatever formal announcement the organization has made about the departure, ideally one that the client has actually drafted themselves.

I offer clients this formula:

1.  Yes, it's true I'm leaving and of course there are some aspects where I feel a bit sad (one reason for 'sadness' is enough, for instance missing the rest of the team, but steer the client away from anything that conveys blame towards anyone else).
2.  I'm looking forward to. . . (could be anything, for instance having time at home, starting with the new employer, taking time to consider what it is I really want to do. . .).
3.  You wish everyone well, including your questioner, and hope to keep in touch.

I often do a little light-hearted role play with the client where I represent a prob-ing, over-curious co-worker who tactlessly presses for more, along the lines of, 'Go on, I'm sure there must be more to it than that'. In the role play the client's job is to smile blandly and just repeat a variant of their script until I, as the nosy questioner, give up. This is good practice for real life where inquisitive colleagues will quickly realize that there is no more to be prised out of the leaver. I emphasize to clients that there should be no exceptions to the rule of saying the same thing to absolutely everyone. When people are told a secret, the wish to tell 'just one other person' can be irresistible and all too soon there is a rival, less positive, story circulating.

The sign that this plan has worked is the point where people start repeating the client's narrative back to them: it has become the authorized version. This formula has proved its value many hundreds of times and I have been to several leaving parties where I have watched in admiration while the client made their little speech based on some variant of it. Many clients have also told me that even where they have initially felt bitterness about their departure, the process of repeating this ver-sion of the truth, (admittedly one that has sometimes been a little massaged) has ultimately convinced even themselves of its 'reality'.

### The party

Slinking away is a bad idea. It feeds suspicion that there is something to be ashamed of, but more importantly, it fails to recognize the psychology of this kind of change. The wider the gap between the formal leaving and the time it takes the client to come to terms with it, the harder it is going to be. A party is a signal, to the client, and to others, that their time in the job has ended. It is a cere-mony and ceremonies speed transition. It invariably involves some warm words, a gift and a sense of being valued. It helps the client and it helps the colleagues they are leaving behind. Normally the organization will fund some kind of gathering but if they do not, colleagues may chip in. Even if it is the simplest and cheapest kind of tea party, with a handpicked group of close colleagues, it is worth doing and if no one else volunteers (unlikely) then the client may want to fund it themselves.

Sometimes the sense of release can be overwhelming and I have known people blow the whole careful strategy of the previous weeks or months by getting drunk at their party or making a reckless and rambling speech where they attempt to be 'witty' at the organization's expense. All this does is embarrass everyone present, just as later it will embarrass the client. If you strongly suspect that something like this could happen, raise the subject of self-management at these events including how to enlist a close friend or family member to act as minder. Where I believe that this could be a risk, I have a few favourite shudder-making YouTube videos that I might share with a client, in the spirit of how not to do it. A short, gracious thank-you speech as a variant on the 'leaving script' is usually plenty.

### Moving on

Where there is time and budget, the client may wish to discuss how to make a positive start in their new role. When you have enjoyed working together they may want to take you with them as their coach or even include further coaching with you as part of their negotiations for the job. The idea of 'the first 100 days' has caught on in thinking about this issue, taken from the way that US presidents are subjected to scrutiny in the same time period. Most of the advice here is about getting clear about expectations, listening, watching, looking for a quick win, avoiding seeming as if 'how we did it in [name of previous organization] was the right way and not making any major decisions too speedily. Some regrets and disillusionment on both sides are inevitable as is a dip in confidence when the client gradually gets to realize what the job actually entails. But this is a big subject in its own right and outside the scope of this book. I recommend Michael Watkins' comprehensive and readable book *The First 90 Days* (2013) to executive clients as an entirely sensible and practical basis for their plan and it is a fertile source of ideas for career coaches too.

## Conclusion

Career coaching is intensely satisfying work. You are with people at turning points in their lives; it is most definitely a whole-person activity and is a rich and complex enterprise for that reason alone. It is possible to know, allowing for a degree of prudent modesty, that you have made a difference because you can see a positive improvement in how the client looks and sounds. You are working towards

**172** COACHING FOR CAREERS

a well-defined outcome most of the time and when the client achieves what they have so earnestly wanted, you can permit yourself a share of the joy.

The newer you are to coaching, the more likely you are to worry about being good enough, especially when clients appear to be entrusting you with something as important as the whole future direction of their lives. When we feel anxiety about our professional competence as coaches, we are inclined to think that the solution is yet more 'tools and techniques'. I have described many such tools and techniques in this book, all of them tried and tested dozens, and in some cases, hundreds of times. Yet ultimately it is just you and your client in that room. Your most important asset is your ability to listen with warmth and without judgement and to ask good questions. In the end that is what will help the client most and what they will remember later. It has sometimes surprised me how much clients have appreciated these apparently simple behaviours. In asking him for feedback after we had finished our programme and when he was well into his new job, one client wrote, 'What made the difference was being a calm compassionate voice of reassurance, reminding me constantly that I was employable, checking in proactively between sessions to see how I was, reminding me to get enough rest and exercise; provoking me occasionally and making me laugh; being so kind and thoughtful: thank you.' So not a word here about the psychometrics we diligently worked through, the detailed feedback I offered him on his CVs, the hours we spent on preparing him for interview or any of the many well-structured 'exercises' we did! Clearly he took all that for granted and of course he was right to do so. In the end it came down, as it always does, to the quality of that essential human connection.

I wish you luck with your own career coaching work. If you have queries, comments or suggestions based on what you have read in this book, please email me: Jenny@JennyRogersCoaching.com.

# References

Bolles, R.N. (2019) *What Color Is Your Parachute?* New York: Ten Speed Press.

Broughton, V. (2017) *Becoming Your True Self: A Handbook for the Journey from Trauma to Healthy Autonomy*. Steyning: Green Balloon Publishing.

Burnett, B. and Evans, D. (2016) *Designing Your Life: Build a Life that Works for You*. London: Chatto & Windus.

Chamorro-Premuzic, T. (2016) Strengths-based coaching can actually weaken you. *Harvard Business Review*, 4 January (available at: https://hbr.org/2016/01/strengths-based-coaching-can-actually-weaken-you).

de Bono, E. (1985) *Six Thinking Hats: An Essential Approach to Business Management*. Boston MA: Little Brown.

Dahl, R. (2009) *Revolting Rhymes*. London: Puffin.

Dickens, C. (2002) *Great Expectations*. London: Penguin Books.

Ehrenreich, B. (2009) *Smile or Die: How Positive Thinking Fooled America and the World*. London: Granta. (Published in the USA as *Bright-Sided: How the Relentless Promotion of Positive Thinking has Undermined America*. New York: Henry Holt and Company).

Eliot, G. (2003) *Middlemarch*. London: Penguin Books.

Erikson, E.H. and Erikson, J.M. (1998) *The Life Cycle Completed: Extended Version*. New York: W.W. Norton & Company.

Frankl, V.E. (1959) *Man's Search for Meaning*. New York: Pocket Books.

Friedman, S. and Laurison, D. (2019) *The Class Ceiling: Why It Pays to Be Privileged*. Bristol: Policy Press.

Gallo, C. (2014) *Talk Like TED*. New York: St Martin's Press.

Graeber, D. (2018) *Bullshit Jobs*. London: Simon & Schuster.

Gratton, L. and Scott, A. (2016) *The 100 Year Life: Living and Working in an Age of Longevity*. London: Bloomsbury.

Herzberg, F. with Mausner, B. and Snyderman, B.B. (1969) *The Motivation to Work*, 2nd edn. New York: John Wiley.

Hill, S. (2017) *Where Did You Learn to Behave Like That? A Coaching Guide for Working with Leaders*. [Not known]: Dialogix with CreateSpace Independent Publishing Platform.

Ibarra, H. (2003) *Working Identity: Unconventional Strategies for Reinventing Your Career*. Boston, MA: Harvard Business School Publishing.

Kahnemann, D. (2011) *Thinking, Fast and Slow*. New York: Penguin Group.

Kingsolver, B. (2018) *Unsheltered*. New York: HarperCollins.

**174** REFERENCES

Lees, J. (2018) *How to Get a Job You Love: 2019–20 Edition*. London: McGraw-Hill Education.

Palmer, E. (2008) The kindness of strangers. *British Medical Journal*, 337: a1993.

Robinson, K. and Aronica, L. (2009) *The Element: How Finding Your Passion Changes Everything*. London: Penguin Books.

Rogers, C. (1956) *Client-Centered Therapy*, 3rd edn. Boston, MA: Houghton-Mifflin.

Rogers, J. (2007a) *Sixteen Personality Types at Work in Organisations*. London/Milton Keynes: Management Futures/ASK Europe.

Rogers, J. (2007b) *Influencing with the Sixteen Types*. London/Milton Keynes: Management Futures/ASK Europe.

Rogers, J. (2011) *Great Answers to Tough CV Problems*. London: Kogan Page.

Rogers, J. (2014) *Facing Redundancy: Surviving and Thriving*. Maidenhead: McGraw-Hill Education.

Rogers, J. (2016) *Coaching Skills: The Definitive Guide to Being a Coach*, 4th edn. Maidenhead: Open University Press.

Rogers, J. (2017) *Building a Coaching Business: Ten Steps to Success*, 2nd edn. London: Open University Press.

Rogers, J. (2017) *Coaching with Personality Type: What Works*. London: Open University Press.

Ryan, R.M. and Deci E.L. (2000) Self-determination theory and the facilitation of intrinsic motivation, social development, and well-being. *American Psychologist*, 55: 68–78.

Schutz, W. (1958) *FIRO: A Three-Dimensional Theory of Interpersonal Behavior*. Nuir Beach, CA. WSA Inc.

Seligman, M.E. and Csikszentmihalyi, M. (2014) *Positive Psychology: An Introduction* (pp. 279–298). In: *Flow and the Foundations of Positive Psychology*. Dordrecht: Springer Netherlands.

Steptoe, A. (2019) Happiness and health. *Annual Review of Public Health*, 40: 4.1–4.21.

Vaughan Smith, J. (2019) *Coaching and Trauma: Moving Beyond the Survival Self*. London: Open University Press.

Waterman, J. and Rogers J. (1997) *Introduction to the FIRO-B Instrument*. Mountain View, CA: Consulting Psychologists Press.

Watkins, M. (2013) *The First 90 Days: Updated and Expanded Proven Strategies for Getting up to Speed Faster and Smarter*. Boston, MA: Harvard Business Review Press.

Wroe, A. (2018) *The Economist Style Guide*, 12th edition. London: Profile Books.

Yalom, I.D. (1980) *Existential Psychotherapy*. New York: Basic Books.

Yates, J. (2014) *The Career Coaching Handbook*. Abingdon: Routledge.

# Index

accents, dealing with 129–30
achievements
  hollow achievements 144
  skills and 83–5
advice
  clinical professionals, advice from 31
  de-cluttering, advice on 32
  employment lawyers, advice from 31
  exercise, advice on 32
  expert advice, suggestions on 31–2
  giving advice 25
  non-directiveness and giving of 25
  reframing as information 25–7
anger 17, 22, 23, 66, 143, 166, 168, 169–70
appearance, looks matter 88–9
applications to career coaching 154–6
Artificial Intelligence 9
assessment centres 125, 133–6
  *see also* full-scale assessment centres
attachment theory 53
attrition 22
austerity, effects of 12
Autonomy, Competence and Emotional
    Connection, Ryan and Deci on 49

backstory
  getting started 50–55
  introduction of 51–3
Bader, Douglas 149
Balance Wheel exercise 49
'banned' words in CVs 89–90
*Becoming Your True Self* (Broughton,
    V.) 53
behaviours to avoid 22–3
Belbin questionnaire 63
'Big Five' questionnaires 63, 64–5
birth rate fall 9–10
blame game, danger in 122–3
Bolles, Richard Nelson 99

brand identity 58–76
  Belbin questionnaire 63
  'Big Five' questionnaires 63, 64–5
  brand and, concepts of 58
  brand discussion 60–65
  brand downsides 59
  'brand essence' jigsaw 75
  brand idea 58–9
  brand values 70
  Career Anchors 63
  career choice questionnaire 63
  change management, skills in 74
  client-coach vocabulary 61–2
  conflict management analysis 63
  differentiation, positivity in 58
  feedback 70–73
  feedback, debriefing 360 feedback 72–3
  feedback, effectiveness of coaching
    and 70–71
  feedback, 360 feedback 71–2
  FIRO-B questionnaire 63, 64
  Five Factor model 65
  Hogan suite of 3 questionnaires 63
  Holland's environments and
    personalities 64
  'human potential' movement 67
  influencing, skills in 74
  instrument choice 62–4
  instrument choice, confusing nature
    of 66
  interpretation, self-awareness and 66
  IPIP-NEO questionnaire 65
  Jung Type Indicator 62
  Jungian personality type instruments
    62
  Keirsey Temperament Sorter 62
  leadership skills 74
  learnt behaviours 67
  management skills 74

## 176 INDEX

marketplace distinctions 58–9
mindspring.uk.com 68
motivation and interpersonal style
  questionnaire 63
multiple questionnaires, use of 66
Myers-Briggs Type Indicator (MBTI)
  62, 63, 64, 65
NEO questionnaire 63, 65
OCEAN (Openness, Conscientiousness,
  Extraversion, Agreeableness,
  Neuroticism) acronym 64–5
OPQ (Occupational Personality
  Questionnaire) 63
organizational skills 74
people as brands 59–60
positive psychology 67
problem-solving skills 73
psychometrics, brand discussion and
  60–65
psychometrics, case against use of 62
psychometrics, case for use of 60–62
psychometrics, getting best out of 65–7
realized strengths 67
reflection, need for 67
self-management skills 74
16 PF questionnaire 63
skills identification framework 73–4
strengths approach 67–9
strengths approach, weaknesses of
  68–9
Strengths Cards 68
Strengths Profiler 67, 68
Strong Interest Inventory 64
SuperStrong 64
team role questionnaire 63
teamwork skills 74
thinking skills 73
Thomas-Kilmann Conflict Mode
  Instrument (TKI) 63
trait-based personality questionnaires
  63
transferable skills 73–4
unrealized strengths 67
values 69–70
Values in Action 68
verbal communication, skills in 74
Virtues, strengths and 68

vitanavis.com 64
Wave 63
weaknesses 67
wrapping it up 74–6
written communication, skills in 73
*Breaking Bad* (TV series) 147
*British Medical Journal* 24
Broughton, Vivian 53
*Building a Coaching Business*
  (Rogers, J.) 37
*Bullshit Jobs* (Graeber, D.) 141
Burnett, B. and Evans, D. 138

Calvinist theology 147
Career Anchors 63
career choice questionnaire 63
career coaches
  advice
    non-directiveness and giving of 25
    reframing as information 25–7
  anger 22
  applications to 154–6
  attrition 22
  behaviours to avoid 22–3
  client issues, change (post 2008) in 1–2
  clients' needs 2–3
    importance of paying attention to
      22–3
  clinical professionals, advice from 31
  congruence, empathy and 17
  contact between sessions 23
  containment 17
  'creativity' coaches, advice from 31
  de-cluttering, advice on 32
  diet, advice on 32
  disagreements, dealing with 27
  effective listening 20–21
  emotion, aim of normalization of 23
  emotion in coaching room,
    management of 21–4
  empathy, capacity for 18
  empathy, foundational skill for 17–19
  empathy, limits of 18–19
  employment lawyers, advice from 31
  executive search consultants, advice
    from 31
  exercise, advice on 32

INDEX **177**

expert advice, suggestions on 31–2
family lawyers, advice from 31
feedback
  positivity in 29
  practical concerns in giving 28–9
  provision of 28–9
feelings, struggles for containment of 21–2
financial advisors, advice from 31
giving advice 25
giving information 24–5
kindness, value of 24
knowledge requirements for 14–15
language, critical importance for 20–21
listening, skill for 19
networking 29–32
nutrition, advice on 32
personal style, advice on 31
presentation skills, advice on 31
promotion processes, need for rigour in 2
questions beginning 'why,' avoidance of 20
recruitment executives, advice from 31
referral suggestions 30
reframing 'advice' as 'information' 25–7
selection processes, need for rigour in 2
self-awareness, empathy and 17–18
small business advisors, advice from 31
special skills of 16–32
specialism of career coaching 1
stress 22
  advice on 32
summarizing, skill for 19–20
therapists, advice from 31
voice skills, advice on 31
web developers, advice from 32
well-being coaches, advice from 32
whole-life perspective, value of 2
*The Career Coaching Handbook* (Yates, J.) 6
careers
  'career,' meaning of 5–6
  career landscape 6–8
  career stages, assumptions about 14

history of, 'thread' identification in 54–5
popular myths about 13–14
qualifications and 14
case studies and exercises
  advice as information, reframing of 26
  backstory 51, 52–3
  brainstorming networks 99
  'brand notes' 75–6
  career coaches, knowledge requirements for 15
  career coaches, special skills of 16
  career coaching, applications for 154–5
  career history 54, 55
  career landscape 5
  contracting 44
  criteria for coaching, establishment of 156
  CV style 82–3, 84–5, 90
  CV work, preparation for 80
  decision environment 50
  decision making 158, 159, 160
  disagreements 27
  emotion in coaching room, management of 21–2
  'fit,' question of 46–7, 48
  giving information 24–5
  'in flow' moments 151
  job hunting 93–4
  life purpose concerns 137–8, 142
  networking 30
  networking, vital importance of 97–9
  note about 3
  people as brands 60
  personal contact, invisible market of 94
  pointless jobs 141–2
  price resistance 35
  privilege and underprivilege 10–11
  psychometrics 61, 65, 69
  research conversations 100
  saying 'no' (and reasons for) 39
  small steps towards 'purpose' 148
  storytelling 122
  truth, importance of 81
  values 70
Cavendish Laboratory 147
centenarians, rise in 9–10

**178** INDEX

Chamorro-Premuzic, Tomas 69
change management, skills in 74
changing world of work 8–15
chronological format for CVs 82, 83–4
clarity on clients' needs, establishment
of 109–10
class and social prejudice 129–30
*The Class Ceiling* (Friedman, S. and
Laurison, D.) 11–12
client-coach vocabulary 61–2
client issues, change (post 2008) in 1–2
client ownership of CV work, importance
of 91–2
clients' needs
career coaches 2–3
clarity on, establishment of 109–10
importance of paying attention to 22–3
clinical professionals, advice from 31
coaching
coaching CV work 78, 79–80
requests for, forms of 2–3
rewards of 3–4
*see also* career coaches
*Coaching and Trauma* (Vaughan Smith,
J.) 53
*Coaching with Personality Type: What
Works* (Rogers, J.) 63–4
coachingandtrauma.com 53
competency-based questions 118, 120–22
confidentiality (and limits of) 44
conflict management analysis 63
congruence, empathy and 17
contact between sessions 23
containment 17
contracting 43–4
'creativity' coaches, advice from 31
crisis points, life purpose and 143–4
Csikszentmihalyi, Mihaly 67, 149
CV/résumé, client in words 77–92
achievements, skills and 83–5
advertising copy with client as
'product,' CV as 78
appearance, looks matter 88–9
'banned' words 89–90
chronological format 82, 83–4
client ownership of CV work,
importance of 91–2

coaching CV work 78, 79–80
covering letter/email 90–91
CV language, phenomenon of 87
*Economist Style Guide* (2018) 88
grammar, spelling and 88
graphic design 88–9
humour 86
hybrid CVs 83–5
interests, effective ways of writing
about 86
length 86–8
management jargon 79
preparation of client for CV work 79–80
purpose of CV/résumé 77–9
representation, written presentation
and 77
'safe pair of hands' trap 78–9
skills-based CVs 82–3, 83–4
SmartWorks 91–2
specialist CVs 85
styles and types of CV 82–5
summary paragraph 89–90
super-caution 79
truth, importance of 80–81
uniqueness, specificity and 80
volunteer experience, personal
interests and 85–6
word magic 86–8

Dahl, Roald 128
Darwin, Charles 139
De Bono, Edward 158–9
de-cluttering, advice on 32
decision environment 48–50
decision time 153–72
applications to career coaching 154–6
concluding comments 171–2
criteria, establishment of 155–6
decision-maker? 164
decision-making, flawed nature of
153–4
decision-making tools 157–61
decision matrices 159–60
delusional optimism 153–4
disappointment 166
due diligence work 162–3
emotion, realism and 163

INDEX **179**

employers' perspectives 164
equilibrium, recovery of 169
fired clients 167
*The First 90 Days* (Watkins, M) 171
flexibility 163–4
formula for leaving 170
goal clarity 164
honesty 163–4
hygiene factors 155
'in flow' exercise 155
leaving process 166–8
'leaving script' 169–70
leaving well 168–71
legal processes 167–8
moving on 171
negotiating the deal 161–3
openness 163–4
partying away 170–71
perfect solutions, rarity of 155
planning fallacy 154
principles, establishment of 168–9
principles that make a difference 163–6
professional competence, anxiety
    about 172
realism in preparation, importance of
    163
redundant clients 167
relationships 164–5, 169
release, sense of 171
reputation 169
revisit to life scan exercise 161
self-doubt 162
six thinking hats decision tool 158–9
small steps, small tasks and 165
SWOT (Strengths, Weaknesses,
    Opportunities, Threats) decision
    tool 159–60
taking control 169
*Thinking, Fast and Slow* (Kahnemann,
    D.) 153
trading 165
trap avoidance 169
VUCA (Volatile, Unpredictable, Chaotic
    and Ambiguous) acronym 156
what's at stake? question 156–61
delusional optimism 153–4
depression, exclusion of 147

*Designing Your Life* (Burnett, B. and
    Evans, D.) 138
Dickens, Charles 138
diet, advice on 32
differentiation, positivity in 58
disagreements, dealing with 27
disappointment, dealing with 166
dramatic turning points in life purpose
    143–4
due diligence work 162–3

*Economist Style Guide* (2018) 88
effective listening 20–21
Ehrenreich, Barbara 140
*The Element: How Finding Your Passion
    Changes Everything* (Robinson, K.
    and Aronica, L.) 146
Eliot, George 7
emotion
  aim of normalization of 23
  in coaching room, management of
    21–4
  emotional needs 49
  emotional needs grid 49–50
  realism and 163
empathy
  capacity for 18
  foundational skill for career coaches
    17–19
  limits of 18–19
employer invitations of questions,
    dealing with 123–4
employers' perspectives, decision-making
    and 164
employment lawyers, advice from 31
engagement questionnaires 44–5
Enlightenment thinking 139
equilibrium, recovery of 169
Erikson, Joan and Erik 141
escapist fantasies 145
*Essential Psychotherapy* (Yalom, I.) 138,
    152
executive search consultants, advice
    from 31
exercise, advice on 32
existential crisis, life purpose and 137
expert advice, suggestions on 31–2

**180** INDEX

Facebook 106
family lawyers, advice from 31
feedback 70–73
  debriefing 360 feedback 72–3
  effectiveness of coaching and 70–71
  positivity in 29
  practical concerns in giving 28–9
  provision of 28–9
  360 feedback 71–2
feelings, struggles for containment of 21–2
films and books, themes in 138–9
financial advisors, advice from 31
financial crisis (2008), effects of 1–2, 12
fired clients 167
FIRO-B questionnaire
  brand identity 63, 64
  getting started 49
*The First 90 Days* (Watkins, M) 171
first session, foundational nature of 42
'fit,' question of 46–8
Five Factor model 65
flexibility, decision-making and 163–4
Frankl, Victor 138
free-form questioning 45
Friedman, S. and Laurison, D. 11–12
full-scale assessment centres 133–6
  advice to clients on 135–6
  case study 134
  development centres 135
  group creativity 134
  group exercises 136
  group meetings 134
  hints and tips for clients on 135–6
  in-tray exercise 134
  job roles, performing tasks central to 134
  leaderless discussion 134
  organizational practice 134–5
  presentation giving 134
  psychometric assessments 135
  role-playing exercises 136
  second interviews 135
future, message from 151

Gallo, Carmine 127
genograms 53–4
getting started 42–57

attachment theory 53
Autonomy, Competence and Emotional
  Connection, Ryan and Deci on 49
backstory 50–55
  introduction of 51–3
Balance Wheel exercise 49
career history, 'thread' identification
  in 54–5
confidentiality (and limits of) 44
contracting 43–4
decision environment 48–50
emotional needs 49
emotional needs grid 49–50
engagement questionnaires 44–5
'exercises,' choice of 48–9
FIRO-B questionnaire 49
first session, foundational nature of 42
'fit,' question of 46–8
free-form questioning 45
genograms 53–4
goal-setting question 57
goals 43, 56–7
Life Scan Wheel exercise 49
Maslow's 'Hierarchy of needs' 49
negativity, dealing with 46
present situation, assessment of 44–6
responses to questions 45–6
reviewing data 55–6
welcome session, personal connection
  and 42–3
'what if?' question 53
wrap-up process 43
*see also* preparation
goals
  getting started on 43, 56–7
  goal clarity 164
  goal-setting question 57
Graeber, David 141
grammar, spelling and 88
graphic design 88–9
Gratton, L. and Scott, A. 10
*Great Expectations* (Dickens, C.) 138
*Groundhog Day* (Harold Ramis film)
  138–9

handshake at interviews 113–14
Herzberg, Frederick 155

higher education, work and 8–9
Hill, Sarah 53
historical perspectives
    how work used to be 6–7
    life purpose 139–40
Hogan suite of 3 questionnaires 63
Holland, John 64
honesty 163–4
host role in interview 114–15
*How to Get a Job You Love*
        (Lees, J.) 138
'human potential' movement 67
humour in CVs 86
*The Hundred-Year Life* (Gratton, L. and
        Scott, A.) 10
hybrid CVs 83–5
hygiene factors 155

Ibarra, Herminia 145
image 110–13
    good dressing, general principles of
        111–12
    make-up 112–13
    safe way to discuss 110–11
'in flow' exercise 155
'in flow' moments 149–51
influencing, skills in 74
information
    giving information 24–5
    informational interviews 99
    reframing advice as 25–7
instrument choice 62–4
    confusing nature of 66
interests, effective ways of writing
        about 86
interpretation, self-awareness and 66
interviews, coaching for 107–24
    bad old days 107–8
    clarity on clients' needs, establishment
        of 109–10
    employer invitations of questions,
        dealing with 123–4
    handshake 113–14
    host role in interview 114–15
    image 110–13
        good dressing, general principles of
            111–12

make-up 112–13
    safe way to discuss 110–11
'looking the part' 110
nervousness
    '7-11 breathing' 115
    body language and 115–16
    conscious relaxation 115
    dealing with 114–16
    manifestations of 116
    normalization of 115
    visualization of success 115
over-confidence 108–9
presence in interviews, issue of 108
question of questions 117–23
    answering critical question,
        four-stage strategy for 119–20
    blame game, danger in 122–3
    competency-based questions 118,
        120–22
    framework for answering
        competency question 120–22
    most critical question 119–20
    personal interests 118
    personal situation 118
    problems and issues in organization/
        job, exploration of 118
    STAR (situation, task, action, result)
        acronym 120
    storytelling technique 121–2
    strengths and weaknesses 118
    verbal fillers 122
    what are you currently doing? 117
    what questions do you have for us?
        119, 123–4
    why do you want this job? 118
research, problems about clients work
    on 116–17
social skills 108
two-way process of interview 114–15
intrinsic satisfaction 144
IPIP-NEO questionnaire 65

job market, structural changes in 9
Judeo-Christian worldview 139
Jung Type Indicators 62
Jungian personality type instruments
    62

**182** INDEX

Kahnemann, Daniel 153–4
Keirsey Temperament Sorter 62
kindness, value of 24
Kingsolver, Barbara 12
Kübler Ross, Elizabeth 23

language, critical importance of 20–21
leadership skills 74
learnt behaviours 67
leaving
  formula for 170
  'leaving script' 169–70
  leaving well 168–71
  partying away 170–71
  process of 166–8
Lees, John 138
legal processes 167–8
length of CV/résumé 86–8
*Life Cycle Completed* (Erikson, E.) 141
life purpose 137–52
  *Breaking Bad* (TV series) 147
  Cavendish Laboratory 147
  crisis points 143–4
  depression, exclusion of 147
  *Designing Your Life* (Burnett, B. and
    Evans, D.) 138
  dramatic turning points 143–4
  *The Element: How Finding Your
    Passion Changes Everything*
    (Robinson, K. and Aronica, L.)
    146
  engagement as answer 152
  Enlightenment thinking 139
  escapist fantasies 145
  *Essential Psychotherapy* (Yalom, I.)
    138, 152
  existential crisis 137
  films and books, themes in 138–9
  finding 'purpose,' false quest in 147
  finding your tribe 146–7
  *Great Expectations* (Dickens, C.) 138
  *Groundhog Day* (Harold Ramis film)
    138–9
  historical perspective 139–40
  hollow achievements 144
  *How to Get a Job You Love* (Lees, J.)
    138

identification of 'in-flow' moments,
    methods for 149–51
'in flow' moments 149–51
intrinsic satisfaction 144
issue of, practical applications for
    coaching on 137
*Life Cycle Completed* (Erikson, E.) 141
life purpose questions 140–43
live stage challenges 140–41
*Man's Search for Meaning* (Frankl, V.)
    138
meaning 138, 143
  discovery of 144–7
meaninglessness 137
mentors 146
message from the future 151
network expansion and finding 146
pointless jobs 141–2
purpose 138, 143
  discovery of 144–7
  giving up as well as starting anew in
    finding 147
quest for, principles and 144–7
*Reach for the Sky* (Douglas Bader
    biopic) 149
'self-concept' 148–9
self-transcendence 144, 147
seriousness of topic 140
small steps 147–8
*Smile or Die* (Ehrenreich, B.) 140
something missing 142–3
transcending yourself 144, 147
trigger points 143–4
Western life view 139
work in past centuries 139–40
*Working Identity* (Ibarra, H.) 145
Life Scan Wheel exercise 49
LinkedIn 95, 104, 106, 117, 146
listening
  effective listening 20–21
  skill for 19
live stage challenges 140–41
longevity 10, 139
'looking the part' for interviews 110

management jargon in CVs 79
management skills, brand identity and 74

INDEX **183**

*Man's Search for Meaning* (Frankl, V.) 138
marketplace distinctions 58–9
Maslow, Abraham 49
meaning
   discovery of 144–7
   life purpose and 138, 143
meaninglessness 137
'meet the staff' sessions 130–31
mentors 146
message from the future 151
*Middlemarch* (Eliot, G.) 7
Milton, John 70
mindspring.uk.com 68
More, Kenneth 149
motivation and interpersonal style
   questionnaire 63
moving on, decision making and 171
multiple questionnaires, use of 66
Murray, Bill 139
Myers-Briggs Type Indicator (MBTI) 62,
   63, 64, 65

negativity, dealing with 46
negotiating the deal 161–3
Nelson, Bob 146
NEO questionnaire 63, 65
nervousness
   '7-11 breathing' 115
   body language and 115–16
   conscious relaxation 115
   dealing with 114–16
   manifestations of 116
   normalization of 115
   visualization of success 115
networking 21, 24–5, 29–32, 95, 104, 146
   brainstorming networks 99
   client's network, drawing up of 98–9
   job searching and 97–8
   network expansion and finding life
      purpose 146
   socialization, networking and 97–8
   vital importance of 97–9
nutrition, advice on 32

OCEAN (Openness, Conscientiousness,
   Extraversion, Agreeableness,
   Neuroticism) acronym 64–5

openness 163–4
OPQ (Occupational Personality
   Questionnaire) 63
organizational skills 74
over-confidence 108–9

Palmer, Dr Eileen 24
partying away 170–71
peope as brands 59–60
perfect solutions, rarity of 155
personal style, advice on 31
planning fallacy 154
pointless jobs 141–2
positive psychology 67
PowerPoint presentations 126
preparation 33–41
   'chemistry' conversation 2–3, 37–8, 40,
      42–3, 56
   of client for CV work 79–80
   client type 34
   clients' needs, determination of 38
   competition 33–4
   engagement, reasons for refusal of
      38–41
   expertise, confidence in 36
   market segmentation 33
   pricing, price resistance and 35–7
   product definition 33–4
   qualifications, need for training
      and 33
   realism in, importance of 163
   reasons to say 'no' 38–41
   selling, fear of 37–8
   target market 36–7
   website 34–5
   *see also* getting started
presence in interviews, issue of 108
present situation, assessment of 44–6
presentation
   content of presentations in assessment
      centres 126–7
   impact of presentation, passion and
      127
   practice for presentations 128
   scrutiny of clients, assessment centres
      and 125–30
   skills of, advice on 31

**184** INDEX

presentations
  seeming too critical in 127–8
principles
  difference-making principles 163–6
  establishment of, decision-making and
    168–9
privilege 10–11
problem-solving skills 73
professional competence, anxiety about
    172
professional jobs in past 7
professional roles 9
promotion processes, need for rigour in 2
pronunciation, dealing with 129–30
psychometrics
  brand discussion and 60–65
  case against use of 62
  case for use of 60–62
  getting best out of 65–7
  as part of assessment 131–3
    ability tests 132–3
    numeracy tests 133
    personality questionnaires 132
    verbal reasoning tests 133
purpose
  of CV/résumé 77–9
  discovery of 144–7
  finding 'purpose,' false quest in 147
  giving up as well as starting anew in
    finding 147
  life purpose 138, 143
  quest for, principles and 144–7

Q&A sessions 131
question of questions 117–23
  answering critical question, four-stage
    strategy for 119–20
  blame game, danger in 122–3
  competency-based questions 118, 120–22
  framework for answering competency
    question 120–22
  most critical question 119–20
  personal interests 118
  personal situation 118
  problems and issues in organization/
    job, exploration of 118
  STAR (situation, task, action, result)
    acronym 120

storytelling technique 121–2
strengths and weaknesses 118
verbal fillers 122
what are you currently doing? 117
what questions do you have for us?
    119, 123–4
why do you want this job? 118
questions beginning 'why,' avoidance of
    20

*Reach for the Sky* (Douglas Bader biopic)
    149
realism in preparation, importance of 163
realized strengths 67
recruitment executives, advice from 31
redundancy
  attitudes to 9
  redundant clients 167
referral suggestions 30
reflection, need for 67
relationships, decision making and 164–5,
    169
representation, written presentation and
    77
reputation 169
research, problems about clients work on
    116–17
responses to questions 45–6
reviewing data 55–6
Robinson, K. and Aronica, L. 146
Rogers, Carl 67
routine work, computers and 8
Ryan, R.M. and Deci, E.L. 49

'safe pair of hands' trap 78–9
Schutz, Will 49
scrutiny of clients, assessment centres
    and 125–36
  accents 129–30
  assessment centres 125, 133–6
  class prejudice 129–30
  content of presentations 126–7
  full-scale assessment centres 133–6
    advice to clients on 135–6
    case study 134
    development centres 135
    group creativity 134
    group exercises 136

group meetings 134
hints and tips for clients on 135–6
in-tray exercise 134
job roles, performing tasks central
to 134
leaderless discussion 134
organizational practice 134–5
presentation giving 134
psychometric assessments 135
role-playing exercises 136
second interviews 135
impact of presentation. passion and 127
'meet the staff' sessions 130–31
PowerPoint presentations 126
practice for presentations 128
presentations 125–30
pronunciation 129–30
psychometrics as part of assessment
131–3
ability tests 132–3
numeracy tests 133
personality questionnaires 132
verbal reasoning tests 133
Q&A sessions 131
seeming too critical in presentations
127–8
slowing down 128–9
storytelling with passion 126–7
search methods and techniques 93–106
client's network, drawing up of 98–9
'elevator speech' 102–3
employer thinking 96–7
executive search consultants 104–5
experiment and learning, allowing time
for 106
fast moving nature of change in 93
headhunters 104–5
informational interviews 99
job search 93–4
job search misunderstandings 94–5
job search strategies that don't work
94–5
multiple approaches 105
networking, job searching and 97–8
networking, vital importance of 97–9
personal brand reinforcement with
social media 106
quality of job advertising 96–7

recruitment agencies 104–5
research interviews/conversations
98–100
direct approaches 101
'elevator' speech 101–3
why the approach works 100–103
social media 105–6
socialization, networking and 97–8
*What Color is Your Parachute?*
(Bolles, R.N.) 99
selection processes, need for rigour in 2
self-awareness, empathy and 17–18
'self-concept' 148–9
self-doubt 162
self-management skills 74
self-transcendence 144, 147
Seligman, Martin 67, 68
six thinking hats decision tool 158–9
16 PF questionnaire 63
skills-based CVs 82–3, 83–4
skills identification framework 73–4
slowing down 128–9
small business advisors, advice from 31
small steps
life purpose 147–8
small tasks and 165
SmartWorks 91–2
*Smile or Die* (Ehrenreich, B.) 140
Smith, Julia Vaughan 53
social skills 108
SPAR (Situation, Problem, Action, Result)
acronym 120
specialist CVs 85
STAR (Situation, Task, Action, Result)
acronym 120
Steptoe, Andrew 140
storytelling technique 121–2
storytelling with passion 126–7
strengths approach
to brand identity 67–9
weaknesses of 68–9
Strengths Cards 68
Strengths Profiler 67, 68
stress 22
advice on 32
Strong Interest Inventory 64
success
career success, secrets of 12–14

**186** INDEX

hidden rules of 11–12
summarizing
    skill for 19–20
    summary paragraph in CV/résumé
        89–90
super-caution 79
SuperStrong 64
SWOT (Strengths, Weaknesses,
        Opportunities, Threats) decision
        tool 159–60

taking control 169
*Talk Like TED* (Gallo, C.) 127
team role questionnaire 63
teamwork skills 74
therapists, advice from 31
*Thinking, Fast and Slow* (Kahnemann,
        D.) 153
thinking skills 73
Thomas-Kilmann Conflict Mode
        Instrument (TKI) 63
*3-D Brain* app 115
trading, decision making and 165
trait-based personality questionnaires
        63
transcending yourself 144, 147
transferable skills 73–4
trap avoidance 169
trigger points 143–4
truth, importance of 80–81
Twitter 106, 117, 124

uniqueness, specificity in CVs and 80
unrealized strengths 67
*Unsheltered* (Kingsolver, B.) 12

values, brand identity and 69–70
Values in Action 68
verbal communication, skills in 74
Virtues, strengths and 68
vitanavis.com 64
voice skills, advice on 31
volunteer experience, personal interests
        and 85–6
VUCA (Volatile, Unpredictable, Chaotic
        and Ambiguous) acronym
    decision time 156
    work 14

Waterman, Judy 64
Watkins, Michael 171
Watson-Glaser test 133
Wave 63
weaknesses, brand identity and 67
web developers, advice from 32
welcome session, personal connection
        and 42–3
well-being coaches, advice from 32
Western life view 139
'what if?' question 53
what's at stake? question 156–61
*Where Did You Learn to Behave Like
        That?* (Hill, S.) 53
whole-life perspective, value of 2
Wikipedia 53
women in work, changing situation for 8
word magic 86–8
work
    Artificial Intelligence 9
    austerity, effects of 12
    birth rate fall 9–10
    centenarians, rise in 9–10
    changing world of 8–15
    financial crisis (2008), effects of 1–2, 12
    higher education and 8–9
    historical perspective, how work used
        to be 6–7
    job market, structural changes in 9
    mid-20th century changes 7–8
    in past centuries 139–40
    professional jobs in past 7
    professional roles 9
    redundancy, attitudes to 9
    routine work, computers and 8
    VUCA (Volatile, Unpredictable, Chaotic
        and Ambiguous) acronym 14
    women in work, changing situation for 8
*Working Identity* (Ibarra, H.) 145
wrap-up process
    brand identity and 74–6
    getting started 43
written communication, skills in 73

Yalom, Irvin 138, 152
Yates, Julia 6

zero-hours contracts 8